ISAAC ASIMOV
PRESENTS
SUPER QUIZ IV

ISAAC ASIMOV

PRESENTS

SUPER QUIZ IV

The Fun Game of Q & A's

BY KEN FISHER

DEMBNER BOOKS • NEW YORK

Dembner Books
Published by Red Dembner Enterprises Corp., 80 Eighth Avenue, New
York, N.Y. 10011
Distributed by W. W. Norton & Company, Inc., 500 Fifth Avenue, New
York, N.Y. 10110

ISBN 0-942637-11-9
ISSN 1041–598X

CONTENTS

QUESTIONS! QUESTIONS!   7

1 / PEOPLE   11

2 / FILMS   53

3 / THE PRINTED WORD   69

4 / WORDS   79

5 / MUSIC   125

6 / GEOGRAPHY   135

7 / DAYS AND DATES   159

8 / POTLUCK   175

QUESTIONS! QUESTIONS!

Working with quiz books, as I have been doing (this is the fourth, as you can tell from the title), I have gained experience with respect to the more worrisome parts of the game.

For instance, nothing on Earth is going to prevent a quizmaster, who in this case is Ken Fisher, with myself as a rather imperfect backstop, from making a mistake now and then. We are human, you see, and bloopers come with the territory.

One time we asked the question: "What is the only nation that has the letters ATE, in that order, in its name?"

The answer we had in mind was "Guatemala," which we confidently expected a lot of people would miss. You can't help thinking of ATE as being pronounced "ayt" and as existing as part of a single syllable. In "Guatemala," however, the ATE is pronounced "ahtuh" and is part of two syllables—so you won't ordinarily think of it.

But then, a reader wrote, quite puzzled, and said: "What about 'The United States of America'? Isn't that a nation and doesn't it have ATE in it?"

Yes, it is, and yes, it does, and that proves that in addition to all the fun you can have in getting the answers to questions posed in this book, you also have the still greater fun of possibly catching us out in an error, which you can then point out in a (we hope) good-natured letter.

I was once caught by a bright twelve-year-old youngster in the game of "seconds." Let me explain the game first. It is quite customary to ask questions involving firsts. You know: "What monarch in British history had the longest reign?" "Who was President of the United States for the shortest period of time?" "What is the largest island on Earth?" The answers are Victoria, William Henry

Harrison, and Greenland, respectively, and you can confidently expect that a good many people will be able to give those answers without batting an eye.

But what if you had asked instead: "What monarch in British history had the second longest reign?" "Who was President of the United States for the second shortest period of time?" "What is the second largest island on Earth?" The answers are George III, James Abram Garfield, and New Guinea, respectively, and you can be sure that the number of people who can answer "seconds" is smaller than those who can answer "firsts." If you're a wise guy, then, you play the game of seconds.

So one time, after I had given a talk, that bright twelve-year-old youngster raised his hand, and I was foolish enough to call on him. (Never call on a twelve-year-old, if you can help it. They are old enough to make you look foolish, and not old enough to know that it's not nice to make a respected sage of ancient vintage look foolish.)

The boy said, "What is the second closest star to Earth, sir?"

I was very gratified to know the answer to that, because everyone knows the closest star but only a few particularly bright astronomers, and I, know the second closest star. I smiled paternally and said, "The second closest star, young man, is Barnard's star, which is only 5.9 light-years from Earth."

The youngster allowed a look of puzzlement to cross his face (he was far gone in the wicked art of dissimulation, that vile creature) and said, "But, in that case, what is the *first* closest star?"

I was surprised he didn't know, but I answered carefully. "The closest of all stars to Earth is a three-star system known as Alpha Centauri. One of its members, Alpha Centauri C, also known as Proxima Centauri, is a bit closer than the other two are. It is only 4.3 light-years from Earth."

The young man looked more puzzled than ever and sprung his trap in a voice filled with innocence. He said, "But I thought the Sun was the closest star to Earth."

At this point I tried to jump off the platform and fall upon the kid and kill him, but I was held back by officious, interfering people.

Please notice, by the way, that in this book, questions are asked that can be answered in one word (occasionally in two or three). Such answers are possible as long as we begin the questions with "When," "Where," "What," and "Who."

"When was the Declaration of Independence signed?" (1776)

"Where is the Taj Mahal located?" (Agra, India)

"What is a brougham?" (a four-wheeled carriage)

"Who signed the Magna Carta" (King John of England)

On the other hand, questions that begin with "Why" and "How" must be avoided because they can only be answered at length, sometimes in the form of a large, fat book; even so, the answers may not be definitive. For instance:

Why did the South lose the American Civil War despite the fact that it had better generals?

How do plant cells convert carbon dioxide and water into food and oxygen?

Even if you know the answers, you will not be overjoyed at finding these questions in a quiz book.

You also won't consider it delightful to be required to answer imperative rather than interrogative remarks. As examples of imperatives, you can have:

Name the factors contributing to the coming of the Great Depression of the 1930s.

Compare and contrast the influence of the automobile on American life in the 1920s and the influence of television on American life in the 1950s.

Please note that questions or imperatives that require long, thoughtful, and uncertain answers may be useful, valuable, and the very stuff of scholarship. They may be the sort of thing that the world's leaders must answer if they are to solve the problems that face humanity. However, one thing they are *not* is fun.

And in this book, we don't ask you to bear the weight of the world on your shoulders. We ask you to have fun.

Isaac Asimov

1 / PEOPLE

SURNAMES: A—I

Freshman Level

1. Henry "Hank" Aaron: Whose home run record did he break on April 8, 1974?
2. President John Adams: What was his relationship to President John Quincy Adams?
3. Louisa May Alcott: Name the novel for which she is best known.
4. Edwin Aldrin: What was his main achievement as an astronaut?
5. Alexander the Great: He succeeded his father, Philip II, as King of———.
6. Muhammad Ali: What was his original name?
7. Steve Allen: He was the first host of this NBC TV show.
8. Woody Allen: This 1977 film won four Academy Awards.
9. Idi Amin: He led a military coup in this country.
10. Roald Amundsen: What was his main claim to fame?

1. Babe Ruth's
2. Father
3. *Little Women*
4. Second on moon
5. Macedonia
6. Cassius Clay
7. *Tonight Show*
8. *Annie Hall*
9. Uganda
10. First to South Pole

Graduate Level: The same ten people are repeated.

11. Aaron: How many home runs did he hit during his major league career?
12. Adams: Who followed him as president?
13. Alcott: Name any two of the four young heroines in *Little Women*.
14. Aldrin: By what nickname was he known?
15. Alexander: Name his most famous teacher.
16. Ali: he first won the world crown from this man (1964).
17. Steve Allen: He starred in the screen biography of this musician (1955).
18. Woody Allen: Name three of his films having one-word titles.

19. Amin: He vowed to build a statue in Kampala honoring this man.
20. Amundsen: Whom did he race to the South Pole?

11. 755
12. Thomas Jefferson
13. Meg, Jo, Beth, Amy
14. Buzz
15. Aristotle
16. Sonny Liston
17. Benny Goodman
18. *Sleeper, Banana, Interiors, Manhattan, Zelig*
19. Adolf Hitler
20. Robert Scott

Ph. D. Level: The same ten people are repeated.

21. Aaron: With what team did he complete his career in 1976?
22. Adams: He died on July 4. What other U.S. Presidents died on July 4?
23. Alcott: What was the family name in *Little Women*?
24. Aldrin: What was the name of his 1973 autobiography?
25. Alexander: Name the King of Persia he defeated in 333 B.C.
26. Ali: Name the other two champions whom he defeated.

27. Steve Allen: Name his wife.
28. Woody Allen: Name the actress who starred with him in *Zelig*.
29. Amin: He allowed hijackers of an Israeli plane to land at this airport.
30. Amundsen: What other first did he accomplish between 1903 and 1906?

21. Milwaukee Brewers
22. Thomas Jefferson/ James Monroe
23. March
24. *Return to Earth*
25. Darius III
26. George Foreman, Leon Spinks
27. Jayne Meadows
28. Mia Farrow
29. Entebbe
30. First to complete Northwest Passage

SURNAMES: A—II

Freshman Level

1. Julie Andrews: She won the Best Actress Oscar in this 1964 film.
2. Mark Antony: He is known for his liaison with this Egyptian queen.
3. Eddie Arcaro: He is best known as a———.
4. Aristotle: He is best remembered as an influential———.
5. Neil Armstrong: Name the year in which he walked on the moon.
6. Louis Armstrong: What musical instrument did he play?
7. Arthur Ashe: He was the first black player to win a major title in this sport.
8. Fred Astaire: Name his best known dancing partner.
9. Charles Atlas: This expression described him before he built himself up.
10. Yasir Arafat: He headed this organization.

1. *Mary Poppins*
2. Cleopatra
3. Jockey
4. Philosopher
5. 1969 (July 20)
6. Trumpet and/or cornet
7. Tennis
8. Ginger Rogers
9. 97 pound weakling
10. PLO

Graduate Level: The same ten people are repeated.

11. Andrews: Name her husband.
12. Antony: Name either of the two men with whom he formed the Triumvirate after Caesar's death.
13. Arcaro: He set a record by winning the Kentucky Derby ———times.
14. Aristotle: He attended Plato's school. Name it.
15. Neil Armstrong: What was the name of the lunar module?
16. Louis Armstrong: What was his nickname?
17. Ashe: In 1975 he won the Wimbledon title. Whom did he defeat?
18. Astaire: Name his first dancing partner.
19. Atlas: This term described his isometric exercizes.
20. Arafat: In 1974 he delivered a speech to this organization.

11. Blake Edwards
12. Octavian, Lepidus
13. Five
14. The Academy
15. Eagle
16. Satchmo
17. Jimmy Connors
18. His sister Adele
19. Dynamic tension
20. U.N. General Assembly

Ph D. Level: The same ten people are repeated.

21. Andrews: She created this Broadway role in *My Fair Lady*.
22. Antony: He committed suicide after losing this battle.
23. Arcaro: He rode the Triple Crown winner twice. Name either horse.
24. Aristotle: What did he advocate as the main tool of investigation?
25. N. Armstrong: He landed on an area of the moon called the———.
26. L. Armstrong: He popularized this style of singing.
27. Ashe: What brought on his retirement in 1980?
28. Astaire: Who was his dancing partner in *Silk Stockings* (1957)?
29. Atlas: In ads he returned to punch the bully who had———.
30. Arafat: In 1982 he was driven from this city by a rival faction.

21. Eliza Doolittle
22. Actium
23. Whirlaway, Citation
24. Logic
25. Sea of Tranquillity
26. Scat
27. Heart attack
28. Cyd Charisse
29. Kicked sand in his face.
30. Beirut

SURNAMES: C—I

Freshman Level

1. Julius Caesar: Translate his famous boast, *Veni, vidi, vici.*
2. James Cagney: He won the Oscar portraying G. M. Cohan in this film.
3. Al Capp: Name the comic-strip character he created.
4. Lewis Carroll: Name his most famous novel.
5. Hoagy Carmichael: Name his most famous song.
6. Johnny Carson: Who is "second banana" on his show?
7. President Carter: Who was his vice-president?
8. Charlemagne: He was king of the———.
9. Geoffrey Chaucer: He was one of England's greatest———.
10. Christopher Columbus: In what community was he born?

1. I came, I saw, I conquered.
2. *Yankee Doodle Dandy*
3. Li'l Abner
4. *Alice in Wonderland*
5. "Stardust"
6. Ed McMahon
7. Walter Mondale
8. Franks
9. Poets
10. Genoa

Graduate Level: The same ten people are repeated.

11. Caesar: He was assassinated on March 15. What day was it on the Roman calendar?
12. Cagney: In 1981 he returned in this film.
13. Capp: What fictional town was the setting for his strip?
14. Carroll: What was the sequel to *Alice in Wonderland?*
15. Carmichael: His "Lamplighter's Serenade" was the first song ever recorded by———.
16. Carson: Whom did he replace as host in 1962?
17. Carter: Whom did he defeat in the presidential election?
18. Charlemagne: He is regarded as the founder of this empire.
19. Chaucer: He is best remembered for these tales.
20. Columbus: Name the three ships used on his voyage.

11. Ides of March
12. *Ragtime*
13. Dogpatch, Kentucky
14. *Through the Looking Glass*
15. Frank Sinatra
16. Jack Paar
17. Gerald Ford
18. Holy Roman Empire
19. *Canterbury Tales*
20. *Nina, Pinta, Santa Maria*

Ph. D. Level: The same ten people are repeated.

21. Caesar: Name the adversary he defeated in Greece in 48 B.C.
22. Cagney: In *Public Enemy* he shoved a grapefruit into her face.
23. Capp: This character was a parody of Dick Tracy.
24. Carroll: He coined the word "chortle" from these two words.
25. Carmichael: Name his autobiography.
26. Carson: He portrays this all-knowing seer.
27. Carter: What was his wife's first name?
28. Charlemagne: Who was his father?
29. Chaucer: His tomb in Westminster Abbey was the first in what is now known as———.
30. Columbus: On October 12, 1492, he landed on this island.

21. Pompey
22. Mae Clark
23. Fearless Fosdick
24. Snort, chuckle
25. *The Stardust Road*
26. Carnac the Magnificent
27. Rosalynn
28. Pepin the Short
29. Poet's Corner
30. San Salvador

SURNAMES: C— II

Freshman Level

1. Nadia Comaneci: What country did she represent at the 1976 Olympics?
2. James Cook: Where was he killed?
3. Nicolaus Copernicus: What was his nationality?
4. Hernan Cortes: He is known as the conqueror of———.
5. Jacques Cousteau: He invented this for underwater breathing.
6. Bing Crosby: Name his best-selling record.
7. George Custer: His "last stand" took place in this battle.
8. Bennett Cerf: He was on this TV show from 1952 to 1966.
9. Prince Charles: Whom did he marry in 1981?
10. Agatha Christie: This play ran in London for over thirty years.

1. Romania
2. Hawaiian Islands
3. Polish
4. Mexico and/or Aztecs
5. SCUBA or Aqualung
6. "White Christmas"
7. Little Bighorn
8. *What's My Line?*
9. Lady Diana Spencer
10. *The Mousetrap*

Graduate Level: The same ten people are repeated.

11. Comaneci: In what city did she gain Olympic fame?
12. Cook: What did he name the islands now called Hawaii?
13. Copernicus: He is credited with founding modern———.
14. Cortes: Who was the Aztec king?
15. Cousteau: He helped develope a submersible boat called a———.
16. Crosby: His unique style of singing was known as———.
17. Custer: He graduated last in his class from this institute.
18. Cerf: He founded this publishing house.
19. Charles: His first child was named———.
20. Christie: She created this Belgian detective.

11. Montreal (1976).
12. Sandwich Islands
13. Astronomy
14. Montezuma (II)
15. Bathyscaphe
16. Crooning
17. West Point
18. Random House
19. William
20. Hercule Poirot

Ph. D. Level: The same ten people are repeated.

21. Comaneci: In what event did she score the Olympics' first perfect score?
22. Cook: He proved these islands were not connected.
23. Copernicus: His famous theory is known by this name.
24. Cortes: He founded this city on Mexico's coast.
25. Cousteau: His book was made into an Oscar-winning film. Name it.
26. Crosby: He won an Oscar in this 1944 film.
27. Custer: He fought in the Civil War at the first battle of———.
28. Cerf: He won the right to publish this James Joyce book in the U.S.A.
29. Charles: He is the first heir to the throne to earn a———.
30. Christie: She created this female sleuth.

21. Uneven parallel bars
22. North and South (New Zealand)
23. Heliocentric theory
24. Veracruz
25. *The Silent World*
26. *Going My Way*
27. Bull Run
28. *Ulysses*
29. University degree
30. Miss Jane Marple

CELEBRITIES: WHO'S WHO?
Last names begin with N.

Freshman Level

1. Star of the film *The Verdict*.
2. He played Spock on TV's *Star Trek*.
3. Known as a leading advocate of consumer affairs.
4. U.S. golfer known as the Golden Bear.
5. He was at the center of the Iran-Contra hearings.
6. He resigned the Presidency in 1974.
7. Country music star who created the "Austin sound."
8. His films include *Prizzi's Honor* and *The Border*.
9. He starred in the film *First Family*.
10. She won the U.S. Tennis Open in 1982.

1. Newman, Paul
2. Nimoy, Leonard
3. Nader, Ralph
4. Nicklaus, Jack
5. North, Oliver
6. Nixon, Richard
7. Nelson, Willie
8. Nicholson, Jack
9. Newhart, Bob
10. Navratilova, Martina

Graduate

11. Quarterback who led the N.Y. Jets to victory in Super Bowl (1969).
12. His films include *Connery Row* and *48 Hours*.
13. Vocalist for Fleetwood Mac.
14. This director was once Elaine May's comedy partner.
15. English actor-singer and star of *Stop the World I Want to Get Off*.
16. Winner of the French Tennis Open in 1983.
17. He was TV's Gomer Pyle.
18. Romanian tennis player once known for his temper tantrums.
19. Her films include *Picnic* and *Jeanne Eagels*
20. Singer-actress who appeared in films *Grease* and *Xanadu*.

11. Namath, Joe
12. Nolte, Nick
13. Nicks, Stevie
14. Nichols, Mike
15. Newley, Anthony
16. Noah, Yannick
17. Nabors, Jim
18. Nastase, Illie
19. Novak, Kim
20. Newton-John, Olivia

Ph. D. Level

21. Russian ballet dancer who defected in 1961.
22. Baseball pitcher who was coleader in National League victories in 1974 and 79.
23. Retired news commentator and author of *A Civil Tongue*.
24. Pianist, conductor, composer who began his career on tour with Paul Whiteman.
25. The Flying Finn of ski jumping.
26. Actor and former disc jockey in Canada. Films include *Airplane*.
27. Third baseman who led the American League in home runs in 1976.
28. She did TV commercials for Anacin and Maxim coffee.
29. Boxer who defeated Ali in 1973.
30. Sly Stallone's ex-wife.

21. Nureyev, Rudolf
22. Niekro, Phil
23. Newman, Edwin
24. Nero, Peter
25. Nykanan, Matti
26. Nielsen, Leslie
27. Nettles, Graig
28. Neal, Patricia
29. Norton, Ken
30. Nielsen, Brigitte

CELEBRITIES: WHO'S WHO?
Last names begin with P

Freshman Level

1. Actor, films include *Scarface* and *Serpico*.
2. She plays Pamela in TV's *Dallas*.
3. Golfer, Masters champion 1958, '60, '62, and '64.
4. President of the Academy of Motion Picture Arts and Sciences, 1967–70.
5. Singer, composer, actress, films include *Nine to Five* and *Rhinestone*.
6. Actor, best known for his role in *Psycho* (1959).
7. Actor, Best Actor Oscar for *Lilies of the Field*, 1963.
8. South African golfer, named to World Golf Hall of Fame.
9. Italian tenor and star of film *Yes, Giorgio*.
10. World champion heavyweight boxer 1956–59 and 1960–62.

1. Pacino, Al.
2. Principal, Victoria
3. Palmer, Arnold
4. Peck, Gregory
5. Parton, Dolly
6. Perkins, Anthony
7. Poitier, Sydney
8. Player, Gary
9. Pavarotti, Luciano
10. Patterson, Floyd

Graduate Level

11. Soccer player, named Athlete of the Century in 1980.
12. Won the MVP of the NFL in 1978 as a running back.
13. Actor, TV series include *Banacek* and *The A Team*.
14. Female entertainer named to Country Music Hall of Fame in 1972.
15. Actress, films include *Heartpeeps* and *Annie*.
16. Comic actor, repertory player on *Saturday Night Live*, 1980–84.
17. Author, editor, TV host, books include *Paper Lion* and *Fireworks*.
18. Canadian actor, films include *Sound of Music*.
19. Pianist from Canada, author of *Jazz Exercises and Pieces*.
20. TV journalist, married to Garry Trudeau.

11. Pelé, Arantes
12. Payton, Walter
13. Peppard, George
14. Pearl, Minnie
15. Peters, Bernadette
16. Piscopo, Joe
17. Plimpton, George
18. Plummer, Christopher
19. Peterson, Oscar
20. Pauley, Jane

Ph. D. Level

21. Violinist from Israel.
22. Golfer, winner of the U.S. Open and Canadian Open in 1976.
23. Actress, films include *Lenny, Superman*, and *The Border*.
24. Soprano, first American to receive Bolshoi medal.
25. Auto racer: Winner of Daytona 500 seven times.
26. Comedic actor, films include *Stir Crazy* and *Blue Collar*.
27. Author of *Inside Las Vegas* and *Fools Die*.
28. Entertainer of the Year in Country Music, 1971.
29. Director, one-time husband of Sharon Tate.
30. Actor, films include *Laura, Shock, The Raven*, and *Dragonwyck*.

21. Perlman, Itzhak
22. Pate, Jerome
23. Perrine, Valerie
24. Peters, Roberta
25. Petty, Richard
26. Pryor, Richard
27. Puzo, Mario
28. Pride, Charley
29. Polanski, Roman
30. Price, Vincent

CELEBRITIES: WHO'S WHO?
Last names begin with T.

Freshman Level

1. The star of the film, *Saturday Night Fever*.
2. She became Prime Minister of Britain in 1979.
3. He was John Boy on TV's *The Waltons*.
4. With husband Ike, she won a grammy in 1972.
5. She won the Oscar for her role in *Butterfield 8*.
6. Her films include *Nine to Five* and *All of Me*.
7. She was the dimpled darling of Depression America.
8. Heavyweight boxing champion 1987–?
9. Golfer, U.S. Open champ 1968 and 1971.

1. Travolta, John
2. Thatcher, Margaret
3. Thomas, Richard
4. Turner, Tina
5. Taylor, Elizabeth
6. Tomlin, Lily
7. Temple, Shirley
8. Tyson, Mike
9. Trevino, Lee

Graduate Level

11. Supermodel who promoted her line of clothes for Sears.
12. He played the police captain on TV's *Hill Street Blues*.
13. The original Sweater Girl.
14. Quarterback who led the Redskins to victory in Super Bowl 17.
15. Broadcasting executive, president of MTM Enterprises.
16. This Canadian's variety series ran opposite Johnny Carson's show.
17. Creator of the comic strip *Doonesbury*.
18. Actress, films include *Sounder* and *The Comedians*.
19. Canada's Prime Minister in the late 1960's, 70's and early 80's.
20. She married Hume Cronym in 1942.

11. Tiegs, Cheryl
12. Travanti, Daniel
13. Turner, Lana
14. Theisman, Joe
15. Tinker, Grant
16. Thicke, Alan
17. Trudeau, Garry
18. Tyson, Cicely
19. Trudeau, Pierre
20. Tandy, Jessica

Ph. D. Level

21. She plays Lucy on TV's *Dallas*.
22. Composer and one-time guitarist for The Who.
23. Former member of The Wailers. He had a hit with "Legalize It."
24. NHL rookie of the year in 1976, with the New York Islanders.
25. Minnesota Viking's quarterback; the NFL's MVP in 1975.
26. The author of *Future Shock*, 1970.
27. His films include *Coma*, *First Family*, and *Heartland*.
28. This interviewer-author's books include *Talking to Myself*, 1970.
29. Named Entertainer of the Year 1976, by the Country Music Association.
30. Country and western entertainer who composed "Hello, Darling," 1970.

21. Tilton, Charlene
22. Townshend, Peter
23. Tosh, Peter
24. Trottier, Bryan
25. Tarkenton, Fran
26. Toffler, Alvin
27. Torn, Rip
28. Terkel, Studs
29. Tillis, Mel
30. Twitty, Conway

GEORGE
Provide the last name of the George.

Freshman Level

1. His late wife was Gracie Allen.
2. America's most famous George.
3. Shot while campaigning and paralyzed.
4. Owner of the N.Y. Yankees, 1973–?
5. British playwright. Nobel Prize in literature 1925.
6. Best Actor Oscar for *Patton*.
7. The Sultan of Swat.
8. Member of the Beatles.
9. Vice president in Ronald Reagan's administration.
10. World heavyweight boxing champ 1973–74.

1. Burns
2. Washington
3. Wallace
4. Steinbrenner
5. Bernard Shaw
6. Scott
7. Herman Ruth
8. Harrison
9. Bush
10. Foreman

Graduate Level

11. Kansas City Royals third baseman, 1973–?
12. Composer of "Rhapsody in Blue."
13. U.S. public-opinion statistician.
14. Best known for gangster roles: *Scarface* 1932.
15. "Toastmaster General of the U.S."
16. Democratic presidential candidate in 1972.
17. The author of *Animal Farm*.
18. President of AFL-CIO, 1955–79.
19. Blind British jazz pianist.
20. The lead role in *Love at First Bite*, 1979.

11. Brett
12. Gershwin
13. Gallup
14. Raft
15. Jessel
16. McGovern
17. Orwell
18. Meany
19. Shearing
20. Hamilton

Ph. D. Level

21. Best known for his plays with Moss Hart.
22. Author of the plan for postwar European relief.
23. Quarterback-kicker for Chicago Bears (1949–58).
24. Developed the Kodak camera.
25. Founded his electric company in 1886.
26. Actor, films include *A Touch of Class*, 1973.
27. Won Best Supporting Actor Oscar in *All About Eve*.
28. Invented the sleeping car for trains.
29. Novelist who had a liaison with Frederic Chopin.
30. Born a slave, he revolutionized Southern agriculture.

21. Kaufman
22. Marshall
23. Blanda
24. Eastman
25. Westinghouse
26. Segal
27. Sanders
28. Pullman
29. Sand
30. Washington Carver

CHARLES, CHUCK, AND CHARLIE (CHARLEY)
Provide the last name.

Freshman Level

1. The beloved Little Tramp.
2. President of France, 1958–69.
3. Developed the point-count system for bridge.
4. Leader of the "family" in the Sharon Tate murders.
5. His plane was *The Spirit of St. Louis*.
6. English actor, husband of Elsa Lanchester.
7. Frankish ruler nicknamed The Hammer.
8. Actor: films include *Death Wish*, 1974.
9. TV's *The Rifleman*, 1957–62.
10. One of the first black country-and-western singers.

1. Chaplin
2. De Gaulle
3. Goren
4. Manson
5. Lindbergh
6. Laughton
7. Martel
8. Bronson
9. Connors
10. Pride

Graduate Level

11. He made a five-year voyage on H.M.S. *Beagle*.
12. His pseudonym was Boz.
13. English essayist (1775–1834).
14. Comedic actor, regular on the game show *Match Game*.
15. Country singer; hits include "Behind Closed Doors."
16. Developed an earthquake scale.
17. Developed Grape-Nuts breakfast cereal.
18. Legendary jazz alto saxophonist, cocreator of bebop.
19. General killed at the siege of Khartoum.
20. Invented the vulcanized-rubber process but died a pauper.

11. Darwin
12. Dickens
13. Lamb
14. Nelson Reilly
15. Rich
16. Richter
17. Post
18. Parker
19. Gordon
20. Goodyear

Ph. D. Level

21. Pioneer of the stockbroking business.
22. Cofounder of a famous medical clinic.
23. Actor, films include *Of Mice and Men* 1940.
24. French singer-actor, films include *Candy* 1968.
25. Stand-up comic, regular on TV's *Switch* 1975-78.
26. English land-estate manager, his name became a word.
27. Actor, films include *Our Man Flint*, 1966.
28. He built the Oakland A's team that won the World Series, 1966–68.
29. Comedic actor, films include *Ruggles of Red Gap*, 1935.
30. A pioneer in development of blended and pasteurized cheese.

21. Merrill
22. Mayo
23. Bickford
24. Aznavour
25. Callas
26. Boycott
27. Coburn
28. Finley
29. Ruggles
30. Kraft

ROBERT, BOB, AND BOBBY
Provide the last name.

Freshman Level

1. Starred with Crosby in many "Road" pictures.
2. Assassinated in his 1968 campaign for presidential nomination.
3. First defenseman to be NHL leading scorer.
4. Winner of decathlon in 1948 and 1952 Olympics.
5. Actor, films include *The Deer Hunter* and *Taxi Driver*
6. Republican presidential candidate 1988.
7. Antarctic explorer beaten to the pole by Amundsen.
8. His movies include *The Sting* and *The Chase.*
9. Author of *A Child's Garden of Verses.*
10. Star of TV's *Father Knows Best.*

1. Hope
2. Kennedy
3. Orr
4. Mathias
5. De Niro
6. Dole
7. Scott
8. Redford
9. Louis Stevenson
10. Young

Graduate Level

11. *Baretta* star.
12. Most famous Scottish poet.
13. Star of *The Music Man.*
14. "Believe it or Not."
15. Actor, films include *The Sting* and *Jaws.*
16. He lost the "Match of the Century" to Billie Jean King.
17. Films include *Night of the Hunter* and *Farewell My Lovely.*
18. U.S. poet and Pulitzer Prize winner.
19. He was married to Natalie Wood.
20. German chemist who invented a burner.

11. Blake
12. Burns
13. Preston
14. Ripley
15. Shaw
16. Riggs
17. Mitchum
18. Frost
19. Wagner
20. Bunsen

Ph. D. Level

21. Called the Canadian Kipling.
22. First arctic explorer to reach the North Pole.
23. As Cleveland Indians pitcher he won twenty or more games six times.
24. Regarded as the first British Prime Minister.
25. He starred in *The Man from U.N.C.L.E.*
26. Star of the TV series *The Detectives* 1959–62.
27. Author of *The Matarese Circle,* 1979.
28. U.S. humorist noted for his comic essays.
29. He killed Jesse James.
30. His law involves changes in the volume of gas.

21. Service
22. Peary
23. Lemon
24. Walpole
25. Vaughn
26. Taylor
27. Ludlum
28. Benchley
29. Ford
30. Boyle

FOUR BY FOUR
All answers are names consisting of a four-letter first name and a four-letter last names. Initials are provided.

Freshman Level

1. Comedian, born John Elroy Sanford.	R.F.	1. Redd Foxx	
2. Canadian singer-composer.	P.A.	2. Paul Anka	
3. Emmy Awards for best actor in comedy series.	A.A.	3. Alan Alda	
4. Killer of Lee Harvey Oswald.	J.R.	4. Jack Ruby	
5. He broke Ty Cobb's hits record.	P.R.	5. Pete Rose	
6. Folk singer, character actor.	B.I.	6. Burl Ives	
7. Actor, originally a Broadway song-and-dance man.	J.G.	7. Joel Grey	
8. Australian singer, one of the *Bee Gees*.	A.G.	8. Andy Gibb	
9. U.S. film director.	J.F.	9. John Ford	
10. Key prosecution witness in Watergate hearings.	J.D.	10. John Dean	

Graduate Level

11. *What's My Line* moderator.	J.D.	11. John Daly	
12. Character actor in many westerns from 1930.	W.B.	12. Ward Bond	
13. Pitcher, winner of AL Cy Young Award, 1971.	V.B.	13. Vida Blue	
14. Folk singer-activist of 1960s.	J.B.	14. Joan Baez	
15. Sergeant Friday of *Dragnet*.	J.W.	15. Jack Webb	
16. Author of *Battle Cry* (1953).	L.U.	16. Leon Uris	
17. Canadian country and western singer.	H.S.	17. Hank Snow	
18. Canadian comedian, did satires on current events.	M.S.	18. Mort Sahl	
19. The Cowardly Lion.	B.L.	19. Bert Lahr	
20. One-time singer with Xavier Cugat.	A.L.	20. Abbe Lane	

Ph. D. Level

21. Built first auto with internal combustion engine.	K.B.	21. Karl Benz	
22. Star of TV series *Life with Father* (1953–55).	L.A.	22. Leon Ames	
23. Dutch actress in films of 1940s and 50s.	N.F.	23. Nina Foch	
24. Grandfather of the Waltons	W.G.	24. Will Geer	
25. Author of western romances.	Z.G.	25. Zane Grey	
26. U.S. playwright, Pulitzer Prize drama, 1937.	M.H.	26. Moss Hart	
27. Swiss psychologist.	C.J.	27. Carl Jung	
28. Stand-up comic.	A.K.	28. Alan King	
29. Swiss surrealist painter.	P.K.	29. Paul Klee	
30. Actor, films include *Tea and Sympathy*.	J.K.	30. John Kerr	

FIVE BY FIVE
All answers are names consisting of a five-letter first name and a five-letter last name. Initials rae provided if needed.

Freshman Level

1. Singer: Hit song "Mack the Knife."	B.D.	1. Bobby Darin
2. Star of *The French Chef* TV show.	J.C.	2. Julia Child
3. Prat fall specialist on *Saturday Night Live* (1975–76).	C.C.	3. Chevy Chase
4. He and his brother Frank became infamous outlaws after the Civil War.	J.J.	4. Jesse James
5. Play and film *Funny Girl* are based on her life.	F.B.	5. Fanny Brice
6. Star of film *The Exorcist*.	L.B.	6. Linda Blair
7. Rock star, actor, films include *Labyrinth*.	D.B.	7. David Bowie
8. Actress, daughter of famous parents of TV comedy series.	L.A.	8. Lucie Arnaz
9. U.S. comedian, filmmaker, actor.	W.A.	9. Woody Allen
10. Actor, songwriter, TV star, comedian.	S.A.	10. Steve Allen

Graduate Level

11. Drummer for The Beatles.	R.S.	11. Ringo Starr
12. One of TV's *The Golden Girls*.	B.W.	12. Betty White
13. U.S. vice-president, 1969–73.	S.A.	13. Spiro Agnew
14. Commanded the Green Mountain Boys.	E.A.	14. Ethan Allen
15. Composer of "Maybellene."	C.B.	15. Chuck Berry
16. Comedian, satirist known for his off-color jokes	L.B.	16. Lenny Bruce
17. Commanded army at capture of Quebec from French.	J.W.	17. James Wolfe
18. Actress best known for her role in *Rocky*.	T.S.	18. Talia Shire
19. Jazz singer, sang with Mahalia Jackson 1945–49.	D.R.	19. Della Reese
20. Author of *On the Beach*.	N.S.	20. Nevil Shute

Ph. D. Level

21. Lead vocalist with Jefferson Airplane (1966–72).	G.S.	21. Grace Slick
22. Rock singer and composer, one-time wife of James Taylor.	C.S.	22. Carly Simon
23. Best known for her role in *The Perils of Pauline*.	P.W.	23. Pearl White
24. U.S. violinist, won Grammy awards in 1971 and 1973.	I.S.	24. Isaac Stern
25. Harmonica player.	L.A.	25. Larry Adler
26. Director responsible for Brigitte Bardot's film start.	R.V.	26. Roger Vadim
27. Author of *The Foxes of Harrow*.	F.Y.	27. Frank Yerby
28. Australian, held world record for mile 1962–65.	P.S.	28. Peter Snell
29. Winner of Indianapolis 500 in 1968 and 1975.	B.U.	29. Bobby Unser
30. Woman outlaw who had a child by outlaw Cole Younger.	B.S.	30. Belle Starr

SIX BY SIX

All answers are names consisting of a six-letter first name and a six-letter last name. Initials are provided.

Freshman Level

1.	Aviation pioneer.	W.W.	1. Wilbur Wright
2.	Blind singer-composer.	S.W.	2. Stevie Wonder
3.	Country music singer-songwriter.	W.N.	3. Willie Nelson
4.	Actor, films include *Magnificent Obsession*.	R.T.	4. Robert Taylor
5.	One-time wife of Bogart and Robards.	L.B.	5. Lauren Bacall
6.	Producer, actor, starred in *Shampoo*.	W.B.	6. Warren Beatty
7.	Composer of "God Bless America."	I.B.	7. Irving Berlin
8.	Alleged ax murderess.	L.B.	8. Lizzie Borden
9.	U.S. "method" actor, starred in *The Men*.	M.B.	9. Marlon Brando
10.	Long-word-loving sportscaster.	H.C.	10. Howard Cosell

Graduate Level

11.	Actor, films include *Citizen Kane*.	J.C.	11. Joseph Cotten
12.	Child actor in *Our Gang* film shorts.	J.C.	12. Jackie Cooper
13.	British actor, films include *Lost Horizon* (1937).	R.C.	13. Ronald Colman
14.	Most famous Roman statesman and general.	J.C.	14. Julius Caesar
15.	Italian operatic lyric tenor.	E.C.	15. Enrico Caruso
16.	Singer, hits include "Music, Music, Music."	T.B.	16. Teresa Brewer
17.	Spanish conquistador, conqueror of Mexico.	H.C.	17. Hernan Cortes
18.	Manager of Dodgers 1954–76.	W.A.	18. Walter Alston
19.	Daughter of Nehru and former Indian prime minister.	I.G.	19. Indira Ghandi
20.	Famous American inventor	T.E.	20. Thomas Edison

Ph. D. Level

21.	Singer, gained fame on *Sing Along with Mitch*. TV show.	L.U.	21. Leslie Uggams
22.	U.S. producer/director, films include *M*A*S*H*	R.A.	22. Robert Altman
23.	English actor, won Oscar for *Disraeli* (1929).	G.A.	23. George Arliss
24.	Films include *Ice Castles* (1979).	R.B.	24. Robby Benson
25.	U.S. dancer with wife Irene pre-1914	V.C.	25. Vernon Castle
26.	A chief justice of the U.S.A.	W.B.	26. Warren Burger
27.	Star of TV's *It Takes a Thief*.	R.W.	27. Robert Wagner
28.	Commentator, *60 Minutes*.	A.R.	28. Andrew Rooney
29.	American Puritan minister involved in Salem witch trials in 1692.	C.M.	29. Cotton Mather
30.	Female British dancer.	J.P.	30. Juliet Prowse

MR.

Freshman Level

1. Captain Kangaroo's friend.	1. Mr. Green Jeans
2. The evil side of a doctor with a split personality.	2. Mr. Hyde
3. TV's talking horse.	3. Mr. Ed
4. Second in command on the starship *Enterprise*.	4. Mr. Spock
5. An actor on TV's *A-Team*.	5. Mr. T.
6. A comic clay character on *Saturday Night Live*.	6. Mr. Bill
7. Host of a children's TV show about the neighborhood.	7. Mr. Rogers
8. Milton Berle's nickname.	8. Mr. Television
9. Jim Backus was the voice of this near-sighted cartoon character.	9. Mr. Magoo
10. Dagwood Bumstead's boss.	10. Mr. Dithers

Graduate Level

11. The owner of the soda fountain on *Sesame Street*.	11. Mr. Hooper
12. This cartoon cat chased after Pixie and Dixie.	12. Mr. Jinks
13. TV's Hazel referred to her employer by this name.	13. Mr. B (Baxter)
14. The supermarket manager who told us not to squeeze the Charmin.	14. Mr. Whipple
15. Nickname of comedian Don Rickles.	15. Mr. Warmth
16. The principal of Riverdale High in Archie comics.	16. Mr. Weatherbee
17. Clifton Webb starred as this man in a series of movies.	17. Mr. Belvedere
18. Wally Cox played this teacher on TV.	18. Mr. Peepers
19. The nickname of Robert A. Taft.	19. Mr. Republican
20. Jeff Chandler portrayed this character on radio's *Our Miss Brooks*.	20. Mr. Boynton

Ph. D. Level

21. The central character of JRR Tolkein's *The Hobbit*.	21. Mr. Bilbo Baggins
22. Tapdancer Bill Robinson's nickname.	22. Mr. Bojangles
23. Oliver Twist asked this man for "more."	23. Mr. Bumble
24. Peter Lorre portrayed this Japanese detective.	24. Mr. Moto
25. Cary Grant built a house in this 1948 movie.	25. *Mr. Blandings Builds His Dream House*
26. Superman's foe from the fifth dimension.	26. Mr. MXYZPTLK
27. Pamela and Jerry solved mysteries under this title.	27. *Mr. and Mrs. North*
28. Hi Flagston's boss in the comic strip *Hi and Lois*.	28. Mr. Foofram
29. James Stewart went to Washington in this 1939 movie.	29. *Mr. Smith Goes to Washington*
30. Henry Fonda had the title role in this 1955 film.	30. *Mister Roberts*

MISS AND MRS.

Freshman Level

1. She sat on a tuffet.
2. Benjamin Braddock (Dustin Hoffman) had an affair with her in *The Graduate*.
3. This 1955 film is about a dearly beloved schoolteacher.
4. The Muppet who is in love with Kermit the Frog.
5. Secretary to James Bond's boss.
6. The setting for this comic strip is Kelly School.
7. Jimmy Durante closed his TV shows by saying goodnight to this woman.
8. Title awarded to one of the contestants in the Miss America Contest.
9. Zsa Zsa Gabor won this title in 1936.
10. Fonzie's nickname for Mrs. Cunningham on TV's *Happy Days*.

1. Miss Muffet
2. Mrs. Robinson
3. *Good Morning Miss Dove*
4. Miss Piggy
5. Miss Moneypenny
6. *Miss Peach*
7. Mrs. Calabash
8. Miss Congeniality
9. Miss Hungary
10. Mrs. C

Graduate Level

11. The spinster in *The Wizard of Oz* who tries to take Toto away from Dorothy.
12. Archie Andrew's teacher at Riverdale High.
13. Title of a movie and TV series: *The Ghost and——*.
14. Herman's Hermits sang this 1965 hit.
15. Greer Garson and Walter Pidgeon star in this 1942 Academy Award-winning movie.
16. Aged female sleuth created by Agatha Christie.
17. Diana Rigg's role in *The Avengers*.
18. Her cow is said to have started the Chicago fire.
19. Cock Robin's sweetheart in "Who Killed Cock Robin?"
20. Proponent of Folger's Coffee in TV commercials.

11. Miss Gulch
12. Miss Grundy
13. *Mrs. Muir*
14. "Mrs. Brown You've Got a Lovely Daughter"
15. *Mrs. Miniver*
16. Miss (Jane) Marple
17. Mrs. Emma Peel
18. Mrs. O'Leary
19. Miss Jenny Wren
20. Mrs. Olson

Ph. D. Level

21. The confidential secretary of Belgian detective Hercule Poirot.
22. Gen. Amos Halftrack's private secretary in *Beetle Bailey*
23. Detective Philo Vance's pet Scottish terrier (novels).
24. Dudley Do-Right's girlfriend.
25. Lucille Ball and William Holden star in this 1949 film.
26. Rita Hayworth plays the title role in this 1953 film.
27. The goat mascot in the TV series *F-Troop*.
28. Sherlock Holmes' housekeeper and landlady.
29. The unmarried ladies in the game of *Clue*.
30. The married woman in the game of *Clue*.

21. Miss Lemon
22. Miss Buxley
23. Miss MacTavish
24. Miss Nell (Fenwick)
25. *Miss Grant Takes Richmond*
26. *Miss Sadie Thompson*
27. Miss Gwendoline
28. Mrs. Hudson
29. Miss Scarlet and Miss Peacock
30. Mrs. White

WHAT'S IN A NAME?
People known by a single name.

Freshman Level

1. Flamboyant U.S. pianist.
2. Greek philosopher condemned to drink hemlock.
3. Roman gladiator who led the Servile War.
4. Japanese Emperor during W.W. II.
5. The founder of Islam.
6. He led the Hebrews out of bondage in Egypt.
7. Greek writer of fables.
8. Most influential philosopher in Chinese history.
9. She rose to fame singing with Sonny Bono.
10. Best remembered for his theorem concerning right-angled triangles.

1. Liberace
2. Socrates
3. Spartacus
4. Hirohito
5. Mohammed
6. Moses
7. Aesop
8. Confucius
9. Cher
10. Pythagoras

Graduate Level

11. Author of the *Iliad* and the *Odyssey*.
12. The father of medicine.
13. He crossed the Alps with elephants.
14. Painter of the Sistine Chapel ceiling.
15. Greek mathematician who compiled the geometrical data of his time.
16. His discoveries ended the influence of Aristotle and Ptolemy on astronomy.
17. Creator of the modern Yugoslav state.
18. Singer during 1950s and 60s with backup group The Belmonts.
19. Greek philosopher who founded a school named the Lyceum.
20. Sultan of Egypt and Syria who negotiated a peace with the Crusaders.

11. Homer
12. Hippocrates
13. Hannibal
14. Michelangelo
15. Euclid
16. Galileo
17. Tito
18. Dion
19. Aristotle
20. Saladin

Ph. D. Level

21. Persian religious reformer and founder of Parsiism.
22. The first president of Indonesia.
23. Author of the *Aeneid*.
24. Actress, films include *Lost Horizon* (1937), wife of Eddie Albert.
25. Greek poet, founder of tragic drama.
26. Babylonian ruler known for his set of laws.
27. Scottish singer of the 1960s, songs include "Mellow Yellow."
28. He searched with a lantern for an honest man.
29. The famous lover of Pierre Abelard.
30. This Greek philosopher's work was in the form of dialogues and epistles.

21. Zoroaster
22. Sukarno
23. Vergil
24. Margo
25. Thespis
26. Hammurabi
27. Donovan
28. Diogenes
29. Héloise
30. Plato

SURNAMES PLEASE

Although there are many possible answers, there is an excellent chance that you will know the correct name.

Freshman Level

1. Elvis———
2. Adolf———
3. Humphrey———
4. Winston———
5. Marilyn———
6. Sigmund———
7. Oral———
8. Charlie———
9. Abraham———
10. Napoleon———

1. Presley
2. Hitler
3. Bogart
4. Churchill
5. Monroe
6. Freud
7. Roberts
8. Chaplin
9. Lincoln
10. Bonaparte

Graduate Level

11. Christopher———
12. Frank———
13. George———
14. Horatio———
15. Dwight———
16. Walt———
17. Albert———
18. Amelia———
19. Clint———
20. Telly———

11. Columbus
12. Sinatra
13. Washington
14. Nelson
15. Eisenhower
16. Disney
17. Einstein
18. Earhart
19. Eastwood
20. Savalas

Ph. D. Level

21. Sissy———
22. Zero———
23. Goldie———
24. Yasir———
25. Mia———
26. Wyatt———
27. Eartha———
28. Yuri———
29. Joel———
30. Lena———

21. Spacek
22. Mostel
23. Hawn
24. Arafat
25. Farrow
26. Earp
27. Kitt
28. Gagarin
29. Grey
30. Horne

MIDDLE NAMES
All the people listed are better known by their middle name. Provide it.

Freshman Level

1. Michael Stallone	(actor)	1. Sylvester
2. Terrence McQueen	(actor)	2. Steve (Stephen)
3. William Gable	(actor)	3. Clark
4. George Newhart	(comedian)	4. Bob (Robert)
5. Marvin Simon	(playwright)	5. Neil
6. George Welles	(actor, director)	6. Orson
7. Margaret Pauley	(newscaster)	7. Jane
8. James Niven	(actor)	8. David
9. Olive Osmond	(singer)	9. Marie
10. Henry Beatty	(actor, director)	10. Warren Beatty

Graduate Level

11. Mary Fawcett	(actress)	11. Farrah
12. Charles Redford	(actor)	12. Robert
13. Eldred Peck	(actor)	13. Gregory
14. Arnold Sevareid	(newscaster)	14. Eric
15. Ernestine Russell	(actress)	15. Jane
16. Patrick O'Neal	(actor)	16. Ryan
17. Thomas Wilson	(U.S. president)	17. Woodrow
18. Stephen Cleveland	(U.S. president)	18. Grover
19. Eleanor Carter	(U.S. first lady)	19. Rosalynn
20. Alfred Runyon	(writer)	20. Damon

Ph. D. Level

21. William Crawford	(actor)	21. Broderick
22. Herbert McLuhan	(educator, writer)	22. Marshall
23. Alfred Cooke	(journalist)	23. Alistair
24. Harold Crane	(U.S. poet)	24. Hart
25. Francis Harte	(U.S. writer)	25. Bret (Brett)
26. Robert Shriver	(attorney)	26. Sargent
27. David Peckinpah	(director)	27. Sam (Samuel)
28. William Rains	(actor)	28. Claude
29. Lynn Ryan	(pitcher)	29. Nolan
30. Arthur Chamberlain	(prime minister)	30. Neville

ENTERTAINERS

For each pair provide the last name which is the same as the first name—e.g.,
Jack———,———Hill. *Answer*: Benny

Freshman Level

1. James———,———Granger
2. James———,———Martin
3. Kirk———,———Fairbanks
4. Minnie———,———Bailey
5. Charlie———,———Little
6. Loretta———,———Redgrave
7. Peggy———,———Remick
8. Elton———,———Wayne
9. George———,———Ford
10. Cass———,——— Gould

1. Stewart
2. Dean
3. Douglas
4. Pearl
5. Rich
6. Lynn
7. Lee
8. John
9. Harrison
10. Elliott

Graduate Level

11. Bob———,———Lange
12. Edward———,——— Schwarzenegger
13. Ray———,———Boyer
14. John———,———Newton
15. Randolph———,———Baio
16. Ron———,———Duff
17. Julie———,——— Brinkley
18. Margaret———,———Wagner
19. Dean———,———Balsam
20. Sandy———,———Morgan

11. Hope
12. Arnold
13. Charles
14. Wayne
15. Scott
16. Howard
17. Christie
18. Lindsay
19. Martin
20. Dennis

Ph. D. Level

21. Harold———,———Bridges
22. Eddie———,———Brooks
23. Beatrice ———,———Treacher
24. Gene———,———Nelson
25. Robert———,———O'Neal
26. Claire———,———Howard
27. Laurence———,———Korman
28. Amanda———,———Edwards
29. Nancy———,———Baker
30. Ruth———,———MacRae

21. Lloyd
22. Albert
23. Arthur
24. Barry
25. Ryan
26. Trevor
27. Harvey
28. Blake
29. Carroll
30. Gordon

NATURAL PEOPLE

Provide the name. Each name consists of a natural object. (No repeat answers.)

Freshman Level

1.	Actor	———Hudson	1. Rock
2.	Actress	Veronica———	2. Lake
3.	Actress	Natalie———	3. Wood
4.	Comedienne	Joan———	4. Rivers
5.	Singer	Dinah———	5. Shore
6.	Film critic	Rex———	6. Reed
7.	Filmmaker, comedian	Mel———	7. Brooks
8.	Country singer	Hank———	8. Snow
9.	Rock musician	Sly———	9. Stone
10.	Pioneer automobile manufacturer	Henry———	10. Ford

Graduate Level

11.	Baseball player	Pete———	11. Rose
12.	English TV personality	David———	12. Frost
13.	Miss America pageant host	Bert———	13. Parks
14.	TV's Alice Kramden	Audrey———	14. Meadows
15.	Actor, director	———Robertson	15. Cliff
16.	Politician	George———	16. Bush
17.	Actor	Raymond———	17. Burr
18.	Actress	Sally———	18. Field
19.	Singer, commedienne	Minnie———	19. Pearl
20.	Actress, singer	Ethel———	20. Waters

Ph. D. Level

21.	Singer	Jerry———	21. Vale
22.	Actor	Claude———	22. Rains
23.	Baseball executive	———Rickey	23. Branch
24.	Singer	Dan———	24. Hill
25.	French novelist	George———	25. Sand
26.	Singer, songwriter	Chuck———	26. Berry
27.	Tennis player	Alice———	27. Marble
28.	Murderer	Jack———	28. Ruby
29.	Singer	Neil———	29. Diamond
30.	Physicist	James———	30. Rainwater

WHOSE IS IT?

Provide the owner—e.g., Ark. *Answer*: Noah's.

Freshman Level

1. Travels
2. Box
3. Ride
4. Mother
5. Cabin
6. Revenge
7. Farm
8. Comet
9. Fables
10. Apple

1. Gulliver's
2. Pandora's
3. Paul Revere's
4. Whistler's
5. Uncle Tom's
6. Montezuma's
7. Old MacDonald's
8. Halley's
9. Aesop's
10. Adam's

Graduate Level

11. Rainbow
12. Heel
13. Last Stand
14. Ferry
15. Peak
16. Mines
17. Island
18. Wake
19. Choice
20. Follies

11. Finian's
12. Achilles'
13. Custer's
14. Harper's
15. Pike's
16. King Solomon's
17. Gilligan's
18. Finnegan's
19. Hobson's
20. Ziegfeld's

Ph. D. Level

21. Fire
22. Dance
23. Choice
24. Bay
25. Bad Boy
26. Chowder
27. Vineyard
28. *Complaint*
29. Inferno
30. Thesaurus

21. St. Elmo's
22. St. Vitus'
23. Dealer's
24. Hudson's
25. Peck's
26. Mrs. Murphy's
27. Martha's
28. *Portnoy's*
29. Dante's
30. Roget's

CAPTAINS

Freshman Level

1. Captain of the pirate ship *Jolly Roger* in *Peter Pan*.
2. Commander of the starship *Enterprise*.
3. Secret identity of Billy Batson.
4. Police captain played by Hal Linden.
5. Famous Scottish pirate.
6. Captain of *HMS Bounty*.
7. Surgeon portrayed by Alan Alda on *MASH*.

8. Bad guy in McDonald commercials.
9. His life was saved by Pocahontas.
10. Their No. 1 hit was *Love Will Keep Us Together.*"

1. Captain Hook
2. Captain James T. Kirk
3. Captain Marvel
4. Captain Barney Miller
5. Captain Kidd
6. Captain William Bligh
7. Captain "Hawkeye" Pierce
8. Captain Crook
9. Captain John Smith
10. Captain and Tennille

Graduate Level

11. Pirate captain who buried the treasure on *Treasure Island*.
12. Regan MacNeil's imaginary playmate in *The Exorcist*.
13. Captain of the submarine *Nautilus*.
14. Captain of the *Caine* in *The Caine Mutiny*.
15. English explorer and navigator (1728–79).
16. Nickname of Wyatt (Peter Fonda) in the film *Easy Rider*.
17. Captain played by Claude Rains in *Casablanca*.

18. Title of a novel by Rudyard Kipling (1897).
19. Errol Flynn's role in 1935 film of the same name.
20. Captain of the *Pequod* in *Moby Dick*.

11. Captain Flint
12. Captain Howdy
13. Captain Nemo
14. Captain Queeg
15. Captain James Cook
16. Captain America
17. Captain (Louis) Renaud
18. *Captains Courageous*
19. Captain Blood
20. Captain Ahab

Ph. D. Level

21. Captain portrayed by Richard Chamberlain in the TV series *Shogun*.
22. Captain of *The Flying Dutchman*.
23. Captain and owner of the *Cotton Blossom* in *Show Boat*.
24. Puppet on the *Kukla, Fran, and Ollie* TV show.
25. Secret identity of Victor (Dom De Luise) in *Cannonball Run*.
26. Comic strip character in cartoon *Wash Tubbs*.
27. Captain of the *Titanic* when she hit an iceberg.
28. Captain of the *Ghost* in *The Sea Wolf*.
29. Christopher Plummer's role in *The Sound of Music*.
30. Title of an Elton John album.

21. Captain John Blackmore
22. Captain Van Straaten
23. Captain Andy (Hawks)
24. Captain Crackie
25. Captain Chaos
26. Captain Easy
27. Captain Edward Smith
28. Captain Wolf Larsen
29. Captain von Trapp
30. "Captain Fantastic"

MAJORS, COLONELS, AND GENERALS

Not all answers are people.

Freshman Level

1. Founder of Kentucky Fried Chicken
2. One of the big three U.S. car manufacturers.
3. Officer in charge of prisoners in Stalag 13 on television.
4. MASH surgeon who had an affair with Margaret Houlihan.
5. Name of a television soap opera.
6. A play by George Bernard Shaw.
7. The Six Million Dollar Man.
8. Commanding officer of the MASH unit played by Harry Morgan.

9. George C. Scott won an Oscar portraying this person.

10. True title of the march whistled in *Bridge over the River Kwai.*

1. Colonel Sanders
2. General Motors
3. Colonel Hogan
4. Major (Frank) Burns
5. *General Hospital*
6. *Major Barbara*
7. Colonel (Steve) Austin
8. Colonel (Sherman) Potter
9. General (George) Patton
10. Colonel Bogey

Graduate Level

11. A 1965 movie starring Charlton Heston.
12. Secret agent played by Robert Conrad in *Wild, Wild West.*
13. Giant sequoia said to be largest living thing.
14. Nickname of 36-inch-tall Charles S. Stratton.
15. Main character of comic strip *Our Boarding House.*
16. Who was the first U.S. General of the Army?

17. Nickname of Napoleon Bonaparte.
18. Name of the red Dodge Charger in *The Dukes of Hazard.*
19. American Civil War officer killed at the battle of Little Big Horn.

20. Superman's enemy in the 1981 film *Superman.*

11. *Major Dundee*
12. Major (James T.) West
13. General Sherman
14. General Tom Thumb
15. Major (Amos) Hoople
16. General Ulysses S. Grant
17. Little Corporal
18. General Lee
19. Colonel (George) Custer
20. General Zod

Ph. D. Level

21. Renegade Green Beret colonel played by Marlon Brando in *Apocalypse Now.*
22. Camp commander in Beetle Bailey comics.

23. Title of a 1942 movie starring Ginger Rogers and Ray Milland.

24. He became the president of Pakistan.
25. Professor Henry Higgin's friend in *My Fair Lady.*

26. Post commander under whom Sergeant Bilko served.
27. Argentine cruiser sunk by British submarine in 1982.
28. Wagonmaster in TV series *Wagon Train*, played by Ward Bond.
29. Name three of the U.S. five-star generals of W.W. II.

30. A famous Confederate locomotive engine.

21. Colonel Kurtz
22. General (Ames T.) Halftrack
23. *The Major and the Minor*
24. General Zia
25. Colonel (Hugh) Pickering
26. Colonel (John T.) Hall
27. General Belgrano
28. Major Seth Adams
29. Arnold, Bradley, Eisenhower, MacArthur, Marshall
30. The General

ADVERSARIES
Name the adversary of the given fictional character.

Freshman Level

1. Lex Luthor	1. Superman
2. Dr. No	2. James Bond
3. Wile E. Coyote	3. Roadrunner
4. Elmer Fudd	4. Bugs Bunny
5. Snidely Whiplash	5. Dudley Do-Right
6. Captain Hook	6. Peter Pan
7. Darth Vader	7. Luke Skywalker
8. The Penguin	8. Batman
9. The Wicked Witch of the East	9. Dorothy
10. Brutus (Bluto)	10. Popeye

Graduate Level

11. Ming the Merciless	11. Flash Gordon
12. Flattop	12. Dick Tracy
13. Sheriff of Nottingham	13. Robin Hood
14. Wo Fat	14. Detective Steve McGarrett
15. Rattop	15. Fearless Fosdick
16. Sylvester Cat	16. Tweety Pie
17. Dr. Silvana	17. Captain Marvel
18. Professor Moriarty	18. Sherlock Holmes
19. The Harlequin	19. The Green Lantern
20. Boris Badenov	20. Rocky and Bullwinkle

Ph. D. Level

21. Captain Esteban Pasquale	21. Zorro
22. Oil Can Harry	22. Mighty Mouse
23. The King of Zing	23. Plastic Man
24. Doctor Octopus	24. Spiderman
25. Doctor Pauli	25. Captain Video
26. The Red Skull	26. Captain America
27. Killer Kane	27. Buck Rogers
28. Mordred	28. King Arthur
29. Butch Cavendish	29. The Long Ranger
30. Lieutenant Philip Gerard	30. Richard Kimble (The Fugitive)

HOME SWEET HOME

Given the address and a clue, identify the resident (TV, radio, and film characters).

Freshman Level

1. 39 Stone Canyon Way — Bedrock — *The Flintstones*
2. 14 Maple Street — Mayberry, NC — Andy Taylor, (*Andy Griffith Show*)
3. 328 Chauncey Street — Bensonhurst, Brooklyn — The Kramdens (*The Honeymooners*)
4. 221B Baker Street — London — Sherlock Holmes
5. 39 Crenshaw Street — Tuckahoe, NY — Maude
6. 79 Wistful Vista — Radio show — Fibber McGee and Molly
7. 704 Hauser Street — Queens, NY — Archie Bunker
8. 211 Pine Avenue — Mayfield — Cleavers (*Leave It to Beaver*)
9. 1619 Pine Street — Boulder, CO — Mork and Mindy
10. 607 Maple Street — Springfield — Andersons (*Father Knows Best*)

Graduate Level

11. 518 Crestview Drive — Beverly Hills — Clampetts (*Beverly Hillbillies*)
12. 119 North Weatherly Street — Minneapolis — Mary Richards (M.T.M. Show)
13. 17 Cherry Tree Lane — London — Bankses (*Mary Poppins*)
14. 1049 Park Avenue — Apt. 1102 — Felix and Oscar (*The Odd Couple*)
15. 51 West 57th Street — Apt. 2A — Mr. Baxter (Lemmon) *The Apartment*)
16. 505 East 50th Street, N.Y. — Apt. 781 — Williamses (*Danny Thomas Show*)
17. 730 Hampton Street — Apt. A (Milwaukee) — Laverne and Shirley
18. 698 Sycamore Road — San Pueblo, CA — Partridge Family
19. 1436 Oak Street — Sacramento, CA — Bradfords (*Eight Is Enough*)
20. 1164 Morning Glory Circle — Westport CT — Samantha Stevens (*Bewitched*)

Ph. D. Level

21. 3100 Willow Road — Los Angeles — The Harts (*Hart to Hart*)
22. 632 Elysian Fields — New Orleans — Stanley and Blanche (*A Streetcar Named Desire*)
23. 9114 South Central — Los Angeles — Fred Sanford (*Sanford and Son*)
24. 3600 Prospect Street — a brick townhouse — Regan MacNeil (*The Exorcist*)
25. 1200 Glenview Road — Los Angeles — Robinsons (*The Graduate*)
26. 27A Wimpole Street — London — Professor Higgins (*My Fair Lady*)
27. 627 Elm Street — Hillsdale, CA — Mitchells (*Dennis the Menace*)
28. 123 Marshall Road — Hydsberg, NY — Baxters (*Hazel*)
29. 148 Bonnie Meadow Road — New Rochelle, NY — Petries (*Dick Van Dyke Show*)
30. 4802 Fifth Avenue — Children's show — Fred Rogers (*Mr. Rogers' Neighborhood*).

IDENTITY CRISIS
Identify each of the given names.

Freshman Level

1. Jack Ruby
2. Lynette Alice Fromme
3. Sally Ride
4. Arthur Murray
5. Xavier Hollander
6. Clyde Beatty
7. Norma Jean Baker
8. Mary Jo Kopechne

9. Pat Garrett
10. Gary Gilmore

1. Killed Lee Harvey Oswald (1963).
2. Attempted to assassinate President Ford (1975).
3. First American woman in space.
4. Originated the Arthur Murray School of Dancing.
5. The Happy Hooker.
6. World-famous circus animal tamer.
7. Real name of Marilyn Monroe.
8. Killed when Edward Kennedy's car ran off bridge at Chappaquiddick (1969).
9. Sheriff who shot and killed Billy the Kid (1881).
10. First to be executed in the U.S. in ten years (1977).

Graduate Level

11. Karen Quinlan

12. Richard Speck
13. Christine Keeler

14. Graham Kerr
15. John Merrick
16. Melvin Dummar

17. John Birch

18. Jimmy Boyd

19. Rasputin
20. James Meredith

11. Her life-support system was cut off but she did not immediately die.
12. Killed eight women in an apartment in 1966.
13. Her affair with British minister of war John Profumo caused a scandal (1963).
14. Cooking expert known as the Galloping Gourmet.
15. Deformed person known as the Elephant Man.
16. Gas station attendant who claimed Howard Hughes had willed part of his estate to him.
17. Considered to be the first American killed by the Communists after W.W. II.
18. Twelve-year old whose record I Saw Mommy Kissing Santa Claus" sold over 2 million copies (1952).
19. Russian monk notorious for his debauchery (1873–1916).
20. First black to attend the University of Mississippi (1961).

Ph. D. Level

21. Edith Cavell
22. Susan B. Anthony
23. Eddie Slovik
24. Louise Joy Brown
25. Bob Keeshan
26. Peter Hurkos

27. Ron Galella
28. Don Dunphy
29. Eddie Feigner

30. Albert De Salvo

21. British nurse in WW I who helped soldiers escape to Holland.
22. Early leader of woman's suffrage movement in U.S.
23. Only U.S. soldier executed for desertion in WW II.
24. World's first test tube baby (1978).
25. Played Clarabell the clown and Captain Kangaroo.
26. Psychic who assisted police departments to solve different crimes.
27. Photographer who hounded Jacqueline Kennedy Onassis.
28. Fight announcer during 1940s and 50s.
29. Softball pitcher with a three man team billed as the King and His Court.
30. The Boston Strangler.

INITIAL WARNINGS

Name the person from the given clue. The initials of the clue are also the initials of the answer—e.g., Proclaiming *Rider*. *Answer* Paul Revere.

Freshman Level

1. Clothing Designer
2. American Cartoonist
3. Munich Swimmer
4. Fantastic Pugilist
5. Baby Specialist
6. Skating Heroine
7. Classic Comedian
8. Great Catcher
9. Baseball Manager
10. Famous Singer

1. Christian Dior
2. Al Capp
3. Mark Spitz
4. Floyd Patterson
5. Benjamin Spock
6. Sonja Henie
7. Charlie Chaplin
8. Gary Carter
9. Billy Martin
10. Frank Sinatra

Graduate Level

11. Cardplaying Genius
12. Premier Figureskater
13. Lyric Performer
14. Lucky Explorer
15. Fourteenth President
16. Union General
17. Foreign Filmmaker
18. Super Pitcher
19. Famous Fascist
20. Running Britisher

11. Charles Goren
12. Peggy Fleming
13. Luciano Pavarotti
14. Leif Ericson
15. Franklin Pierce
16. Ulysses Grant
17. Federico Fellini
18. Satchel Paige
19. Francisco Franco
20. Roger Bannister

Ph. D. Level

21. American Composer
22. Innovative Dancer
23. Afflicted Poet
24. Rock Star
25. Master Barrister
26. Leading Industrialist
27. Hitler's Henchman
28. Boston Baseman
29. Cartoonist Supreme
30. Courageous Captain

21. Aaron Copland
22. Isadora Duncan
23. Alexander Pope
24. Rod Stewart
25. Melvin Belli
26. Lee Iacocca
27. Heinrich Himmler
28. Bill Buckner
29. Charles Schulz
30. Christopher Columbus

POSTAL CODE INITIALS

The new two-letter postal code of the given state matches the initials of the person in the answer. A clue is provided—e.g., Alabama: syndicated advice columnist. *Answer:* Ann Landers.

Freshman Level

1. Alabama:	*People Are Funny*	1. Art Linkletter
2. Alaska:	Expert on sex	2. Alfred Kinsey
3. Colorado:	Archie Bunker	3. Carroll O'Connor
4. Delaware:	Roy Rogers	4. Dale Evans
5. Florida:	"Mule Train"	5. Frankie Laine
6. Georgia:	The singing cowboy	6. Gene Autry
7. Kansas:	"God Bless America"	7. Kate Smith
8. Minnesota:	Woman tennis champion	8. Martina Navratilova
9. North Carolina:	Hit songs include "Nature Boy"	9. Nat "King" Cole
10. North Dakota:	Hit songs include "Sweet Caroline"	10. Neil Diamond

Graduate Level

11. South Dakota:	Spanish surrealist painter	11. Salvador Dali
12. Montana:	Samuel Langhorne Clemens	12. Mark Twain
13. Nebraska:	He sang with Jeanette Macdonald	13. Nelson Eddy
14. New Mexico:	Famous U.S. postwar writer	14. Norman Mailer
15. Iowa:	Prolific author of fiction and non-fiction	15. Isaac Asimov
16. Maryland:	German-U.S. actor-singer	16. Marlene Dietrich
17. Ohio:	With Stan Laurel	17. Oliver Hardy
18. South Carolina:	Runner, set three world records in 1979	18. Sebastian Coe
19. Illinois:	One-time wife of Howard Duff	19. Ida Lupino
20. Oregon:	U.S. evangelist	20. Oral Roberts

Ph. D. Level

21. Vermont:	First woman in space	21. Valentina Tereshkova
22. Arizona:	Chairman emeritus of Famous Players/Paramount, 1935–76	22. Adolph Zukor
23. Arkansas:	*The Fountainhead*	23. Ayn Rand
24. California:	English prime minister, 1945– 52	24. Clement Atlee
25. Connecticut:	Country and western performer-composer	25. Conway Twitty
26. Hawaii:	First English actor ever knighted	26. Henry Irving
27. Louisiana:	Satchmo	27. Louis Armstrong
28. Massachusetts:	He defeated Brutus and Cassius	28. Marc Antony
29. Missouri:	Sister of Donny	29. Marie Osmond
30. Oklahoma:	Popular Soviet gymnast	30. Olga Korbut

DUST TO DUST
What caused the premature death?

Freshman Level

1. James Dean	(1931–1955)	1. Auto crash
2. Sal Mineo	(1939–1976)	2. Stabbed to death
3. Grace Kelly	(1929–1982)	3. Auto crash
4. John Belushi	(1949–1982)	4. Overdosed
5. John Lennon	(1940–1980)	5. Murder
6. Natalie Wood	(1938–1981)	6. Drowned accidentally
7. Janis Joplin	(1943–1970)	7. Overdosed
8. T. E. Lawrence	(1888–1935)	8. Motorbike crash
9. Rock Hudson	(1925–1987)	9. AIDS
10. Karen Silkwood	(1952–1974)	10. Car accident (or murder)

Graduate Level

11. Ernie Kovacs	(1919–1962)	11. Car crash
12. Marvin Gaye	(1939–1984)	12. Shot to death by his father
13. Sam Cooke	(1935–1964)	13. Shot to death (justifiable homicide)
14. Charles Boyer	(1899–1978)	14. Shot himself
15. Rudolph Valentino	(1895–1926)	15. Peritonitis (caused by bleeding ulcer)
16. Buddy Holly	(1936–1959)	16. Airplane crash
17. Jimi Hendrix	(1942–1970)	17. Overdosed
18. Harry Houdini	(1874–1926)	18. Advanced case of appendicitis
19. Russ Columbo	(1907–1933)	19. Accidentally shot with old dueling pistol
20. Inger Stevens	(1934–1970)	20. Overdosed

Ph. D. Level

21. Jack Cassidy	(1927–1976)	21. Burned to death in house fire
22. Lord Byron	(1788–1824)	22. Malarial fever
23. Jim Morrisson	(1943–1971)	23. Heart attack
24. Carl "Alfalfa" Switzer	(1926–1959)	24. Shot to death (justifiable homicide)
25. John Keats	(1795–1821)	25. Tuberculosis
26. Jean Harlow	(1911–1937)	26. Kidney failure (inflamed gall bladder)
27. George Reeves	(1914–1959)	27. Suicide by shooting indicated
28. Isadore Duncan	(1878–1927)	28. Broken neck (scarf caught in car wheel)
29. Percy Shelley	(1792–1822)	29. Drowned when boat capsized
30. Margaret Mitchell	(1900–1949)	30. Hit-and-run accident

NOTORIOUS PEOPLE

Freshman: Name the person.

1. He assassinated President Lincoln.
2. He assassinated President Kennedy.
3. He assassinated Robert Kennedy.
4. He attempted to assassinate President Reagan in 1981.
5. He led members of the People's Temple to commit suicide (1979).
6. Outlaw who executed daring bank and train robberies from 1866.
7. She joined the symbionese Liberation Army in 1974.
8. She married Hitler.
9. American abolitionist who captured Harpers Ferry October 16, 1859.
10. Attempted to blow up the English Parliament building (1604).

1. John Wilkes Booth
2. Lee Harvey Oswald
3. Sirhan Sirhan Bishara
4. John Hinckley
5. James Warren Jones
6. Jesse James
7. Patricia Hearst
8. Eva Braun
9. John Brown
10. Guy Fawkes

Graduate Level: Name the person.

11. Shot and killed Martin Luther King, Jr.
12. Traitor who tried to surrender West Point to the British (1780).
13. The first U.S. citizen to be executed for espionage (1953).
14. Convicted of murder at My Lai massacre.
15. The first Grand Wizard of the Ku Klux Klan.
16. He shot his attackers on the New York subway.
17. Nazi doctor called the Angel of Death.
18. Convicted of kidnapping and killing of Lindbergh's son.
19. This Englishman was the self-proclaimed "worst man in the world."
20. U.S. bank robber with "Pretty Boy" Floyd and "Baby Face" Nelson.

11. James Earl Ray
12. Benedict Arnold
13. Julius Rosenberg
14. Lieutenant William Calley
15. Nathan Bedford Forrest
16. Bernard Goetz
17. Josef Mengele
18. Bruno Hauptmann
19. Aleister Crowley
20. John Dillinger

Ph. D. Level: Give the reason for the notoriety.

21. Gavrilo Princip. (1914)
22. Nat Turner (1831)
23. Sara Jane Moore (1975)
24. Mary Mallon (1905–1915)
25. Leon Czolgosz (1901)
26. Mehmet Ali Agca (1981)
27. Nathan Leopold (1924)
28. Charles Whitman (1966)
29. Wayne Williams (1981)
30. Peter Sutcliffe (1975–81)

21. Assassinated Archduke Francis Ferdinand.
22. Led the only widespread slave revolt in U.S. history.
23. Attempted to assassinate President Ford.
24. "Typhoid Mary"—knowingly spread her illness.
25. Fatally wounded President William McKinley.
26. Shot and wounded Pope John Paul II.
27. In the Crime of the Century he murdered a fourteen-year old.
28. Shot and killed sixteen from tower at University of Texas.
29. Guilty in the "murdered children of Atlanta" case.
30. The Yorkshire Ripper—thirteen women murdered.

ADOLF HITLER

Freshman Level

1. In what country was he born?
2. What was his ambition as a young man?
3. He won this prestigious medal during WWI
4. In 1923 Hitler led a revolt now known as the———.

5. During imprisonment he wrote this book.
6. What is the translation of the title?
7. Who took dictation for him while in prison?
8. In his book he wanted *Lebensraum* for the German people. What is it?
9. What did he name his new party?

10. By what name were its members known?

1. Austria
2. To be an artist
3. Iron Cross
4. Munich Beer Hall Putsch
5. *Mein Kampf*
6. My struggle
7. Rudolf Hess
8. Living space
9. National Socialist German Workers' Party
10. Nazis

Graduate Level

11. What emblem did Hitler adopt?
12. He set up a private army of elite guards, the *Schutzstaffel* known as the———.
13. Who was the chief Nazi propagandist?
14. Who became the party's chief executioner?
15. This woman was Hitler's mistress.
16. By what name did Hitler refer to his government?

17. Hitler's secret police were called the———.
18. What title did Hitler give himself?
19. His airforce was known by this name.
20. Who commanded the air force?

11. The swastika
12. SS or Blackshirts
13. Joseph Goebbels
14. Heinrich Himmler
15. Eva Braun
16. The Third Reich (Empire)
17. Gestapo
18. *Führer* (leader)
19. *Luftwaffe* (Air Weapon)
20. Herman Goering

Ph. D. Level

21. The German parliament building was burned in 1933. What was it called?
22. Today the "Final Solution of the Jewish Question" goes by this name.
23. Hitler's lightninglike military attacks were called———.
24. He undertook construction of a network of superhighways called———.
25. Whom did he replace as leader of the government?
26. Hitler and Chamberlain signed this agreement in 1938.
27. Britain and France declared war on Germany when Hitler attacked this country in 1939.
28. Germany's defeat here reversed Hitler's advance to the east.
29. This man refused to carry out Hitler's order to institute a scorched-earth policy in Germany.
30. Whom did Hitler appoint as his successor prior to his death?

21. The *Reichstag*
22. The Holocaust
23. *Blitzkrieg* (Lightning War)
24. *Autobahnen*
25. Paul von Hindenburg
26. Munich Pact
27. Poland
28. Stalingrad (now Volgograd)
29. Albert Speer
30. Admiral Karl Doenitz

PRESIDENTS AND FIRST LADIES: Nicknames

Freshman Level: Presidents.

1. Ike	1. Dwight D. Eisenhower
2. Tricky Dickie	2. Richard M. Nixon
3. Dutch	3. Ronald Reagan
4. Old Hickory	4. Andrew Jackson
5. Rough Rider	5. Theodore Roosevelt
6. Silent Cal	6. Calvin Coolidge
7. The Peace President	7. Woodrow Wilson
8. Old Rough and Ready	8. Zachary Taylor
9. Father of His Country	9. George Washington
10. Old Tippecanoe	10. William Henry Harrison

Graduate Level: Presidents.

11. Illinois Baboon	11. Abraham Lincoln
12. The Beast of Buffalo	12. Grover Cleveland
13. That Man in the White House	13. Franklin Roosevelt
14. Man of Independence	14. Harry Truman
15. His Rotundity	15. John Adams
16. Little Magician	16. Martin Van Buren
17. Jemmy	17. James Madison
18. Old Veto	18. John Tyler
19. Handsome Frank	19. Franklin Pierce
20. Long Tom	20. Thomas Jefferson

Ph. D. Level: First Ladies.

21. Lady Bird	21. Claudia Johnson
22. Lemonade Lucy	22. Lucy Hayes
23. Dolley	23. Dorothy Madison
24. Pat	24. Thelma Nixon
25. The Duchess	25. Florence Harding
26. Mrs. President	26. Abigail Adams
27. Public Enemy Number One	27. Eleanor Roosevelt
28. Jackie	28. Jacqueline Kennedy
29. Mamie	29. Marie Eisenhower
30. The Last Lady of the Land	30. Bess Truman

ELECTED PRESIDENTS
Name the elected presidents in reverse order. The year (s) of election is given.

Freshman Level

1. 1988
2. 1980 and 1984
3. 1976
4. 1968 and 1972
5. 1964
6. 1960
7. 1952 and 1956
8. 1948
9. 1932, 1936, 1940, 1944
10. 1928

1.
2. Ronald Reagan
3. Jimmy Carter
4. Richard Nixon
5. Lyndon Johnson
6. John Kennedy
7. Dwight Eisenhower
8. Harry Truman
9. Franklin D. Roosevelt
10. Herbert Hoover

Graduate Level

11. 1924
12. 1920
13. 1912 and 1916
14. 1908
15. 1904
16. 1896 and 1900
17. 1892
18. 1888
19. 1884
20. 1880

11. Calvin Coolidge
12. Warren Harding
13. Woodrow Wilson
14. William Taft
15. Theodore Roosevelt
16. William McKinley
17. Grover Cleveland
18. Benjamin Harrison
19. Grover Cleveland
20. James Garfield

Ph. D. Level

21. 1876
22. 1868 and 1872
23. 1860 and 1864
24. 1856
25. 1852
26. 1848
27. 1844
28. 1840
29. 1836
30. 1828 and 1832

21. Rutherford Hayes
22. Ulysses Grant
23. Abraham Lincoln
24. James Buchanan
25. Franklin Pierce
26. Zachary Taylor
27. James Polk
28. William Harrison
29. Martin Van Buren
30. Andrew Jackson

PRESIDENTIAL RUNNER-UPS

The year(s) and winner are provided. Name the runner up. (Give the initials as a hint if needed.)

Freshman Level

1.	1988		1.
2.	1984	Ronald Reagan	2. Walter Mondale
3.	1980	Ronald Reagan	3. Jimmy Carter
4.	1976	Jimmy Carter	4. Gerald Ford
5.	1972	Richard Nixon	5. George McGovern
6.	1968	Richard Nixon	6. Hubert Humphrey
7.	1964	Lyndon Johnson	7. Barry Goldwater
8.	1960	John Kennedy	8. Richard Nixon
9.	1952–1956	Dwight Eisenhower	9. Adlai Stevenson
10.	1948	Harry Truman	10. Thomas Dewey

Graduate Level

11.	1944	F. D. Roosevelt	11. Thomas Dewey
12.	1940	F. D. Roosevelt	12. Wendell Wilkie
13.	1936	F. D. Roosevelt	13. Alfred Landon
14.	1932	F. D. Roosevelt	14. Herbert Hoover
15.	1912	Woodrow Wilson	15. Theodore Roosevelt and William Taft
16.	1908	William Taft	16. William J. Bryan
17.	1896–1900	William McKinley	17. William J. Bryan
18.	1892	Grover Cleveland	18. Benjamin Harrison
19.	1888	Benjamin Harrison	19. Grover Cleveland
20.	1884	Grover Cleveland	20. James Blaine

Ph. D. Level

21.	1860	Abraham Lincoln	21. Stephen A. Douglas
22.	1844	James K. Polk	22. Henry Clay
23.	1836–1840	Martin Van Buren	23. William H. Harrison
24.	1832	Andrew Jackson	24. Henry Clay
25.	1828	Andrew Jackson	25. John Quincy Adams
26.	1824	John Quincy Adams	26. Andrew Jackson
27.	1820	James Monroe	27. John Quincy Adams
28.	1800	Thomas Jefferson	28. Aaron Burr
29.	1796	John Adams	29. Thomas Jefferson
30.	1789–1792	George Washington	30. John Adams

PRESIDENTIAL FIRSTS, U.S.A.

Freshman Level

1. First elected under the Constitution.	1. G. Washington
2. First to be assassinated.	2. A. Lincoln
3. First who was a Catholic.	3. J. Kennedy
4. First whose son became president.	4. John Adams
5. First to resign while in office.	5. R. Nixon
6. First to have been divorced.	6. R. Reagan
7. First elected for a fourth term.	7. F. D. Roosevelt
8. First whose assassination was attempted.	8. A. Jackson
9. First elected for two nonconsecutive terms.	9. G. Cleveland
10. First to reside in the White House.	10. John Adams

Graduate Level

11. First born beyond the boundaries of the original thirteen states.	11. A. Lincoln
12. First to be married in the White House.	12. G. Cleveland
13. First whose grandson became president.	13. W. H. Harrison
14. First to visit a European country while in office.	14. W. Wilson
15. First to fly in an airplane.	15. T. Roosevelt
16. First to fly in a helicopter.	16. D. Eisenhower
17. First to be seen on television.	17. F. D. Roosevelt
18. First to receive fewer popular and electoral votes than his opponent.	18. J. Q. Adams
19. First to use a telephone.	19. J. Garfield
20. First who was a bachelor.	20. J. Buchanan

Ph. D. Level

21. First to be born a citizen of the U.S.	21. M. Van Buren
22. First to be married while in office.	22. J. Tyler
23. First to pitch a ball to open the baseball season.	23. W. Taft.
24. First to be buried in the National Cemetery at Arlington, Va.	24. W. Taft.
25. First to be born on Independence Day.	25. C. Coolidge
26. First to ride on a railroad train.	26. A. Jackson
27. First to broadcast by radio.	27. W. Harding
28. First who was wholly a first-generation American because all of his forebears were foreign-born.	28. A. Jackson
29. First to call the President's House the White House.	29. T. Roosevelt
30. First to celebrate his silver wedding anniversary at the White House.	30. R. Hayes

LITTLE-KNOWN PRESIDENTIAL FACTS

Freshman Level

1. He invented the revolving chair and a pedometer.
2. The only president who was a published poet.
3. The first to have electricity in the White House.
4. He originated the phrase "lunatic fringe."
5. The only president to have worked as a male model.
6. He practiced his putting on the White House lawn.
7. He suffered from malaria, smallpox, pleurisy, and dysentery all before he was thirty.
8. After his son's death his wife persuaded him to participate in several séances in the White House.
9. His mother had been briefly interned in a Federal "camp" during the Civil War.
10. The only president to visit all fifty states while in office.

1. Thomas Jefferson
2. John Quincy Adams
3. Benjamin Harrison
4. Theodore Roosevelt
5. Gerald Ford
6. Dwight D. Eisenhower
7. George Washington
8. Abraham Lincoln
9. Harry S. Truman
10. Richard Nixon

Graduate Level

11. A special bathtub was installed to accommodate his bulk.
12. In addition to Greek and Latin he knew French, Italian, Spanish, and German.
13. He used to spar in the White House gym.
14. The only president to graduate from the Annapolis Naval Academy.
15. He held poker games twice a week.
16. The first left-handed president.
17. He brought Hercules his black slave to the capital to act as master chef.
18. His numerous colorful nicknames included "Petticoat Pet."
19. He produced the most grandchildren (forty-eight) and great grandchildren (one hundred-six).
20. The only president to obtain a patent.

11. William H. Taft
12. Thomas Jefferson
13. Theodore Roosevelt
14. Jimmy Carter
15. Warren G. Harding
16. James Garfield
17. George Washington
18. Martin Van Buren
19. William H. Harrison
20. Abraham Lincoln

Ph. D. Level

21. The first to be the subject of a serious impeachment attempt.
22. During most of his life he made his own clothes.
23. Most of his upper jaw was secretly removed when a cancerous growth was found.
24. He suffered his first nervous breakdown at age twenty-two.
25. His stinginess provoked the White House chef to quit.
26. Only president to face enemy gunfire while in office.
27. He swam in the buff in the Potomac every morning.
28. He destested the sight of blood; even in rare meat.
29. His favorite diversion was Sunday night hymn-singing.
30. At his death his stamp collection fetched more than $200,000.

21. John Tyler
22. Andrew Jackson
23. Grover Cleveland
24. Warren G. Harding
25. Calvin Coolidge
26. James Madison
27. John Quincy Adams
28. Ulysses S. Grant
29. Rutherford B. Hayes
30. F. D. Roosevelt

THE HALL OF FAME
For Great Americans, New York City

Freshman Level: Authors.

1. He wrote under the pen name "Mark Twain."

2. Author of *The Deerslayer.*

3. Philosopher, poet, essayist, whose poems include "The Problem."
4. Author of *The Scarlet Letter.*
5. Poet, essayist who named *The Atlantic Monthly.*
6. Author of "Rip Van Winkle."
7. Poet who wrote "The Village Blacksmith."

8. Political philosopher who wrote *Common Sense.*
9. His poems include "The Raven."
10. Author of *Uncle Tom's Cabin.*

1. Samuel Langhorne Clemens
2. James Fenimore Cooper
3. Ralph Waldo Emerson

4. Nathaniel Hawthorne
5. Olilver Wendell Holmes
6. Washington Irving
7. Henry Wadsworth Longfellow
8. Thomas Paine
9. Edgar Allan Poe
10. Harriet Beecher Stowe

Graduate Level: Inventors and Explorers.

11. First to patent and exploit the telephone.
12. Invented the electric light bulb.
13. First to develop a practical steamship.
14. Invented the first practical sewing machine.
15. Invented the first practical telegraph.
16. Invented the air brake.
17. Invented the cotton gin.
18. He is credited with flying the first heavier-than-air machine.
19. Admitted to the Hall of Fame in 1955, his brother in 1965.
20. The most famous frontiersman of colonial times.

11. Alexander Graham Bell
12. Thomas Alva Edison
13. Robert Fulton
14. Elias Howe
15. Samuel F. B. Morse
16. George Westinghouse
17. Eli Whitney
18. Orville Wright
19. Wilbur Wright
20. Daniel Boone

Ph. D. Level: Scientists.

21. Discovered the Ice Age.
22. Illustrated *The Birds of America.*
23. Worked out details of chemical thermodynamics and statistical mechanics.
24. Botanist, major contributor to knowledge of N.A. plants.
25. Physicist, invented electric relay, discovered self-induction.
26. His nickname is "Pathfinder of the Seas."

27. The first U.S. winner of the Nobel Prize in physics (1907).

28. Astronomer, known for her study of sunspots.
29. Astronomer, famous for his studies of the motion of heavenly bodies.
30. Revolutionized the uses for peanuts.

21. Louis Agassiz
22. John James Audubon
23. Josiah Willard Gibbs

24. Asa Gray
25. Joseph Henry
26. Matthew Fontaine Maury

27. Albert Abraham Michelson

28. Maria Mitchell
29. Simon Newcomb

30. George Washington Carver

THE SENATE
Name the state each senator represents (period of service is indicated).

Freshman Level

1.	1969–93	Robert J. Dole	1. Kansas
2.	1963–93	Daniel K. Inouye	2. Hawaii
3.	1962–89	Edward M. Kennedy	3. Massachusetts
4.	1985–91	Paul Simon	4. Illinois
5.	1973–91	Joseph R. Biden, Jr.	5. Delaware
6.	1985–91	Albert Gore, Jr.	6. Tennessee
7.	1977–89	Daniel P. Moynihan	7. New York
8.	1973–91	Jesse Helms	8. North Carolina
9.	1956–91	Strom Thurmond	9. South Carolina
10.	1957–89	William Proxmire	10. Wisconsin

Graduate Level

11.	1979–91	Gordon J. Humphrey	11. New Hampshire
12.	1976–93	John H. Glenn, Jr.	12. Ohio
13.	1971–91	John W. Warner	13. Virginia
14.	1979–91	Bill Bradley	14. New Jersey
15.	1971–89	Lawton Chiles	15. Florida
16.	1972–91	Sam Nunn	16. Georgia
17.	1977–89	John Heinz	17. Pennsylvania
18.	1979–91	Howard T. Heflin	18. Alabama
19.	1969–93	Alan Cranston	19. California
20.	1961–91	Claiborne Pell	20. Rhode Island

Ph. D. Level

21.	1971–89	Robert T. Stafford	21. Vermont
22.	1947–89	John C. Stennis	22. Mississippi
23.	1979–91	William S. Cohen	23. Maine
24.	1971–91	J. Bennett Johnston	24. Louisiana
25.	1975–93	Wendell H. Ford	25. Kentucky
26.	1979–91	Carl Levin	26. Michigan
27.	1977–89	John C. Danforth	27. Missouri
28.	1973–91	Pete V. Domenici	28. New Mexico
29.	1987–93	Barbara A. Mikulski	29. Maryland
30.	1975–93	Lloyld Bentsen	30. Texas

1987 NEWSMAKERS

Freshman Level

1. *Time* magazine's man of the year.
2. The winners of the World Series.
3. Talk of a possible split put this royal couple in the news.
4. Thousands flocked to Graceland to commemorate the tenth anniversary of his death.
5. This would-be president dropped out of the campaign, then jumped back in, then faded out again.
6. She lost the No. 1 spot despite winning at Wimbledon and the U.S. Open.
7. This Marine colonel was featured at the Iran-Contra hearings.
8. He had skin cancer removed from his nose and intestinal polyps examined.
9. His PTL empire crashed.
10. Robert Bork failed in his bid to join this prestigious body.

1. Mikhail Gorbachev
2. Minnesota Twins
3. Di and Charles
4. Elvis Presley
5. Gary Hart
6. Martina Navratilova
7. Oliver North
8. President Reagan
9. Jim Bakker
10. U.S. Supreme Court

Graduate Level

11. Peter Holm failed to get a big alimony check from this woman.
12. She was the femme fatale in the Gary Hart episode.
13. He returned to the ring to defeat Marvin Hagler.
14. Why was London's King's Cross subway station in the news?
15. Young Jessica McClure was trapped for fifty-eight hours. Where?
16. An Iraqi missile hit this U.S. ship killing thirty-seven.
17. Why was the *Herald of Free Enterprise* in the news?
18. This document-shredding secretary got herself a Hollywood agent.
19. This CBS anchor man had an embarrassing six-minute no-show.
20. Mary Beth Whitehead was the surrogate mother of this baby, known by a single letter.

11. Joan Collins
12. Donna Rice
13. Sugar Ray Leonard
14. Fire killed thirty-one
15. A dry well (Texas)
16. USS *Stark*
17. British ferry capsized, killing 135
18. Fawn Hall
19. Dan Rather
20. Baby M

Ph. D. Level

21. He admitted that he had smoked pot and lost his shot at the Supreme Court.
22. After a frolic with a preacher, she let it all out in *Playboy*.
23. This Democratic presidential contender borrowed one too many famous speeches.
24. Became U.S. Supreme Court Chief Justice.
25. Little Cecilia Cichan was in the news. Why?
26. Six-year old illegally adopted Elizabeth Steinberg was the year's most innocent victim. Why?
27. This aging golfer shot a hole-in-one and won $175,000 at a Palm Springs tournament.
28. AIDS victim Gaetan Dugas was nicknamed————.
29. He became the "planet's fastest human."
30. The Butcher of Lyons was sentenced to life imprisonment.

21. Douglas Ginsberg
22. Jessica Hahn
23. Joseph Biden
24. William Rehnquist
25. Sole survivor of Detroit air crash
26. Beaten to death
27. Lee Trevino
28. Patient Zero
29. Ben Johnson
30. Klaus Barbie

1987 FAREWELLS
Name the individual who passed away in 1987. The age is given.

Freshman Level

1. TV's Ralph Kramden (seventy-one).
2. Singer, dancer, actor, best known as Walter Mitty (seventy-four).
3. Pianist whose trademark was a candelabrum (sixty-seven).
4. An American dancer, actor (eighty-eight).
5. An actress who was married and divorced five times (sixty-eight).
6. Dick Martin's partner on *Laugh In* (sixty-five).
7. The father on TV's *Bonanza* (seventy-two).
8. Actor involved in landmark "palimony" case (sixty-three).
9. This American drummer played with many big bands (sixty-nine).
10. In 1973 he won an Oscar, a Tony, and an Emmy (sixty).

1. Jackie Gleason
2. Danny Kaye
3. Liberace
4. Fred Astaire
5. Rita Hayworth
6. Dan Rowan
7. Lorne Green
8. Lee Marvin
9. Buddy Rich
10. Bob Fosse

Graduate Level

11. He had the title role in *The Music Man* (sixty-eight).
12. The scarecrow in *The Wizard of Oz* (eighty-three).
13. Director of the CIA since 1981 (seventy-four).
14. Director of *The Maltese Falcon* and *The African Queen* (eighty-one).
15. A noted Spanish guitarist (ninety-four).
16. He introduced the Thunderbird and the Mustang.
17. The inspiration for *The Sound of Music* (eighty-two).
18. She won an Oscar in the 1985 film *The Trip to Bountiful* (sixty-two).
19. The leading exponent of pop art (fifty-eight).
20. Controversial coach of the Ohio State Football team (seventy-four).

11. Robert Preston
12. Ray Bolger
13. William Casey
14. John Huston
15. Andres Segovia
16. Henry Ford II
17. Maria Von Trapp
18. Geraldine Page
19. Andy Warhol
20. Woody Hayes

Ph. D. Level

21. Orchestra leader who composed "Blues on Parade" (seventy-four).
22. Host of a syndicated talk show (sixty-six).
23. U.S. Violin virtuoso who had been a child prodigy (eighty-six).
24. She asked, "Where's the beef?"
25. Best known as Brigid O'Shaughnessy in *The Maltese Falcon* (eighty-one).
26. Chicago's first black major (sixty-five).
27. A playwright, congresswoman, ambassador, and the instigator of *Life* magazine.
28. Probably the finest black writer of his time (sixty-three).
29. Famous for his line of Williwear casual clothes (thirty-nine).
30. *Chorus Line* was his record-breaking Broadway Show (forty-four).

21. Woody Herman
22. David Susskind
23. Jascha Heifetz
24. Clara Peller
25. Mary Astor
26. Harold Washington
27. Clare Boothe Luce
28. James Baldwin
29. Willi Smith
30. Michael Bennett

2 / FILMS

ONE-WORD FILM TITLES

Words of similar meanings are given. Provide the one-word title—e.g., Burglar, robber. *Answer: Thief.*

Freshman Level

1. Terminal, aerodrome
2. Conquest, triumph
3. Chrysalis, hatchery
4. Cookout, outing
5. Stranger, foreigner
6. Ape man, Neanderthal
7. Absent, lost
8. Parenthood, fatherhood
9. Lubricant, salve
10. Departure, emigration

1. *Airport*
2. *Victory*
3. *Cocoon*
4. *Picnic*
5. *Alien*
6. *Caveman*
7. *Missing*
8. *Paternity*
9. *Grease*
10. *Exodus*

Graduate Level

11. Disguise, facial covering
12. Onlooker, beholder
13. Mandibles, bones that support the teeth
14. Screwball, loony
15. Colossus, behemoth
16. Excuse, apology
17. Coffee shop, canteen
18. Renown, notability
19. Colleagues, associates
20. Chevrons, bands

11. *Mask*
12. *Witness*
13. *Jaws*
14. *Psycho*
15. *Giant*
16. *Alibi*
17. *Diner*
18. *Fame*
19. *Partners*
20. *Stripes*

Ph. D. Level

21. Imprint, brand
22. Praise, encomium
23. Lattice, grid
24. Salvation, extrication
25. Bewitched, enchanted
26. Doubt, mistrust
27. Pageant, caravan,
28. Ground, terrain
29. Nightclub, café
30. Knoll, sand hill

21. *Tattoo*
22. *Tribute*
23. *Network*
24. *Deliverance*
25. *Spellbound*
26. *Suspicion*
27. *Cavalcade*
28. *Country*
29. *Cabaret*
30. *Dune*

BIOPICS—1
Name the main character portrayed in the given film and the actor/actress who played the role.

Freshman Level

1. *Lust for Life*	1. Vincent Van Gogh	Kirk Douglas
2. *Fear Strikes Out*	2. Jim Piersall	Anthony Perkins
3. *Raging Bull*	3. Jake La Motta	Robert De Niro
4. *A Song to Remember*	4. Frederic Chopin	Cornel Wilde
5. *Birdman of Alcatraz*	5. Robert Stroud	Burt Lancaster
6. *Funny Girl*	6. Fanny Brice	Barbra Streisand
7. *Lady Sings the Blues*	7. Billie Holiday	Diana Ross
8. *The Pride of the Yankees*	8. Lou Gehrig	Gary Cooper
9. *Man of 1000 Faces*	9. Lon Chaney, Sr.	James Cagney
10. *The Agony and the Ecstasy*	10. Michelangelo	Charlton Heston

Graduate Level

11. *I Want to Live*	11. Barbara Graham	Susan Hayward
12. *Stars and Stripes Forever*	12. John Philip Sousa	Clifton Webb
13. *Pride of St. Louis*	13. Dizzy Dean	Dan Dailey
14. *With a Song in My Heart*	14. Jane Froman	Susan Hayward
15. *Young Man with a Horn*	15. Bix Beiderbecke	Kirk Douglas
16. *Somebody up There Likes Me*	16. Rocky Graziano	Paul Newman
17. *Swanee River*	17. Stephen Foster	Don Ameche
18. *Till the Clouds Roll By*	18. Jerome Kern	Robert Walker
19. *Gentleman Jim*	19. Jim Corbett	Errol Flynn
20. *Your Cheatin' Heart*	20. Hank Williams	George Hamilton

Ph. D. Level

21. *I Aim at the Stars*	21. Wernher von Braun	Curt Jurgens
22. *The Moon and Sixpence*	22. Gauguin	George Sanders
23. *The Winning Team*	23. Grover Cleveland Alexander	Ronald Reagan
24. *Moulin Rouge*	24. Henride Toulouse-Lautrec	José Ferrer
25. *Song Without End*	25. Franz Liszt	Dirk Bogarde
26. *Deep in My Heart*	26. Sigmund Romberg	José Ferrer
27. *Interrupted Melody*	27. Marjorie Lawrence	Eleanor Parker
28. *Too Much, Too Soon*	28. Diana Barrymore	Dorothy Malone
29. *The Great White Hope*	29. Jack Johnson	James Earl Jones
30. *The Magic Bow*	30. Paganini	Stewart Granger

BIOPICS—II
Name the actor/actress who portrayed the real-life person

Freshman Level

1. *Houdini*
2. *Lenny*
3. *The Glen Miller Story*
4. *The Jackie Robinson Story*
5. *The Great Caruso*
6. *The Babe Ruth Story*
7. *W. C. Fields and Me*
8. *The Jolson Story*
9. *The Buster Keaton Story*
10. *Bonnie and Clyde*

1. Tony Curtis
2. Dustin Hoffman
3. James Stewart
4. Jackie Robinson
5. Mario Lanza
6. William Bendix
7. Rod Steiger
8. Larry Parks
9. Donald O'Connor
10. Faye Dunaway, Warren Beatty

Graduate Level

11. *Jeanne Eagels*
12. *The Stratton Story*
13. *The Gene Krupa Story*
14. *Marco*
15. *The Helen Morgan Story*
16. *Story of Will Rogers*
17. *Amadeus*
18. *The Great Ziegfeld*
19. *Freud*
20. *Sergeant York*

11. Kim Novak
12. James Stewart
13. Sal Mineo
14. Desi Arnaz, Jr.
15. Ann Blyth
16. Will Rogers, Jr.
17. Tom Hulce
18. William Powell
19. Montgomery Clift
20. Gary Cooper

Ph. D. Level

21. *Madame Curie*
22. *The Story of Louis Pasteur*
23. *The Story of Vernon and Irene Castle*

24. *Dr. Ehrlich's Magic Bullet*
25. *Scott of the Antarctic*
26. *Christopher Columbus*
27. *Edison the Man*
28. *Gable and Lombard*

29. *The Story of Alexander Graham Bell*
30. *Young Tom Edison*

21. Greer Garson
22. Paul Muni
23. Fred Astaire, Ginger Rogers
24. Edward G. Robinson
25. John Mills
26. Fredric March
27. Spencer Tracy
28. James Brolin, Jill Clayburgh
29. Don Ameche
30. Mickey Rooney

FILM ROLES
Given the actor/actress and the role, name the movie.

Freshmen Level

1. Henry Fonda as Tom Joad.
2. Dustin Hoffman as Michael Dorsey.
3. Katharine Hepburn as Ethel Thayer.
4. John Travolta as Tony Manero.
5. Ethyl Merman as Annie Oakley.
6. Woody Allen as Alvy Singer.
7. Humphrey Bogart as Charlie Allnut.
8. Richard Dreyfuss as Elliott Garfield.
9. Marlon Brando as Terry Malloy.
10. Gene Hackman as Jimmy Doyle.

1. *The Grapes of Wrath*
2. *Tootsie*
3. *On Golden Pond*
4. *Saturday Night Fever*
5. *Annie Get Your Gun*
6. *Annie Hall*
7. *The African Queen*
8. *The Goodbye Girl*
9. *On the Waterfront*
10. *The French Connection*

Graduate Level

11. Burt Lancaster as Sergeant Milton Warden.
12. Robert De Niro as Rupert Pupkin.
13. Jack Lemon as Ensign Frank Pulver.
14. William Hurt as Ned Racine.
15. Paul Newman as Eddie Felson.
16. John Wayne as Sergeant John Stryker.
17. Sidney Poitier as Mark Thackeray.
18. Peter O'Toole as Alan Swann.
19. Robert Redford as Roy Hobbs.
20. Spencer Tracy as Father Edward Flanagan.

11. *From Here to Eternity*
12. *The King of Comedy*
13. *Mister Roberts*
14. *Body Heat*
15. *The Hustler*
16. *Sands of Iwo Jima*
17. *To Sir, with Love*
18. *My Favorite Year*
19. *The Natural*
20. *Boys Town*

Ph. D. Level

21. Elizabeth Taylor as Gloria Wandrous.
22. James Stewart as Macauley "Mike" Connor.

23. Kirk Douglas as Midge Kelly.
24. Jane Fonda as Kimberly Wells.
25. Edward G. Robinson as Little John Sarto.
26. Warren Beatty as Joe Pendleton.
27. Bruce Dern as Captain Bob Hyde.
28. Faye Dunaway as Diana Christensen.
29. Gregory Peck as Robert Thorn.
30. Dustin Hoffman as Babe Levy.

21. *Butterfield 8*
22. *The Philadelphia Story*
23. *Champion*
24. *The China Syndrome*
25. *Brother Orchid*
26. *Heaven Can Wait*
27. *Coming Home*
28. *Network*
29. *The Omen*
30. *Marathon Man*

FILMS WITH SOMETHING IN COMMON

Freshman Level

1. *The Seven Year Itch, Bus Stop, Niagara.*
2. *Champions, Phar Lap, National Velvet.*
3. *A Night to Remember, The Hindenberg, San Francisco.*
4. *Donald's Vacation, Crazy over Daisy, Commando Duck.*
5. *Bwana Devil, House of Wax, Dial M for Murder.*
6. *The Spy Who Loved Me, For Your Eyes Only, Thunderball.*
7. Cliff Robertson in *PT 109*, Ralph Bellamy in *Sunrise at Campobello.*
8. *Adam's Rib, Pat and Mike, Guess Who's Coming to Dinner?*
9. John Wayne in *True Grit*, Kirk Douglas in *The Vikings*
10. Marlon Brando in *The Teahouse of the August Moon*, Jennifer Jones in *Love Is a Many Splendored Thing.*

1. Marilyn Monroe
2. Horse racing
3. Real-life disasters
4. Donald Duck films
5. 3.-D films
6. James Bond films
7. Played U.S. Presidents

8. Tracy and Hepburn
9. Wore an eye patch
10. Portrayed Orientals

Graduate Level

11. *A Patch of Blue, Charly, Coming Home.*
12. *Days of Wine and Roses, The Lost Weekend, Arthur.*
13. *With a Song in My Heart, I'll Cry Tomorrow, Funny Girl.*
14. Mickey Rooney in *The Black Stallion*, Burt Lancaster in *Atlantic City*, Marlon Brando in *The Godfather.*
15. Lee Marvin in *Cat Ballou*, George Hamilton in *Zorro, the Gay Blade*, Peter Sellers in *The Prisoner of Zenda.*
16. Tony Curtis in *Some Like It Hot*, Dustin Hoffman in *Tootsie*
17. Albert Finney in *Annie*, Yul Brynner in *The King and I.*
18. *Mary Poppins, Chitty, Chitty Bang Bang, The Thief of Bagdad.*
19. *Moon Pilot, Island at the Top of the World, Third man on the Mountain.*
20. *Lifeboat, Rear Window, Marnie.*

11. People with handicaps
12. Alcoholics
13. Real-life singers
14. Comeback stars

15. Twin parts

16. Dressed as women
17. Bald headed
18. Unusual method of flight

19. Walt Disney Studio films

20. Hitchcock films

Ph. D. Level

21. *It's a Great Feeling, Prisoner of War, Hellcats of the Navy.*
22. Charlton Heston in *The Ten Commandments*, Orson Wells in *Citizen Kane*, Burt Lancaster in *Birdman of Alcatraz.*
23. Robert DeNiro in *Angel Heart*, Ray Walston in *Damn Yankees*, Walter Huston in *All That Money Can Buy.*
24. *Destination Tokyo, On the Beach, Ice Station Zebra.*
25. *The Poseidon Adventure, Butch Cassidy and the Sundance Kid, Nashville.*
26. *Quo Vadis, The Sand Pebbles, The Turning Point.*

27. *The King and I, West Side Story, My Fair Lady.*

28. *Planet of the Apes, On the Beach, World Without End.*

29. *Steamboat Willie, A Trip to the Moon, The Jazz Singer.*
30. Orson Welles in *Citizen Kane*, Clint Eastwood in *Play Misty for Me*, Warren Beatty in *Heaven Can Wait.*

21. Ronald Reagan films
22. Actors age a lot

23. Portrayed the Devil

24. Set on submarines
25. Best Song Oscars

26. Nominated for eight Oscars but won none.
27. Songs dubbed (by Marni Nixon)

28. Set in aftermath of WWIII

29. Movie firsts
30. Actors directed themselves

FILM FIRST

Freshman Level

1. The first movie to win the Best Picture Oscar.
2. The first color film to win Best Picture Oscar.
3. The first feature-length cartoon.

4. The first actress depicted on a postage stamp.
5. The first film musical.
6. The first talking cartoon.
7. The first black to win an Oscar.

8. The first issue of this movie fan magazine was in 1912.
9. Charlie Chaplin's first sound film (music but no dialogue).
10. First actor and son to receive Oscars for the same film.

1. *Wings*
2. *Gone with the Wind*
3. *Snow White and the Seven Dwarfs*
4. Grace Kelly
5. *The Jazz Singer*
6. *Steamboat Willie*
7. Hattie McDaniel (*GWTW*)
8. *Photoplay*
9. *City Lights*
10. Walter and John Huston *Treasure of Sierra Madre*)

Graduate Level

11. The first film presented in 3-D.
12. The first color film presented in 3-D.
13. The first film presented in Cinemascope.
14. The first science fiction film.
15. John C. Rice and May Irwin were the first to do this on film.
16. America's first film serial.
17. The first western film with a plot and featuring a holdup.

18. The first movie premiere festivities to be televised.
19. The first film to be screened at the White House.
20. The first to receive Best Actor Oscars.

11. *Bwana Devil*
12. *House of Wax*
13. *The Robe*
14. *A Trip to the Moon*
15. *Kiss* (1896)
16. *The Perils of Pauline*
17. *The Great Train Robbery*
18. Opening of *GWTW*
19. *Birth of a Nation*
20. Emil Jannings and Janet Gaynor.

Ph. D. Level

21. The first western starring John Wayne.
22. The first film presented simultaneously in major cities throughout the world.
23. Thomas Edison's Black Maria was the first of these in the United States.
24. The first musical movie with a completely original score.

25. The first all-talking film in color.
26. The first all-talking film.
27. The first color cartoon.

28. The first film produced with Dolby Sound.
29. The first closeup was of Fred Ott doing this.
30. The first Western hero.

21. *The Big Trail*
22. *On the Beach*
23. Motion Picture Studio
24. *The Broadway Melody*
25. *On with the Show*
26. *Lights of New York*
27. *The Debut of Thomas Kat*
28. *The Quiet Revolution*
29. Sneezing
30. Bronco Billy Anderson

SCIENCE-FICTION FILMS
Complete the title

Freshman Level

1. 1971 – *A Clockwork*——
2. 1977 – *Close Encounters of the*——
3. 1968 – *Planet of the*——
4. 1966 – *Fantastic*——
5. 1959 – *On the*——
6. 1973 – *Soylent*——
7. 1977 – *Star*——
8. 1960 – *The Time*——
9. 1902 – *Trip to the*——
10. 1907 – *Twenty Thousand Leagues*——

1. *Orange*
2. *Third Kind*
3. *Apes*
4. *Voyage*
5. *Beach*
6. *Green*
7. *Wars*
8. *Machine*
9. *Moon*
10. *Under the Sea*

Graduate Level

11. 1954 – *Creature from the*——
12. 1957 – *The Incredible*——
13. 1953 – *Invaders from*——
14. 1953 – *It Came from*——
15. 1974 – *The Land That*——
16. 1968 – *The Night of the*——
17. 1971 – *The Omega*——
18. 1966 – *The Reluctant*——
19. 1957 – *Twenty Million Miles to*——
20. 1968 – *2001: A*——

11. *Black Lagoon*
12. *Shrinking Man*
13. *Mars*
14. *Outer Space*
15. *Time Forgot*
16. *Living Dead*
17. *Man*
18. *Astronaut*
19. *Earth*
20. *Space Odyssey*

Ph. D. Level

21. 1956 – *World Without*——
22. 1951 – *When Worlds*——
23. 1972 – *Silent*——
24. 1976 – *The Man Who*——
25. 1963 – *The Man With the*——
26. 1976 – *Logan's*——
27. 1974 – *It's*——
28. 1956 – *Invasion of the*——
29. 1965 – *Fahrenheit*——
30. 1951 – *The Day the Earth*——

21. *End*
22. *Collide*
23. *Running*
24. *Fell to Earth*
25. *X-Ray Eyes*
26. *Run*
27. *Alive*
28. *Body Snatchers*
29. *451*
30. *Stood Still*

U.S. MOVIE BOX OFFICE CHAMPS

Name the number one star for the given year(s). The first twenty are men. The final ten are top female stars. Initials are provided.

Freshman Level: Male Stars

1. 1978–79	B.R.	1.	Burt Reynolds
2. 1977	S.S.	2.	Sylvester Stallone
3. 1974–75–76	R.R.	3.	Robert Redford
4. 1972–73	C.E.	4.	Clint Eastwood
5. 1950,51,54,63,71	J.W.	5.	John Wayne
6. 1969–70	P.N.	6.	Paul Newman
7. 1968	S.P.	7.	Sydney Poitier
8. 1967	L.M.	8.	Lee Marvin
9. 1965–66	S.C.	9.	Sean Connery
10. 1964	J.L.	10.	Jack Lemmon

Graduate Level: Male Stars

11. 1957,59,60,61	R.H.	11.	Rock Hudson
12. 1958	G.F.	12.	Glenn Ford
13. 1956	W.H.	13.	William Holden
14. 1955	J.S.	14.	James Stewart
15. 1953	G.C.	15.	Gary Cooper
16. 1949	B.H.	16.	Bob Hope
17. 1944–45–46–47–48	B.C.	17.	Bing Crosby
18. 1939–40–41	M.R.	18.	Mickey Rooney
19. 1936–37–38	C.G.	19.	Clark Gable
20. 1933–34–35	W.R.	20.	Will Rogers

Ph. D. Level: Female Stars

21. 1979	J.F.	21.	Jane Fonda
22. 1978	D.K.	22.	Diane Keaton
23. 1977,75,74,73,72,70	B.S.	23.	Barbra Streisand
24. 1969	K.H.	24.	Katherine Hepburn
25. 1967–68	J.A.	25.	Julie Andrews
26. 1957–58–61–66	E.T.	26.	Elizabeth Taylor
27. 1952–59–60–62–63–64–65	D.D.	27.	Doris Day
28. 1953–54–56	M.M.	28.	Marilyn Monroe
29. 1955	G.K.	29.	Grace Kelly
30. 1947–48–49–50–51	B.G.	30.	Betty Grable

QUOTATIONS
Identify the speaker and the film (original speaker only, please).

Freshman Level

1. Love means never having to say you're sorry.
2. Frankly, my dear, I don't give a damn.
3. Louis, I think this is the beginning of a beautiful relationship.
4. You ain't heard nothing yet.
5. La-dee-dah.
6. I'm mad as hell and I'm not going to take it any more.
7. May the force be with you.
8. Go ahead, make my day.
9. Supercalifragilisticexpialidocious.
10. Make him an offer he can't refuse.

1. Ryan O'Neal: *Love Story*
2. Clark Gable: *Gone with the Wind*
3. Humphrey Bogart: *Casablanca*
4. Al Jolson: *The Jazz Singer*
5. Diane Keaton: *Annie Hall*
6. Peter Finch: *Network*
7. Alec Guinness: *Star Wars*
8. Clint Eastwood: *Dirty Harry*
9. Julie Andrews: *Mary Poppins*
10. Marlon Brando: *The Godfather*

Graduate Level

11. After all, tomorrow is another day.
12. Where the devil are my slippers, Eliza?
13. Look Ma—top of the world!
14. Row well and live.
15. Where's the rest of me?
16. Is this the end of Rico?

17. Come up and see me sometime.
18. Here's looking at you, kid!
19. That's the dumbest thing I ever heard.
20. Well, Tillie, when the hell are we going to get some dinner?

11. Vivien Leigh: *Gone with the Wind*
12. Rex Harrison: *My Fair Lady*
13. James Cagney: *White Heat*
14. Jack Hawkins: *Ben Hur*
15. Ronald Reagan: *King's Row*
16. Edward G. Robinson: *Little Caesar*
17. Mae West: *Diamond Lil*
18. Humphrey Bogart: *Casablanca*
19. Ryan O'Neal: *What's Up Doc?*
20. Spencer Tracy: *Guess Who's Coming to Dinner*

Ph. D. Level

21. Yes I killed him. And I'm glad, I tell you. Glad, glad, glad!
22. Excuse me while I slip into something more comfortable.
23. I don't need a spear, it's only a young lion.
24. That's not the northern lights, that's Manderley!
25. This Tartar woman is for me—and my blood says, "Take her."
26. The arrangement of the features of your face is not entirely repulsive to me.
27. Oh, Jerry, don't let's ask for the moon, we have the stars.
28. Hello, everybody. This is Mrs. Norman Maine.
29. Always the same. People come, people go. Nothing ever happens.
30. If you want anything, all you have to do is whistle.

21. Bette Davis: *The Letter*
22. Jean Harlow: *Hell's Angels*
23. Victor Mature: *Samson and Delilah*
24. Laurence Olivier: *Rebecca*
25. John Wayne: *The Conqueror*
26. Greta Garbo: *Ninotchka*
27. Bette Davis: *Now Voyager*
28. Janet Gaynor: *A Star Is Born*
29. Jean Hersholt and/or Lewis Stone: *Grand Hotel*
30. Lauren Bacall: *To Have and Have Not*

CRYPTIC FILM TITLES—I

The title is written in synonymous terms. Provide the original title—e.g., The hellfire of imposing height. *Answer: The Towering Inferno*

Freshman Level: All answers are two-word titles.

1. Common individuals.
2. Brought forth the day before today.
3. Lofty midday.
4. A small city belonging to male children.
5. The natural satellite of the earth made of cellulose pulp.
6. Compassionate kindnesses.
7. Fulminating adult male of cattle.
8. Authentic pluck.
9. Returning to one's residence.
10. Duplicate torso.

1. *Ordinary People*
2. *Born Yesterday*
3. *High Noon*
4. *Boys Town*
5. *Paper Moon*
6. *Tender Mercies*
7. *Raging Bull*
8. *True Grit*
9. *Coming Home*
10. *Body Double*

Graduate Level: All answers are three-word titles.

11. The taciturn adult male.
12. A paired existence.
13. Conserve the large carnivorous Asian cat.
14. Positioned upon a small gilded lake.
15. Ancient two-wheeled vehicles of burning luminosity.
16. The leave-taking maiden.
17. The female descendant of a digger of carbon fuel.
18. The pursuer of various hoofed mammals.
19. Mothlike insects are unfettered.
20. Passion for being.

11. *The Quiet Man*
12. *A Double Life*
13. *Save the Tiger*
14. *On Golden Pond*
15. *Chariots of Fire*
16. *The Goodbye Girl*
17. *Coal Miner's Daughter*
18. *The Deer Hunter*
19. *Butterflies Are Free*
20. *Lust for Life*

Ph. D. Level: All answers are four-word titles.

21. Starting at this place to an endless extent of time.
22. The juicy edible berries from vines of violent fury.
23. Space at the pinnacle.
24. The entirety of the male adults belonging to the chief.

25. A tinge of elegance.
26. It occurred during a single nocturnal period.

27. It is my desire to remain in existence.
28. Spots located in the cardiac region.
29. Large satiny white flowers from the grassland.
30. Transcribed on the current of air.

21. *From Here to Eternity*
22. *The Grapes of Wrath*
23. *Room at the Top*
24. *All the President's Men*

25. *A Touch of Class*
26. *It Happened One Night*

27. *I Want to Live*
28. *Places in the Heart*
29. *Lillies of the Field*
30. *Written on the Wind*

CRYPTIC FILM TITLES—II

Freshman Level

1. The tint of cash.
2. Offspring belonging to an inferior deity.

3. Twelve months of perilous existence.

4. The resonance of melodies.
5. The realm deals a blow in return.

6. Exterminators of apparitions.
7. The bright green wooded area.
8. The peculiar pair.
9. Return to the time yet to come.
10. The twenty-four-hour period during which the planet did not move.

1. *The Color of Money*
2. *Children of a Lesser God*
3. *The Year of Living Dangerously*
4. *The Sound of Music*
5. *The Empire Strikes Back*
6. *Ghostbusters*
7. *The Emerald Forest*
8. *The Odd Couple*
9. *Back to the Future*
10. *The Day the Earth Stood Still*

Graduate Level

11. The pigment lavender.
12. Conditions of affection.
13. The gilded youngster.
14. Paramount ordnance.
15. Attractive in a pale hue of crimson.
16. Hostile attackers of the misplaced Biblical chest.
17. A military functionary and a man of sound character.

18. The morning meal association.
19. The laborer capable of supernatural actions.
20. Obscene rhythmic movement to music.

11. *The Color Purple*
12. *Terms of Endearment*
13. *The Golden Child*
14. *Top Gun*
15. *Pretty in Pink*
16. *Raiders of the Lost Ark*
17. *An Officer and a Gentleman*
18. *The Breakfast Club*
19. *The Miracle Worker*
20. *Dirty Dancing*

Ph. D. Level

21. Merciless humans.
22. Maxilla and mandibles.
23. Stay in an erect position in close proximity to yours truly.
24. Unnaturalized foreign residents.
25. Within the warmth of the nocturnal period.

26. The abode of God can be set aside for the moment.
27. A garment pouch replete with amazing events.
28. In a green tract of public land without shoes or socks.
29. The twelve-month period preferred by this person.
30. Flat-topped items of furniture that are isolated from each other.

21. *Ruthless People*
22. *Jaws*
23. *Stand by Me*
24. *Aliens*
25. *In the Heat of the Night*
26. *Heaven Can Wait*
27. *A Pocketful of Miracles*
28. *Barefoot in the Park*
29. *My Favorite Year*
30. *Separate Tables*

ENIGMATIC FILM TITLES
Explain the title— e.g., *Play It Again Sam. Answer:* The song "As Time Goes By."

Freshman Level

1. *Guess Who's Coming to Dinner?*
2. *M*A*S*H*
3. *The African Queen*
4. *The Pink Panther*
5. *E.T.*
6. *A Tale of Two Cities*
7. *Twelve Angry Men*
8. *La Dolce Vita*
9. *Brief Encounter*
10. *The China Syndrome*

1. A white daughter's black fiancé
2. Mobile Army Surgical Hospital
3. The name of the boat
4. A priceless diamond
5. The extraterrestrial
6. Paris and London
7. A jury
8. The sweet life
9. Two married people meet in a train station café
10. A nuclear meltdown that theoretically could burn through the earth to China.

Graduate Level

11. *Quo Vadis*
12. *The Man with the Golden Arm*
13. *Fahrenheit 451*
14. *The Most Dangerous Game*
15. *F.X.*
16. *Five Easy Pieces*
17. *The Scarlet Letter*
18. *Bringing up Baby*
19. *The Trouble with Harry*
20. *Gentleman's Agreement*

11. Where are you going?
12. A drug addict who injects drugs
13. Temperature at which paper (books) burns
14. Hunting of human beings
15. Special effects
16. Five easily played musical selections
17. Letter A to be worn publicly by an adultress
18. Baby is a pet leopard.
19. Harry is dead. Trouble disposing of corpse
20. An unspoken agreement that Jews will not be accepted.

Ph. D. Level

21. *The Taxi Dancer*
22. *The Big Easy*
23. *The Man Who Loved Cat Dancing*
24. *Every Frenchman Has One*
25. *The Ox-Bow Incident*
26. *X, Y, and Zee*
27. *Two Seconds*
28. *Time Bandits*
29. *King's Row*
30. *Portnoy's Complaint*

21. Girl in a dime-a-dance emporium
22. Nickname for New Orleans
23. Name of his deceased Indian wife
24. A liver
25. Lynching of three innocent men in the Ox-Bow Valley
26. A Widow, Mr. Blakeley, and Mrs. Zee Blakeley
27. Time it takes for a person to die in electric chair
28. Dwarfs steal God's map of the universe
29. Name of midwestern town that provides setting
30. Guilt caused by strict Jewish upbringing and eventual impotence

BEST PICTURE OSCAR
Two or three of the films nominated for the given year are provided. Name the winner.

Freshman Level

1.	1983	*The Right Stuff, Terms of Endearment, Tender Mercies*	1.	TOE
2.	1981	*On Golden Pond, Raiders of the Lost Ark, Chariots of Fire*	2.	COF
3.	1979	*Kramer vs. Kramer, Apocalypse Now, Norma Rae*	3.	KVK
4.	1978	*Midnight Express, The Deer Hunter, Coming Home*	4.	TDH
5.	1977	*Star Wars, Annie Hall, The Goodbye Girl*	5.	AH
6.	1973	*The Exorcist, American Graffiti, The Sting*	6.	TS
7.	1972	*Cabaret, Deliverance, The Godfather*	7.	TG
8.	1971	*The French Connection, Fiddler on the Roof, A Clockwork Orange*	8.	TFC
9.	1970	*M*A*S*H, Airport, Patton*	9.	P
10.	1969	*Butch Cassidy and the Sundance Kid, Midnight Cowboy*	10.	MC

Graduate Level

11.	1968	*Funny Girl, Oliver, The Lion in Winter, Romeo and Juliet*	11.	O
12.	1967	*Bonnie and Clyde, The Graduate, In the Heat of the Night*	12.	ITHOTN
13.	1958	*Separate Tables, Cat on a Hot Tin Roof, Gigi*	13.	G
14.	1957	*Witness for the Prosecution, The Bridge on the River Kwai, Twelve Angry Men*	14.	TBOTRK
15.	1956	*Around the World in 80 Days, Giant, The King and I*	15.	ATWI80D
16.	1955	*Picnic, Mister Roberts, Marty*	16.	M
17.	1954	*On the Waterfront, The Caine Mutiny, Three Coins in the Fountain*	17.	OTW
18.	1953	*The Robe, Shane, From Here to Eternity*	18.	FHTE
19.	1952	*High Noon, Moulin Rouge, The Greatest Show on Earth*	19.	TGSOE
20.	1951	*Quo Vadis, A Streetcar Named Desire, An American in Paris*	20.	AAIP

Ph. D. Level

21.	1950	*Father of the Bride, Born Yesterday, All About Eve*	21.	AAE
22.	1948	*Hamlet, Johnny Belinda, Treasure of Sierra Madre*	22.	H
23.	1947	*Great Expectations, Crossfire, Gentleman's Agreement*	23.	GA
24.	1946	*The Yearling, The Razor's Edge, The Best Years of Our Lives*	24.	TBYOOL
25.	1945	*The Lost Weekend, Mildred Pierce, Spellbound*	25.	TLW
26.	1943	*For Whom the Bell Tolls, Heaven Can Wait, Casablanca*	26.	C
27.	1942	*King's Row, The Magnificent Ambersons, Mrs. Miniver*	27.	MM
28.	1941	*How Green Was My Valley, Citizen Kane, The Maltese Falcon*	28.	HGWMV
29.	1940	*The Grapes of Wrath, Rebecca, The Great Dictator*	29.	R
30.	1939	*The Wizard of Oz, Gone with the Wind, Of Mice and Men*	30.	GWTW

FILM DIRECTORS
Name the film director (use the initial clues only if needed).

Freshman Level

1. *Jaws, Indiana Jones and the Temple of Doom*	S.P.	1. Steven Spielberg
2. *American Graffiti, Star Wars*	G.L.	2. George Lucas
3. *Annie Hall, Sleeper*	W.A.	3. Woody Allen
4. *The Godfather, Apocalypse Now*	F.F.C.	4. Francis Ford Coppola
5. *Cabaret, All That Jazz*	B.F.	5. Bob Fosse
6. *The Ten Commandments, The Greatest Show on Earth*	C.B.D.	6. Cecil B. DeMille
7. *Darling Lili, 10*	B.E.	7. Blake Edwards
8. *Citizen Kane, The Magnificent Ambersons*	O.W.	8. Orson Welles
9. *Fanny and Alexander, The Seventh Seal*	I.B.	9. Ingmar Bergman
10. *Lifeboat, Psycho*	A.H.	10. Alfred Hitchcock

Graduate Level

11. *Gandhi, A Bridge Too Far*	R.A.	11. Richard Attenborough
12. *The Graduate, Catch–22*	M.N.	12. Mike Nichols
13. *The Maltese Falcon, The Treasure of Sierra Madre*	J.H.	13. John Huston
14. *The Apartment, Irma la Douce*	B.W.	14. Billy Wilder
15. *The Man with the Golden Arm, Exodus*	O.P.	15. Otto Preminger
16. *The Grapes of Wrath, Stagecoach*	J.F.	16. John Ford
17. *Mrs. Miniver, The Best Years of Our Lives*	W.W.	17. William Wyler
18. *Rosemary's Baby, Tess*	R.P.	18. Roman Polanski
19. *Fiddler on the Roof, In the Heat of the Night*	N.J.	19. Norman Jewison
20. *The Last Picture Show, What's Up Doc?*	P.B.	20. Peter Bogdanovich

Ph. D. Level

21. *One Flew over the Cuckoo's Nest, Amadeus*	M.F.	21. Milos Forman
22. *Tootsie, The Electric Horseman*	S.P.	22. Sydney Pollack
23. *The Deer Hunter, Heaven's Gate*	M.C.	23. Michael Cimino
24. *The Sound of Music, The Sand Pebbles*	R.W.	24. Robert Wise
25. *The Raging Bull, Taxi Driver*	M.S.	25. Martin Scorsese
26. *On the Beach, Judgment at Nuremberg*	S.K.	26. Stanley Kramer
27. *Lust for Life, Some Came Running*	V.M.	27. Vincente Minnelli
28. *Born Yesterday, A Star is Born*	G.C.	28. George Cukor
29. *A Tree Grows In Brooklyn, On the Waterfront*	E.K.	29. Elia Kazan
30. *It's a Wonderful Life, Mr. Smith Goes to Washington*	F.C.	30. Frank Capra

SWAN SONGS: Last Films of Stars

Given the year and the title of the film, provide the name of the actor or actress (cameo rolls don't count).

Freshman Level

1. *Giant*, 1956
2. *The Misfits*, 1960

3. *Network*, 1976
4. *Guess Who's Coming to Dinner?* 1967
5. *The Harder They Fall*, 1956
6. *On Golden Pond*, 1981
7. *S.O.B.*, 1981
8. *Witness for the Prosecution*, 1957
9. *The Shootist*, 1976
10. *Soylent Green*, 1973

1. James Dean
2. Clark Gable and/or Marilyn Monroe
3. Peter Finch
4. Spencer Tracy
5. Humphrey Bogart
6. Henry Fonda
7. William Holden
8. Tyrone Power
9. John Wayne
10. Edward G. Robinson

Graduate Level

11. *Ragtime*, 1981
12. *Advise and Consent*, 1962
13. *High Society*, 1956
14. *Ride the High Country*, 1962
15. *The Iceman Cometh*, 1973
16. *Ship of Fools*, 1965
17. *The Carpetbaggers*, 1964
18. *House of Evil*, 1968
19. *Inn of the Sixth Happiness*, 1958
20. *Sextette*, 1978

11. James Cagney
12. Charles Laughton
13. Grace Kelly
14. Randolph Scott
15. Frederic March
16. Vivien Leigh
17. Alan Ladd
18. Boris Karloff
19. Robert Donat
20. Mae West

Ph. D. Level

21. *To Be or Not To Be*, 1942
22. *Cuban Rebel Girls*, 1959
23. *The Patsy*, 1964
24. *The Private Life of Don Juan*, 1934
25. *The Defector*, 1966
26. *The Wrath of God*, 1972
27. *Walk, Don't Run*, 1966
28. *I Could Go on Singing*, 1963
29. *Trog*, 1970
30. *How To Be Very Very Popular*, 1955

21. Carole Lombard
22. Errol Flynn
23. Peter Lorre
24. Douglas Fairbanks Sr.
25. Montgomery Clift
26. Rita Hayworth
27. Cary Grant
28. Judy Garland
29. Joan Crawford
30. Betty Grable

3 / THE PRINTED WORD

CHARACTERS IN LITERATURE
Name the book in which the character appears.

Freshman Level

1. Tiny Tim
2. Quasimodo
3. Captain William Bligh
4. D'Artagnan
5. Becky Thatcher
6. Long John Silver
7. Tinker Bell
8. Scarlett O'Hara
9. Ichabod Crane
10. Simon Legree

1. *A Christmas Carol*
2. *The Hunchback of Notre Dame*
3. *Mutiny on the Bounty*
4. *The Three Musketeers*
5. *Tom Sawyer*
6. *Treasure Island*
7. *Peter Pan*
8. *Gone with the Wind*
9. "The Legend of Sleepy Hollow"
10. *Uncle Tom's Cabin*

Graduate Level

11. Sancho Panza
12. Chingachgook
13. Ishmael
14. Fagin
15. Tweedledum and Tweedledee
16. Heathcliff
17. Captain Nemo

18. Willy Loman
19. Madame Defarge
20. Pip

11. *Don Quixote*
12. *The Last of the Mohicans*
13. *Moby Dick*
14. *Oliver Twist*
15. *Through the Looking Glass*
16. *Wuthering Heights*
17. *Twenty Thousand Leagues Under the Sea*

18. *Death of a Salesman*
19. *A Tale of Two Cities*
20. *Great Expectations*

Ph. D. Level

21. Uriah Heep
22. Blanche DuBois
23. Tom Joad
24. David Balfour
25. Allan Quatermain
26. Parris Mitchell
27. Hugh Conway
28. Lennie Small
29. Jody Baxter
30. Tom Canty

21. *David Copperfield*
22. *A Streetcar Named Desire*
23. *The Grapes of Wrath*
24. *Kidnapped*
25. *King Solomon's Mines*
26. *King's Row*
27. *Lost Horizon*
28. *Of Mice and Men*
29. *The Yearling*
30. *The Prince and the Pauper*

CHILDREN'S LITERATURE
Given the author and a clue, provide the title.

Freshman Level

1.	Robert Browning	Rats are led out of town	1. *The Pied Piper of Hamelin*
2.	Hans Rey	A mischievous monkey	2. *Curious George*
3.	Carlo Collodi	A wooden marionette	3. *(The Adventures of) Pinocchio*
4.	Robert L. Stevenson	A pirate story	4. *Treasure Island*
5.	Johann D. Wyss	A shipwrecked family	5. *The Swiss Family Robinson*
6.	Hardie Gramatky	A small tugboat accepts responsibility	6. *Little Toot*
7.	Dr. Seuss	Food provides the title	7. *Green Eggs and Ham*
8.	Eric Knight	A devoted collie dog	8. *Lassie Come Home*
9.	Johanna Spyri	A girl in an Alpine village	9. *Heidi*
10.	Mark Twain	A boy with a brother named Sydney	10. *Tom Sawyer*

Graduate Level

11.	Pamela Travers	A nursemaid blows in on the east wind	11. *Mary Poppins*
12.	E. B. White	A spider saves a pig's life	12. *Charlotte's Web*
13.	Felix Salten	A deer in the forest	13. *Bambi*
14.	Beatrix Potter	About a rabbit	14. *(The Tale of) Peter Rabbit*
15.	Wanda Gag	Plenty of felines	15. *Millions of Cats*
16.	Louisa May Alcott	Meg, Jo, and Beth	16. *Little Women*
17.	Lois Lenski	Lots of little things	17. *The Little Auto* (Train, Farm, etc)
18.	Charlotte Bronte	About a girl's romance	18. *Jane Eyre*
19.	Marjorie Flak	A duck escapes from a Chinese houseboat	19. *(The Story about) Ping*
20.	Sir James Barrie	A boy refuses to grow up	20. *Peter Pan*

Ph. D. Level

21.	Jack London	A sled dog in the Klondike	21. *The Call of the Wild*
22.	Hugh Lofting	An amazing physician	22. *(The Story of) Doctor Dolittle*
23.	C. S. Lewis	The land of Narnia	23. *The Lion, the Witch, and the Wardrobe*
24.	Holling C. Holling	A little canoe makes a trip	24. *Paddle-to-the-Sea*
25.	Mary Dodge	About life in the Netherlands	25. *Hans Brinker (The Silver Skates)*
26.	R. and F. Atwater	About pets kept in a refrigerator	26. *Mr. Popper's Penguins*
27.	Jean De Brunhoff	The adventures of an elephant	27. *(The Story of) Babar, the Little Elephant*
28.	Helen Bannerman	A heroic boy in India	28. *(The Story of) Little Black Sambo*
29.	Sheila Burnford	three house pets in the Canadian wilderness	29. *The Incredible Journey*
30.	Kenneth Grahame	The owner of Toad Hall	30. *The Wind in the Willows*

PROVERBS

Freshman Level

1. The half is better than——
2. Give a man enough rope and——
3. Do not throw pearls——
4. The opera isn't over till——
5. One man's loss is——
6. Imitation is the sincerest——
7. The tree is known by——
8. You can have too much——
9. Many a true word——
10. There are two sides——

1. the whole.
2. he will hang himself.
3. before swine.
4. the fat lady sings.
5. another man's gain.
6. form of flattery.
7. its fruit.
8. of a good thing.
9. is spoken in jest.
10. to every question.

Graduate Level

11. The hand that rocks the cradle——
12. From the sublime to the ridiculous——
13. A watched pot——
14. It is a wise child that——
15. You cannot get blood——
16. A barking dog——
17. If you want peace you must——
18. Nothing is certain but——
19. The nearer the bone——
20. There's many a slip——

11. rules the world.
12. is only a step.
13. never boils.
14. knows its own father.
15. from a stone.
16. never bites.
17. prepare for war.
18. death and taxes.
19. the sweeter the meat.
20. 'twixt cup and lip.

Ph. D. Level

21. You cannot run with the hare——
22. When poverty comes in at the door——
23. Put your trust in God, and——
24. 'Tis better to have loved and lost——
25. Better to be an old man's darling than——
26. Believe nothing of what you hear——
27. He who rides a tiger——
28. A nod is as good as a wink to——
29. You never miss the water——
30. The mills of God grind slowly, yet they——

21. and hunt with the hounds.
22. love flies out of the window.
23. keep your powder dry.
24. than never to have loved at all.
25. a young man's slave.
26. and only half of what you see.
27. is afraid to dismount.
28. a blind horse.
29. till the well runs dry.
30. grind exceeding small.

QUOTATIONS
Provide the final word of each quotation.

Freshman Level

1. The way to a man's heart is through his———.
2. When in doubt tell the———.
3. The most wasted day of all is that on which we have not———.
4. There is nothing permanent except———.
5. He that talks to himself, speaks to a———.
6. The only thing some people do is to grow———.
7. One may return to the place of his birth; he cannot go back to his———.
8. A liar should have a good———.
9. Any one can hold the helm when the sea is———.
10. His only fault is that he has no———.

1. stomach
2. truth
3. laughed
4. change
5. fool
6. older
7. youth

8. memory
9. calm
10. fault

Graduate Level

11. I can resist everything except———.
12. Nobody ever forgets where he buried a———.
13. We all have strength enough to endure the misfortunes of———.
14. Libraries are not made; they———.
15. When the candles are out, all women are———.
16. When angry count four; when very angry———.
17. Never find your delight in another's———.
18. A closed mouth gathers no———.
19. Usually we praise only to be———.
20. No one gets rich quickly if he is———.

11. temptation
12. hatchet
13. others

14. grow
15. fair
16. swear
17. misfortune
18. feet
19. praised
20. honest

Ph. D. Level

21. Woman's virtue is man's greatest———.
22. Obscurity often brings———.
23. Be good and you will be———.
24. You can tell the character of every man when you see how he receives———.
25. No good deed goes———.
26. Old women should not seek to be———.
27. Nothing great was every achieved without———.
28. Marriage is popular because it combines the maximum of temptation with the maximum of———.
29. The test of a man or a woman's breeding is how they behave in a———.
30. Most women are not so young as they are———.

21. invention
22. safety
23. lonesome
24. praise

25. unpunished
26. perfumed
27. enthusiasm
28. opportunity

29. quarrel

30. painted

QUOTATIONS FROM SHAKESPEARE
Name the play from which the quotation is derived.

Freshman Level

1. To be or not to be: that is the question.
2. What's in a name?
3. Is this a dagger which I see before me?
4. Et tu, Brute!
5. How sharper than a serpent's tooth it is to have a thankless child!
6. The quality of mercy is not strain'd.
7. Some are born great, some achieve greatness, and some have greatness thrust upon them.
8. Kindness in women, not their beauteous looks, shall win my love.
9. O! beware, my lord, of jealousy; It is the green-eyed monster which doth mock The meat it feeds on:
10. My salad days, When I was green in judgment.

1. *Hamlet*
2. *Romeo and Juliet*
3. *Macbeth*
4. *Julius Caesar*
5. *King Lear*
6. *Merchant of Venice*
7. *Twelfth Night*
8. *The Taming of the Shrew*
9. *Othello*
10. *Antony and Cleopatra*

Graduate Level: The same ten plays are repeated.

11. A pair of star-cross'd lovers.
12. The path is smooth that leadeth on to danger.
13. If you prick us, do we not bleed?
14. Then come kiss me, sweet and twenty, Youth's a stuff will not endure.
15. Friends, Romans countrymen, lend me your ears;
16. O! that this too too solid flesh would melt,
17. How poor are they that have not patience!
18. The prince of darkness is a gentleman.
19. Fair is foul, and foul is fair:
20. Though it be honest, it is never good To bring bad news.

11. *Romeo and Juliet*
12. *The Taming of the Shrew*
13. *The Merchant of Venice*
14. *Twelfth Night*
15. *Julius Caesar*
16. *Hamlet*
17. *Othello*
18. *King Lear*
19. *Macbeth*
20. *Antony and Cleopatra*

Ph. D. Level: Ten different plays. No repeats.

21. A horse! a horse! my kingdom for a horse!
22. The huge army of the world's desires.
23. The fashion wears out more apparel than the man.
24. All the world's a stage, And all the men and women merely players.
25. The course of true love never did run smooth.
26. Better three hours too soon than a minute too late.
27. I am a man whom Fortune hath cruelly scratched.
28. O, what may man within him hide, Though angel on the outward side!
29. O brave new world, That has such people in't!
30. How use doth breed a habit in a man!

21. *King Richard III*
22. *Love's Labour's Lost*
23. *Much Ado About Nothing*
24. *As You Like It*
25. *A Midsummer Night's Dream*
26. *Merry Wives of Windsor*
27. *All's Well That Ends Well*
28. *Measure for Measure*
29. *The Tempest*
30. *The Two Gentlemen of Verona*

DEFINITIONS

The speaker and his quotation are given; to what does the quotation refer? All answers are one word.

Freshman Level

1. Karl Marx	"The opium of the people"	1.	Religion
2. George Meredith	"The last thing civilized by man"	2.	Women
3. Walter Landon	"Silent conversation"	3.	Books
4. O.K. Bovard	"Cow pasture pool"	4.	Golf
5. Oscar Wilde	"the name everyone gives to their mistakes"	5.	Experience
6. Voltaire	"an opinion without judgment"	6.	Prejudice
7. Charles Montesquieu	"the right to do what the laws allow"	7.	Liberty
8. Oscar Wilde	"the diary we all carry about with us"	8.	Memory
9. William Shakespeare	"the food of love"	9.	Music
10. Herbert Spencer	"organized knowledge"	10.	Science

Graduate Level

11. Henry Beecher	"the river of life in this world"	11.	Love
12. Herbert Spencer	"that which man is always trying to kill, but which ends up killing him"	12.	Time
13. William Shakespeare	"a stuff will not endure"	13.	Youth
14. Oliver Wendell Holmes	"what we pay for civilized society"	14.	Taxes
15. Ralph Waldo Emerson	"the first wealth"	15.	Health
16. Ernst Toller	"propaganda of the victors"	16.	History
17. Sir Thomas Browne	"the art of God"	17.	Nature
18. Ambrose Bierce	"a period of cheating between two periods of fighting"	18.	Peace
19. Juvenal	"the holiest of our gods"	19.	Wealth
20. Ambrose Bierce	"a ship big enough to carry two in fair weather but only one in foul."	20.	Friendship

Ph. D. Level

21. Will Durant	"the nucleus of civilization"	21.	Family
22. Joseph Joubert	"truth in action"	22.	Justice
23. Thomas Carlyle	"the dismal science"	23.	Economics
24. Robert Ingersoll	"places where pebbles are polished and diamonds are dimmed"	24.	Colleges (schools)
25. Henry Thoreau	"life near the bone"	25.	Poverty
26. Ambrose Bierce	"consisting of a master, a mistress, and two slaves, making in all two"	26.	Marriage
27. Ralph Waldo Emerson	"the archives of history"	27.	Language
28. Ralph Waldo Emerson	"a little fire, a little food, and an immense quiet"	28.	Hospitality
29. Matthew Arnold	"literature in a hurry"	29.	Journalism
30. Ralph Waldo Emerson	"the amassed thought and experience of innumerable minds"	30.	Knowledge

MYTHS AND LEGENDS

Freshman Level

1. He was killed by an arrow shot into his heel.
2. For how long was Troy besieged by the Greeks?
3. This Greek god had horns, a tail, and goat's feet.
4. Prometheus was punished for giving this to man.
5. This creature was half-man and half-horse.
6. This sculptor fell in love with his own statue of Aphrodite.
7. Who cut the Gordian Knot?
8. This Greek heroine was hatched from an egg.
9. This mountain was sacred to Apollo and the Muses.
10. What bird was associated with the goddess Athena?

1. Achilles
2. Ten years
3. Pan
4. Fire
5. Centaur
6. Pygmalion
7. Alexander the Great
8. Helen of Troy
9. Parnassus
10. Owl

Graduate Level

11. When Odysseus returned home he was recognized by Argos. Who or what was Argos?
12. On returning home from Troy he was killed by his wife and her lover.
13. She challenged Athena to surpass her at weaving.
14. In Greek mythology Pandora was the first———.
15. The Chimaera was composed of these three animals.
16. What was Medusa, Stheno, and Euryale collectively known as?
17. What did Daedalus construct for Minos?
18. What yearly payment did King Minos of Crete demand?

19. The Egyptian god Anubis had the head of this animal.
20. Who was the father of the Nine Muses?

11. His dog
12. Agamemnon
13. Arachne
14. woman on earth
15. lion, goat, serpent
16. The three Gorgons
17. The Labyrinth
18. Seven men and women for the Minotaur
19. Jackal
20. Zeus

Ph. D. Level

21. In Roman myths who opened the gates of heaven each day for the sun god Apollo?
22. For what crime(s) did Oedipus blind himself?
23. He was forced to kiss the hands that had killed his sons.
24. Who was the divine messenger in the *Iliad?*
25. He tried to fly with wings of wax and feathers but the sun melted the wax and he fell to his death.
26. Hera, Aphrodite, and Athena asked him to judge which of them was the fairest.
27. Why was Orpheus unsuccessful in his attempt to bring Eurydice back from the underworld?
28. Who agreed to hold up the heavens for Atlas?
29. In Greek mythology who were Clotho, Lachesis and Atropos?
30. What are "splendor," "mirth," and "good cheer" collectively known as?

21. Aurora
22. Patricide and incest
23. Priam
24. Iris
25. Icarus
26. Paris (Prince of Troy)
27. He broke the condition not to look back.
28. Heracles (Hercules)
29. The Three Fates
30. The Three Graces

PULITZER PRIZES IN LETTERS
Name the author. Provide the initials as a hint if necessary.

Freshman Level-Fiction

1.	1983	*The Color Purple*	A.W.	1.	Alice Walker
2.	1982	*Rabbit Is Rich*	J.U.	2.	John Updike
3.	1980	*The Executioner's Song*	N.M.	3.	Norman Mailer
4.	1976	*Humboldt's Gift*	S.B.	4.	Saul Bellow
5.	1961	*To Kill a Mockingbird*	H.L.	5.	Harper Lee
6.	1953	*The Old Man and the Sea*	E.H.	6.	Ernest Hemingway
7.	1952	*The Caine Mutiny*	H.W.	7.	Herman Wouk
8.	1940	*The Grapes of Wrath*	J.S.	8.	John Steinbeck
9.	1937	*Gone with the Wind*	M.M.	9.	Margaret Mitchell
10.	1932	*The Good Earth*	P.B.	10.	Pearl S. Buck

Graduate Level-Drama

11.	1940	*The Time of Your Life*	W.S.	11.	William Saroyan
12.	1943	*The Skin of Our Teeth*	T.W.	12.	Thornton Wilder
13.	1949	*Death of a Salesman*	A.M.	13.	Arthur Miller
14.	1955	*Cat on a Hot Tin Roof*	T.W.	14.	Tennessee Williams
15.	1957	*Long Day's Journey into Night*	E.O.	15.	Eugene O'Neill
16.	1967	*A Delicate Balance*	E.A.	16.	Edward Albee
17.	1973	*That Championship Season*	J.M.	17.	Jason Miller
18.	1979	*Buried Child*	S.S.	18.	Sam Shepard
19.	1981	*Crimes of the Heart*	B.H.	19.	Beth Henley
20.	1987	*Fences*	A.W.	20.	August Wilson

Ph. D. Level-Fiction

21.	1919	*The Magnificent Ambersons*	B.T.	21.	Booth Tarkington
22.	1926	*Arrowsmith*	S.L.	22.	Sinclair Lewis
23.	1928	*The Bridge of San Luis Rey*	T.W.	23.	Thornton Wilder
24.	1939	*The Yearling*	M.R.	24.	Marjorie K. Rawlings
25.	1943	*Dragon's Teeth*	U.S.	25.	Upton Sinclair
26.	1958	*A Death in the Family*	J.A.	26.	James Agee
27.	1960	*Advise and Consent*	A.D.	27.	Allen Drury
28.	1963	*The Reivers*	W.F.	28.	William Faulkner
20.	1984	*Ironweed*	W.K.	29.	William Kennedy
30.	1987	*A Summons to Memphis*	P.T.	30.	Peter Taylor

BOOKS OF GREAT INFLUENCE

Freshman Level

1. The fundamental book of Christianity.
2. The sacred text of Islam.
3. Karl Marx's case against the capitalist system.
4. The basis of religious authority for traditional Judaism.
5. Alexis de Tocqueville's classic political work.
6. Set in Denmark, perhaps Shakespeare's most influenctial play.
7. Harriet Beecher Stowe's anti-slavery novel.
8. Preacher John Bunyan's classic novel.
9. His book, *The Common Sense Book of Baby and Child Care*, had considerable impact.
10. Emily Post's classic book on proper behavior.

1. The Bible
2. *The Koran*
3. *Das Kapital*
4. *Talmud*
5. *Democracy in America*
6. *Hamlet*
7. *Uncle Tom's Cabin*
8. *Pilgrim's Progress*
9. Benjamin Spock
10. *Etiquette*

Graduate Level

11. Thomas Paine's famous pamphlet calling for independence.
12. Adam Smith's economic treatise.
13. Henry Thoreau's essay against unjust government.
14. Plato's book devoted to the meaning of justice.
15. Sigmund Freud's earliest major work (1900).
16. *Relativity, the Special and General Theories.*
17. Darwin's book about "natural selection."
18. Translated title: *Anatomical Exercise on the Motion of the Heart and Blood in Animals.* Author?
19. Edward Bellamy's Utopian and socialist novel about the year 2000.
20. Rachel Carson's book increased concern with ecology.

11. *Common Sense*
12. *Wealth of Nations*
13. *Civil Disobedience*
14. *Republic*
15. *The Interpretation of Dreams*
16. Albert Einstein
17. *The Origin of Species*
18. William Harvey
19. *Looking Backward*
20. *Silent Spring*

Ph. D. Level

21. A. T. Mahan's book showing the interrelationship of naval and political history.
22. English geographer H. J. Mackinder's analyses of the interrelationships of geography and politics.
23. *Essay on the Principle of Population.*
24. An anthropological odyssey by James Frazer.
25. Translated title: *Mathematical Principles of Natural Philosophy.* Author?
26. Dr. Alfred Kinsey's classic studies.
27. R. H. Dana's novel on sailing and sailors.
28. Upton Sinclair's novel about the Chicago stockyards.
29. Translated title: *Concerning the Revolution of the Heavenly Spheres.*
30. Oswald Spengler's book pictured history as a series of cycles of rising and falling civilizations.

21. *The Influence of Sea Power upon History*
22. *The Geographical Pivot of History*
23. Thomas Malthus
24. *The Golden Bough*
25. *Sir Isaac Newton*
26. *Sexual Behavior in the Human Male* and *Female*
27. *Two Years Before the Mast.*
28. *The Jungle*
29. Nicolaus Copernicus
30. *The Decline of the West*

4 / WORDS

BIG THINGS
All answers contain the word "big."

Freshman Level

1. The bell in the clock tower of the House of Parliament in London.
2. An organization serving boys without fathers.
3. A term designating a circus.
4. A hunting term applied to large animals.
5. A popular McDonalds hamburger.
6. Nickname of racehorse Man-O'War.
7. Nickname of New York City
8. The Sasquatch is also known by this name.
9. A wild sheep of North America.
10. Name for the permanent members of the U.N. Security Council.

1. Big Ben
2. Big Brothers
3. Big Top
4. Big game
5. Big Mac
6. Big Red
7. Big Apple
8. Big Foot
9. Bighorn
10. Big Five

Graduate Level

11. A large German cannon used in WWI
12. The ultimate ruler in George Orwell's novel *1984*.
13. These small-sized cartoon and photograph books were once very popular.
14. "Walk softly but carry a ———."
15. Guy Lombardo, Glen Miller, and Lawrence Welk all had one.
16. Expression for creation of the universe.
17. Jimmy Dean's No. 1 hit song of 1961.
18. American slang for a prison.
19. Film nominated for Best Picture Oscar for 1983.
20. Another name for this 7-star constellation is Ursa Major or Great Bear.

11. Big Bertha
12. Big Brother
13. Big little books
14. Big stick
15. Big band
16. Big Bang
17. "Big Bad John"
18. Big house
19. *Big Chill*
20. The Big Dipper

Ph. D. Level

21. He was killed in an air crash along with Buddy Holly.
22. Nickname of the Missouri River.
23. A nickname for Tennessee.
24. Nickname of pitcher Walter Johnson
25. Nickname of NBA basketball player Elvin Hayes.
26. Bogart and Becall starred in this 1946 film.
27. The Four Seasons' No. 1 hit song of 1962.
28. A group in the empire of Lilliput, in Swift's *Gulliver's Travels*.
29. Carl Sandburg called Chicago the "City of the———."
30. An expression denoting the New York Stock Exchange.

21. The Big Bopper
22. Big Muddy
23. Big Bend State
24. The Big Train
25. Big E
26. *The Big Sleep*
27. "Big Girls Don't Cry"
28. Big-Endians
29. Big Shoulders
30. Big Board

LITTLE BY LITTLE
All answers contain the word "little."

Freshman Level

1. One of Robin Hood's men.
2. Nickname of Charles Chaplin.
3. She lost her sheep.
4. Who put Pussy in the well?
5. She went into the woods to visit her grandmother.
6. He sings for his supper.
7. TV series starring Michael Landon.

8. Who laughed when the cow jumped over the moon?
9. Her dog's name is Sandy.
10. He was asked to blow his horn.

1. Little John
2. Little Tramp
3. Little Bo Peep
4. Little Johnny Green
5. Little Red Riding Hood
6. Little Tom Tucker
7. *Little House on the Prairie*
8. The little dog
9. Little Orphan Annie
10. Little Boy Blue

Graduate Level

11. Dustin Hoffman portrayed the title character in this 1970 film.
12. Edward G. Robinson portrayed this Chicago gangster in a 1930 movie.
13. The are made of "frogs and snails and puppy dog tails."
14. His father's name was Jumbo and his mother's name was Mumbo.
15. Red Ryder's sidekick.
16. The Jolly Green Giant's tiny helper.
17. Statue in Copenhagen Harbor.
18. They were originally named Our Gang.
19. A baseball organization for boys twelve and younger.
20. The North Star is in this constellation.

11. *Little Big Man*
12. *Little Caesar*
13. Little boys
14. Little Black Sambo
15. Little Beaver
16. Little Sprout
17. The Little Mermaid
18. The Little Rascals
19. Little League baseball
20. Little Dipper

Ph. D. Level

21. The capital city of Arkansas.
22. Code name of the bomb dropped at Hiroshima.
23. Nickname of Stephen Arnold Douglas
24. Freddie Bartholomew portrayed this character in a 1936 movie.
25. Comic-strip girl friend of Tubby.
26. This was the pseudonym of rock 'n' roll singer Richard Penniman.
27. The Italian Swiss Colony character featured on TV Commercials.
28. Nickname (translations) of New York City Mayor Fiorello La Guardia.
29. Nickname of tennis champion Maureen Connally.
30. Pseudonym of Catherine Devine who danced at the Chicago World's Fair in 1893.

21. Little Rock
22. Little Boy
23. Little Giant
24. Little Lord Fauntleroy
25. Little Lulu
26. Little Richard
27. Little Old Winemaker
28. The Little Flower
29. Little Mo
30. Little Egypt

LITTLE
Complete the "little" expression.

Freshman Level

1. Little Bo-Peep has———.
2. Little things mean———.
3. Mary had a———.
4. O Little Town of———.
5. Thank heaven for———.
6. Little pitchers have———.
7. Try a little———.
8. Little Boy Blue, come———.
9. Those little white———.
10. Daddy's little———.

1. lost her sheep
2. a lot
3. little lamb
4. Bethlehem
5. little girls
6. big ears
7. tenderness
8. blow your horn
9. lies
10. girl

Graduate Level

11. It only hurts for———.
12. Where, oh where, has my———.
13. Say a little———.
14. The battle of Little———
15. Little strokes fell———.
16. There was a little girl and she had———.
17. A little learning is———.
18. Little Jack Horner———.
19. Men who know much———.
20. Little boys are made of———.

11. a little while
12. little dog gone?
13. prayer, for me
14. Bighorn
15. great oaks
16. a little curl
17. a dangerous thing
18. sat in a corner
19. say little
20. snips and snails

Ph. D. Level

21. Suffer the little———.
22. I had a little pony———.
23. Little boats should keep———.
24. The fog comes on———.
25. Every little movement has a meaning———.
26. Little Polly Flinders———.
27. Great oaks from———.
28. Little Sisters of———.
29. In my little corner———.
30. You gotta give a little, take a little, let your———.

21. children to come unto me
22. his name was Dapple Grey
23. near shore
24. little cat feet
25. of its own
26. sat among the cinders
27. little acorns grow
28. the Poor
29. of the world
30. poor heart break a little

WHAT'S NEW
All answers contain the word "new."

Freshman Level

1. January 1.
2. Team that has won the most World Series.
3. The Western Hemisphere.
4. This sweeps clean.
5. An island country consisting of two main islands.
6. The Empire State.
7. The capital of India.
8. Its capital city is Trenton.
9. Home of the famous French Quarter.
10. The forty-seventh state to enter the Union.

1. New Year's Day
2. New York Yankees
3. New World
4. New broom
5. New Zealand
6. New York
7. New Delhi
8. New Jersey
9. New Orleans
10. New Mexico

Graduate Level

11. FDR promised this to the American public.
12. It became Canada's tenth province in 1949.
13. The Granite State.
14. Name for the northeast section of the U.S.A.
15. Its motto is, "All the news that's fit to print."
16. Yale University is here.
17. The capital of this Canadian province is Fredericton.
18. Part of the Bible.
19. Rhode Island city.
20. The world's second largest island.

11. A New Deal
12. Newfoundland
13. New Hampshire
14. New England
15. New York Times
16. New Haven
17. New Brunswick
18. New Testament
19. Newport
20. New Guinea

Ph. D. Level

21. Poem inscribed on the pedestal of the Statue of Liberty.
22. A Pacific Island 1,000 miles northeast of Sydney, Australia.
23. A 1971 film starring Walter Matthau and Elaine May.
24. A chain of about eighty islands in the Pacific.
25. A Sigmund Romberg–Oscar Hammerstein musical.
26. A No. 1 hit song by the Eagles (1971).
27. The Neolithic Age.
28. This Tom Jones' song went to No. 3 in 1965.

29. Nassau is on this island.
30. Magazine seen floating in the opening scene of the movie *Lifeboat* (1944).

21. "The New Colossus"
22. New Caledonia
23. *A New Leaf*
24. New Hebrides
25. *New Moon*
26. "New Kid in Town"
27. New Stone Age
28. "What's New Pussy-cat?"
29. New Providence
30. *The New Yorker*

OLD
All answers contain the word "old."

Freshman Level

1. Geyser in Yellowstone National Park.
2. In the children's song he had a farm.
3. In nursery rhymes he called for "his fiddlers three."
4. Term for an unmarried mature woman.
5. A 1957 Disney classic about a dog.
6. A term for the U.S. flag.
7. Hammerstein–Kern song about the Mississippi River.
8. Her cupboard was bare.
9. The first thirty-nine books of the Bible.
10. Name for Europe, Asia and Africa collectively.

1. Old Faithful
2. Old MacDonald
3. Old King Cole
4. Old Maid
5. *Old Yellow*
6. Old Glory
7. "Old Man River"
8. Old Mother Hubbard
9. Old Testment
10. Old World

Graduate Level

11. An Ernest Hemingway novel about a Cuban fisherman.
12. Pattie Page's 1957 hit song.
13. Nickname of President Zachary Taylor.
14. A popular Stephen Foster song.
15. Nickname of General G. S. Patton.
16. A cocktail made of whiskey, bitters, sugar, and soda.
17. A dominant, usually conservative element of a political party.
18. New Hamsphire's most famous landmark.
19. Jerry Falwell's weekly TV show.
20. This brought Frosty the Snowman to life.

11. *The Old Man and the Sea*
12. "Old Cape Cod"
13. Old Rough and Ready
14. "My Old Kentucky Home"
15. Old Blood and Guts
16. Old Fashioned
17. Old guard
18. Old Man of the Mountains
19. *Old Time Gospel Hour*
20. Old silk hat

Ph. D. Level

21. Nickname of Captain Queeg in the movie *Caine Mutiny*.
22. Nickname of champion boxer Archie Moore.
23. The camel shown on the package of Camel cigarettes.
24. Tom Mix's sidekick.
25. *Three Dog Night* had this hit song in 1971.
26. The Central Criminal Court of the City of London.
27. Nickname of President Andrew Jackson.
28. Theater in London famous for its Shakespearean productions.
29. The Paleolithic period.
30. Nickname for U.S.S. *Constitution*

21. Old Yellowstain
22. Old Mongoose
23. Old Joe
24. Old Wrangler
25. "Old Fashioned Love Song"
26. Old Bailey
27. Old Hickory
28. Old Vic
29. Old Stone Age
30. Old Ironsides

THREE'S A CROWD
All answers contain the word "three."

Freshman Level

1. They lost their mittens.
2. Their houses were made of straw, sticks, and bricks.
3. Their motto was, "All for one, one for all."
4. Goldilocks visited their house.
5. In poker it beats two pair.
6. The farmer's wife cut off their tails.
7. The butcher, the baker, and the candlestick maker.
8. A 1987 film starring Steve Martin and Chevy Chase.
9. Airplane landing in which the two main wheels and tail wheel touch the ground simultaneously.
10. A race in which contestants run in pairs with adjacent legs bound together.

1. Three Little Kittens
2. Three Little Pigs
3. Three Musketeers
4. The Three Bears
5. Three of a kind
6. Three Blind Mice
7. Three men in a Tub
8. *The Three Amigos*
9. Three-point landing
10. Three-legged race

Graduate Level

11. Reading, writing, and arithmetic.
12. Larry, Curly, and Moe.
13. Gasper, Melchior, and Balthasar.
14. A 1954 film about three American secretaries in Rome.
15. A song title that gives you the time of day.
16. TV show starring John Ritter.
17. "Mack the Knife" is in this opera.
18. a 1987 film starring Tom Selleck and Ted Danson.
19. Bwana Devil was a film that used this visual trickery.
20. Faith, hope, and charity are known by this name.

11. The Three R's
12. The Three Stooges
13. The Three Wise Men
14. *Three Coins in a Fountain*
15. "Three o'Clock in the Morning"
16. *Three's Company*
17. *Three Penny Opera*
18. *Three Men and a Baby*
19. 3-D
20. Three theological virtues

Ph. D. Level

21. Home of the Pittsburgh Pirates baseball team.
22. Nuclear power plant near Harrisburg, Pennsylvania.
23. 1975 Robert Redford movie.
24. No. 1 hit of 1959 by the Browns.
25. Joanne Woodward won an Oscar in this 1957 film.
26. Book by Jerome K. Jerome, made into a 1956 movie.
27. Their No. 1 hit of 1971 was "Joy to the World."
28. The three men cast by Nebuchadnezzar into the fiery furnace and delivered by an angel.
29. A city in southwest Michigan.
30. No.1 hit of 1978 by the Commodores.

21. Three Rivers Stadium
22. Three Mile Island
23. *Three Days of the Condor*
24. "Three Bells"
25. *Three Faces of Eve*
26. *Three Men in a Boat*
27. Three Dog Night
28. Three Holy children
29. Three Rivers
30. "Three Times a Lady"

SMALL-OLD-BLACK

Freshman Level: All answers start with "small."

1. Tam or cap	1. Small hat
2. Sip	2. Small drink
3. Twig	3. Small branch
4. Memo	4. Small note
5. Gherkin	5. Small pickle
6. Tart	6. Small pie
7. Fob	7. Small pocket
8. Bistro	8. Small restaurant
9. Mat	9. Small rug
10. Cot	10. Small bed

Graduate Level: All answers start with "old."

11. Jalopy	11. Old car
12. Hag	12. Old woman
13. Chestnut	13. Old joke
14. Salt	14. Old sailor
15. Nag	15. Old horse
16. Fogy	16. Old person
17. Rags	17. Old clothes
18. Scrap	18. Old iron/metal
19. Senescence	19. Old age
20. An adage	20. Old saying

Ph. D. Level: All answers start with "black."

21. Bubonic	21. Black plague/death
22. Necromancy	22. Black magic
23. Slate	23. Blackboard
24. Twenty-one	24. Blackjack
25. Shiner	25. Black eye
26. General Pershing	26. Black Jack
27. Poisonous spider	27. Black widow
28. It surrounds the Crimean Peninsula	28. Black Sea
29. Reject	29. Blackball
30. Extortion	30. Blackmail

RED, WHITE AND BLUE

All answers contain one of the words, "red," "white," or "blue."

Freshman Level

1. An organization that works to relieve suffering.
2. The president's official residence.
3. Symbol of the Toronto baseball team.
4. Used instead of paint for basement walls.
5. The Children of Israel crossed it.
6. The world's largest animal.
7. The many technicalities found in a bureaucracy.
8. Capital city of the Yukon Territory.
9. Laws designed to enforce morality.
10. It's outside the Kremlin.

1. Red Cross
2. White House
3. Blue Jay
4. Whitewash
5. Red Sea
6. Blue whale
7. Red tape
8. Whitehorse
9. Blue laws
10. Red Square

Graduate Level

11. Its located in Capri.
12. Government report or policy statement.
13. Nickname for Kentucky.
14. The eastern ranges of the Appalachian Mountains.
15. Name for British soldiers during the eighteenth and nineteenth centuries.
16. Organization to pay expenses of hospitalized illness.
17. A missile range in New Mexico.
18. A famous chief of the Oglala Sioux.
19. A birth condition resulting from a defective heart or lung.
20. A famous football star.

11. Blue Grotto
12. White Paper
13. Bluegrass State
14. Blue Ridge Mountains
15. Redcoats
16. Blue Cross
17. White Sands
18. Red Cloud
19. Blue baby
20. Red Grange

Ph. D. Level

21. Nickname for Delaware.
22. The Dutch Method produces the best grade of this.
23. Another name for harebells.
24. A cloudy vision experienced when flying loops, spins, etc.
25. The famous Old Man of the Mountain is in this range.
26. The state flower of Texas.
27. They are also known as "blowflies."
28. It is also called the Judas Tree.
29. A flowing spring at Castalia in Ohio.
30. Erythrocytes

21. Blue Hen State
22. White lead
23. Bluebells-of-Scotland
24. Red-out
25. White Mountains
26. Bluebonnet
27. Bluebottle (fly)
28. Redbud
29. Blue Hole
30. Red blood cells

CATS
All answers start with the word "cat."

Freshman Level

1. The larva of a butterfly.
2. Domesticated bovine animals.
3. The seat of a bishopric.
4. A lists of names, objects, etc. in alphabetical order.
5. A machine for hurling stones, etc.
6. A cord used for stringing musical instruments.
7. A major world religion.
8. A herb enjoyed by cats.
9. A disaster, a calamity.
10. An huge underground place of burial.

1. caterpillar
2. cattle
3. cathedral
4. catalog
5. catapult
6. catgut
7. Catholicism
8. catnip
9. catastrophe
10. catacomb

Graduate Level

11. An island southwest of Los Angeles.
12. Steep rapids of great size.
13. An archaic name for China.
14. An outline of the principles of a religious creed.
15. A narrow walking space, as at the side of a bridge.
16. The part of an electron tube from which electrons escape.
17. A shrill whistle expressing derision.
18. A boat having twin hulls.
19. One who provides food for social functions.
20. A tank at the entrance to a drain or sewer, to retain matter that might block the flow.

11. Catalina
12. cataract
13. Cathay
14. catechism
15. catwalk
16. cathode
17. catcall
18. catamaran
19. caterer
20. catch basin

Ph. D. Level

21. Inflammation of the mucous membrane in the throat.
22. A dry white wine made from an American red grape.
23. A purifying of the emotions.
24. The name for a group of rapidly growing shade trees.
25. A substance used to speed up or retard a chemical reaction.
26. A condition in which a person loses the desire to move.
27. A slender tube for introduction into body cavities.
28. Another name for the mountain lion.
29. Any violent upheaval or change.
30. Without qualification, absolute.

21. catarrh
22. catawba
23. catharsis
24. catalpa
25. catalyst
26. catalepsy
27. catheter
28. catamount
29. cataclysm
30. categorical

WORDS BEGINNING WITH "im"

Freshman Level

1. Not full grown.
2. That which cannot happen.
3. Put in danger.
4. Unlikely to be true.
5. Exempt, not susceptible.
6. Living forever.
7. A person who moves into a new country.
8. Plunge into a liquid.
9. One who is weak in mind.
10. Not relevant.

1. immature
2. impossible
3. imperil
4. improbable
5. immune
6. immortal
7. immigrant
8. immerse
9. imbecile
10. immaterial

Graduate Level

11. Instrument, utensil.
12. A deceiver, a cheat.
13. Not suitable, wrong.
14. Fair, just, showing no favor.
15. Coming at once, without delay.
16. Creation of the mind.
17. Anything that adds value or makes better.
18. A sudden inclination.
19. Push forward, drive.
20. Necessary, urgent.

11. implement
12. impostor
13. improper
14. impartial
15. immediate
16. imagination
17. improvement
18. impulse
19. impel
20. imperative

Ph. D. Level

21. Without previous thought or preparation.
22. Driving force.
23. Not having power, helpless.
24. Able to resist attack.
25. Defective.
26. Not noticeable.
27. Rudely bold, forward.
28. An obstacle, hindrance.
29. Acting hastily, rashly, or with sudden feeling.
30. Unexpressed but inferable.

21. impromptu
22. impetus
23. impotent
24. impregnable
25. imperfect
26. imperceptible
27. impudent
28. impediment
29. impetuous
30. implicit

WORDS ENDING IN "or"

Freshman Level

1.	One who plays a part in a play or movie.	1.	actor
2.	An unmarried man.	2.	bachelor
3.	A physician.	3.	doctor
4.	A mistake.	4.	error
5.	One who creates something new.	5.	inventor
6.	One who pays a call, a guest.	6.	visitor
7.	One who supervises publication.	7.	editor
8.	One who leads an orchestra.	8.	conductor
9.	A hoisting machine or lift.	9.	elevator
10.	Highest elected official of a state.	10.	governor

Graduate Level

11.	One who starts something new.	11.	originator
12.	One who gathers or obtains something.	12.	collector
13.	A person or device that guards.	13.	protector
14.	A person having exclusive ownership to anything.	14.	proprietor
15.	In England, a lawyer who advises clients.	15.	solicitor
16.	One trained to direct the course of a ship, aircraft, etc.	16.	navigator
17.	Any alcoholic beverage; especially distilled spirits.	17.	liquor
18.	A man experienced in warfare.	18.	warrior
19.	One who owes something.	19.	debtor
20.	A keyboard machine that adds, subtracts, multiplies, etc.	20.	calculator

Ph. D. Level

21.	Any trembling, quivering effect.	21.	tremor
22.	A condition in which the senses are greatly dulled.	22.	stupor
23.	One who gives help or confers a benefit.	23.	benefactor
24.	An apparatus for the artificial hatching of eggs.	24.	incubator
25.	One who makes himself responsible for the debit of another.	25.	sponsor.
26.	One who keeps others down by harsh use of force.	26.	dictator
27.	One who acts between disputing parties.	27.	mediator
28.	A lack of energy or enthusiasm.	28.	languor
29.	One who remains alive.	29.	survivor
30.	A type of coffee pot in which boiling water filters down through finely ground coffee.	30.	percolator

WORDS ENDING IN "ice"

Freshman Level

1. A staple food	1. rice
2. Small cubes used in games	2. dice
3. A crafty scheme or plan	3. device
4. Small rodents	4. mice
5. The cost	5. price
6. An immoral habit	6. vice
7. A thin, broad piece cut off from a larger piece	7. slice
8. An alternative	8. choice
9. Suggestion	9. advice
10. The power of speech	10. voice

Graduate Level

11. To do or perform repeatedly	11. practice
12. A substance used to flavor food	12. spice
13. A civil department to enforce the law	13. police
14. The flavor of a black candy	14. licorice
15. The rendering of what is due or merited	15. justice
16. A giving up of some desired thing	16. sacrifice
17. An instant	17. trice
18. To attract by arousing hope	18. entice
19. The brink of a cliff	19. precipice
20. A beginner	20. novice

Ph. D. Level

21. A moist mass applied to a sore	21. poultice
22. Greed	22. avarice
23. Upper portion of a woman's dress	23. bodice
24. An opening into a cavity	24. orifice
25. A tendency to make a sudden change of mind	25. caprice
26. The crowning top of an entablature	26. cornice
27. A place of rest or shelter	27. hospice
28. A preparation for cleaning the teeth	28. dentifrice
29. A diseased condition of the liver, yellowness of the skin	29. jaundice
30. A large and imposing building	30. edifice

WORDS ENDING IN "ive"

Freshman Level

1. An engine used to pull freight trains.
2. Having the ability to induce someone to do something.
3. Grossly offensive, causing feelings of disgust.
4. Inclined to much chatter.
5. Resembling the style of early times.
6. Typical of a group.
7. Large in size, ponderous, and heavy.
8. Obnoxious, disgusting, unpleasant, disagreeable.
9. In mathematics greater than zero.
10. Tending to choose carefully.

1. locomotive
2. persuasive
3. repulsive
4. talkative
5. primitive
6. representative
7. massive
8. offensive
9. positive
10. selective

Graduate Level

11. Not acting, working, or operating; inactive, inert.
12. Something related as a story.
13. Having a strong desire for complete domination of another person.
14. A substance added to food to retard spoilage.
15. Striving for or favoring reform.
16. Inclined to take something in.
17. Having a desire to shield or defend from attack.
18. Inclined to give an answer or reply.
19. Judgment of facts with regard to their importance.
20. Elevated to the highest degree.

11. passive
12. narrative
13. possessive
14. preservative
15. progressive
16. receptive
17. protective
18. responsive
19. perspective
20. superlative

Ph. D. Level

21. Having a revengeful spirit.
22. Subject to change, experimental.
23. Perceived or learned without conscious reasoning.
24. Expressing a subdued sadness, mournful.
25. Not easily noticed; not standing out.
26. A verbal mood that offers supposition.
27. Preventing the sale, purchase, etc., of something.
28. Anticipated; looking toward the future.
29. Following in sequence, consecutive.
30. Relating to each of those under consideration.

21. vindictive
22. tentative
23. intuitive
24. plaintive
25. unobtrusive
26. subjunctive
27. prohibitive
28. prospective
29. successive
30. respective

WORDS ENDING IN "ity"

Freshman Level

1. More than half	1. majority
2. Information intended to promote	2. publicity
3. Distinctive qualities of an individual	3. personality
4. A current or charge of energy	4. electricity
5. A famous person	5. celebrity
6. Quickness in movement	6. agility
7. Virginity or celibacy	7. chastity
8. An income paid yearly	8. annuity
9. Transmission of characteristics from parents to offspring.	9. heredity
10. A gift of money for services, a tip	10. gratuity

Graduate Level

11. The right to command or act.	11. authority
12. A place, region, etc.	12. locality
13. The state of being able to withstand wear	13. durability
14. Full physical development	14. maturity
15. An institution for higher education.	15. university
16. Maximum ability to contain something	16. capacity
17. The state of having the same abilities, power, etc.	17. equality
18. The state of having a resemblance to something else	18. similarity
19. The state of being lower in quality or worth	19. inferiority
20. An abnormally shaped part of the body	20. deformity

Ph. D. Level

21. An expression having more than one meaning	21. ambiguity
22. Using an excess of words	22. verbosity
23. Lack of understanding	23. stupidity
24. The state of having the same abilities, powers, etc.	24. equality
25. The attraction of the earth's mass for bodies at or near its surface	25. gravity
26. Responsibility for damages	26. liability
27. Extreme fatness	27. obesity
28. The state of using an excess of words	28. verbosity
29. A trade relation allowing mutual interchange	29. reciprocity
30. State of being excellent, worthy, or esteemed	30. dignity

ANIMAL WORDS
All answers are the names of animals.

Freshman Level

1. The black ——— of the family.
2. That's a ——— of another color.
3. The ———'s share.
4. Take the ——— by the horns.
5. To put on the ———.
6. A ——— in a poke.
7. A pretty kettle of ———
8. ——— of a feather
9. Let the ——— out of the bag.
10. To cast pearls before ———.

1. sheep
2. horse
3. lion
4. bull
5. dog
6. pig
7. fish
8. birds
9. cat
10. swine

Graduate Level

11. Till the ——— come home.
12. A ——— song.
13. A road ———
14. Be a ——— for work.
15. A lame ———.
16. ——— business.
17. A red ———.
18. A ——— in the ointment.
19. Some day the ——— will turn.
20. To cook one's ———.

11. cows
12. swan
13. hog
14. bear
15. duck
16. monkey
17. herring
18. fly
19. worm
20. goose

Ph. D. Level: Provide the animal name which is used as verb with the given meaning.

21. To mimic
22. To trick by cunning
23. To eat voraciously
24. To trail persistently
25. To tamper with
26. To be evasive
27. To engage in prankish play
28. To pester
29. To move forward with a side to side motion
30. To thrash

21. ape
22. fox
23. wolf
24. dog
25. monkey
26. weasel
27. horse
28. badger
29. snake
30. whale

ANIMAL WORDS

Place an animal's name in front of the given word(s) to make another word—e.g., house. *Answer:* doghouse

Freshman Level

1. pen, session	1. Bull
2. fight, tag	2. Dog
3. hole, trot	3. Fox
4. hand, lick	4. Cow
5. call, gut	5. Cat
6. business, wrench	6. Monkey
7. play, sense	7. Horse
8. dance, charmer	8. Snake
9. line, hive	9. Bee
10. ball, eaten	10. Moth

Graduate Level

11. express	11. Pony
12. wife	12. Fish
13. trap	13. Mouse
14. feed	14. Chicken
15. pecked	15. Hen
16. tent	16. Pup
17. pen	17. Pig
18. neck	18. Turtle
19. lily	19. Tiger
20. hearted	20. Lion

Ph. D. Level

21. pace	21. Snails
22. wood	22. Worm
23. eyed	23. Eagle or hawk
24. tears	24. Crocodile
25. board	25. Beaver
26. browed	26. Beetle
27. tie	27. Hog
28. bar	28. Crow
29. court	29. Kangaroo
30. dip	30. Sheep

ANIMAL EXPRESSIONS
All answers contain the name of an animal.

Freshman Level

1. One who imitates someone else
2. Insincere grief
3. By the most direct route
4. A small amount of money
5. In disfavor especially with one's spouse
6. Depend on something which is not yet certain

7. An overanxious employee, student, etc.
8. Zero, nothing
9. Be patient
10. Suspect treachery

1. copycat
2. crocodile tears
3. as the crow flies
4. chicken feed
5. in the doghouse
6. count your chickens before they hatch
7. eager beaver
8. goose egg
9. hold your horses
10. smell a rat

Graduate Level

11. Reveal a secret
12. Avoid, escape from
13. Take the shortest possible route
14. To continue or nurse ill feeling toward
15. An obscure contestant in a race, who may surprise
16. Out of one's element
17. One who deceives by guileless exterior

18. A long time, forever

19. Remain unconcerned, calm
20. A group discussion covering several trivial topics

11. let the cat out of the bag
12. duck out
13. make a beeline for
14. bear a grudge
15. dark horse
16. fish out of water
17. wolf in sheep's clothing
18. till the cows come home
19. not to bat an eye
20. bull session

Ph. D. Level

21. To set aside consideration of
22. The largest part
23. Foolishness or unethical dealing
24. Something purchased without being examined
25. A convict
26. Something that's hard to believe
27. Speak frankly and forcefully
28. A useless or unmanageable gift
29. Pretend to be dead or asleep
30. To discover through careful investigation

21. pigeonhole
22. lion's share
23. monkey business
24. pig in a poke
25. jailbird
26. cock-and-bull story
27. talk turkey
28. white elephant
29. play possum
30. Ferret out

EDIBLE EXPRESSIONS
All answers contain the name of a food.

Freshman Level

1. The chief person in a group.
2. Indulge in youthful excesses.
3. Pretend dislike for something unobtainable.
4. Exactly alike.
5. Savings set aside for one's old age.
6. To save or store up.
7. Enjoy two opposite advantages from a single thing.

8. Laugh at, mock.
9. The best available.
10. Complain.

1. top banana
2. sow your wild oats
3. sour grapes
4. two peas in a pod
5. nest egg
6. salt away
7. have one's cake and eat it too
8. give the raspberry
9. cream of the crop
10. beef about

Graduate Level

11. To understand what attitude is most advantageous.

12. Only through experience can something be tested.

13. Disclose a secret.
14. Nonsense.
15. A great treasure to someone.
16. Be unsuccessful, fail.
17. Carry off the prize, prove superior to.
18. Something designed to deceive.
19. To seek to ingratiate oneself.
20. Succeed in some project, be triumphant.

11. know on which side one's bread is buttered
12. proof of the pudding is in the eating
13. spill the beans
14. baloney
15. the apple of one's eye
16. lay an egg
17. take the cake
18. red herring
19. butter up
20. bring home the bacon

Ph. D. Level

21. Accept with serious reservations.

22. Anything easy to do.
23. An extra dividend or bonus.
24. Something easy such as money received for little or no work.
25. Chop up into fine pieces.
26. Be upset, worried.
27. The higher social class.
28. The period of one's youth.
29. Displease, attend, irritate.
30. Worry about something unalterable.

21. take with a grain of salt
22. duck soup/easy as pie
23. frosting on the cake
24. gravy train
25. make mincemeat of
26. in a stew
27. upper crust
28. salad days
29. go against the grain
30. cry over spilled milk

BODY PARTS

Freshman Level

1. —— watch
2. —— grease
3. cigarette ——
4. rule of ——
5. lump in the ——
6. —— in cheek
7. —— relative
8. a —— for news
9. community ——
10. —— the music

1. wrist
2. elbow
3. butt
4. thumb
5. throat
6. tongue
7. blood
8. nose
9. chest
10. face

Graduate Level

11. —— the mark
12. cod —— oil
13. out on a ——
14. well turned ——
15. pot —— stove
16. —— of clay
17. stiff upper ——
18. all —— on deck
19. the long —— of the law
20. rule with an iron ——

11. toe
12. liver
13. limb
14. ankle
15. belly
16. feet
17. lip
18. hands
19. arm
20. fist

Ph. D. Level

21. nothing but skin and ——
22. the —— that launched a thousand ships
23. keep your —— crossed
24. tough as ——
25. word of ——
26. —— room
27. —— a ride
28. kick up your ——
29. let your —— down
30. —— the bill

21. bones
22. face
23. fingers
24. nails
25. mouth
26. elbow
27. thumb
28. heels
29. hair
30. foot

MAKE

Freshman Level: All answers are 3-letter words.

1. Make an effort
2. Make fun of
3. Make less bright
4. Make a request
5. Make a choice
6. Make damp
7. Make firm
8. Make imitation of
9. Make irate
10. Make note of

1. try
2. rib
3. dim
4. ask/beg
5. opt
6. wet
7. fix/tie
8. ape
9. vex/irk
10. jot

Graduate Level: All answers are 4-letter words.

11. Make arrangements
12. Make docile
13. Make well
14. Make eyes
15. Make the first move
16. Make less dense
17. Make angry
18. Make written corrections
19. Make a sweater
20. Make a botch of

11. plan
12. tame
13. cure
14. leer/ogle
15. lead/open
16. thin
17. rile
18. edit
19. knit
20. flub

Ph. D. Level: All answers are 5-letter words.

21. Make late
22. Make lustrous
23. Make merry
24. Male amends
25. Make broader
26. Make cloth
27. Make even and flat
28. Make glad
29. Make haste
30. Make way

21. delay
22. shine
23. revel
24. atone
25. widen
26. weave
27. level
28. amuse/cheer
29. hurry/speed
30. yield

CROSSWORD PUZZLERS: 3 letter words

All answers are three-letter words.

Freshman Level

1. Born
2. Yes (French)
3. Female sheep
4. Resort
5. Lamprey
6. Swamp
7. Wreath (Hawaiian)
8. Fish eggs
9. Herd: whales
10. Coin (Japanese)

1. Née
2. Oui
3. Ewe
4. Spa
5. Eel
6. Bog, fen
7. Lei
8. Roe
9. Pod, gam
10. Yen, sen

Graduate Level

11. Turkish cap
12. Australian bird
13. Age
14. Dry (French)
15. Piece out
16. Revolver (slang)
17. Right: cause to turn
18. Sailor
19. Salt
20. Hare: female

11. Fez
12. Emu
13. Era
14. Sec
15. Eke
16. Gat
17. Gee
18. Tar, gob
19. Sal
20. Doe

Ph. D. Level

21. Food (Hawaiian)
22. High (music)
23. Newt
24. Lettuce
25. Biblical high priest
26. Toward the stern
27. Wing
28. Pseudonym: Dickens'
29. Spread grass for drying
30. Witticism

21. Poi
22. Alt
23. Eft
24. Cos
25. Eli
26. Aft
27. Ala
28. Boz
29. Ted
30. Mot

CURRENT WORDS I

All answers are a two-part term—some hyphenated words, some solid compounds, some two-word phrases. Many are slang terms. Letter clues are provided—e.g., A bar at which drinks are served free (O.B.). *Answer:* open bar.

Freshman Level

1. A motor vehicle for driving on sand beaches (D.B.)
2. One who leaves a party early. (P.P.)
3. Social activity after a day's skiing (A.S.).
4. To withdraw from conventionial society (D.O.).
5. Food that can be eaten without utensils (F.F.).
6. To plead poverty as an excuse (P.M.).
7. Printed record produced automatically by a computer (P.O.).
8. To avoid work or responsibility (G.O.).
9. Out of the range of a motion picture or television camera (O.C.).
10. A feature that automatically counteracts the effect of a malfunction (F.S.).

1. dune buggy
2. party pooper
3. après ski
4. drop out
5. finger food
6. poor-mouth
7. printout
8. goof off
9. off camera
10. fail-safe

Graduate Level

11. An excess: beyond what is required (O.K.)
12. Involved, often deliberately ambiguous language (D.S.).
13. To deemphasize (D.P.).
14. A system allowing employees to choose their own working hours (F.T.)
15. Slang term for a psychiatric hospital (F.F.).
16. Distress caused by rapid changes (F.S.).
17. A stategy for achieving an object (G.P.).
18. A health spa (F.F.).
19. To withdraw from reality by taking drugs (F.O.).
20. An informal group discussion (R.S.).

11. overkill
12. doublespeak
13. downplay
14. flex time
15. funny farm
16. future shock
17. game plan
18. fat farm
19. freak out
20. rap session

Ph. D. Level

21. To dress up, prettify (G.U.).
22. The state of being well-off (F.C.).
23. A cinematic movement characterized by improvisation (N.W.).
24. To wrap (a product) in clear plastic to form a tightly fitting package (S.W.).
25. The hierarchical interrelationships existing within a group (P.S.).
26. Extending of service beyond current limits (O.R.).
27. An unstructured group designed to develop open emotional ties (E.G.).
28. A detailed report recommending a course of action on an issue (P.P.).
29. Advocating a persistently firm course of action (H.L.).
30. Permitting access to stored data in any order desired (R.A.).

21. gussy up
22. fat city
23. New Wave
24. shrink-wrap
25. power structure
26. outreach
27. encounter group
28. position paper
29. hard line
30. random access

CURRENT WORDS II

All answers are a two-part term—some hyphenated words, some solid compounds, some two-word phrases. Many are slang terms. Letter clues are provided.

Freshman Level

1. A period of time during which bar prices are reduced (H.H.).
2. A western film produced by Italians (S.W.).
3. To swim in the nude (S.D.).
4. Something, as a story, that is obviously a cheap copy or imitation of something else (R.O.).
5. A traveling bag for use in air travel (F.B.).
6. Something that enhances and satisfies one's own self (E.T.).
7. A bag for carrying food home from a restaurant (D.B.).
8. Designed to prevent tampering or breaking by children (C.P.).
9. The practice of carrying one's lunch to work in a bag (B.B.).
10. An alcoholic drink served without ice (S.U.).

1. happy hour
2. spaghetti western
3. skinny-dip
4. rip-off
5. flight bag
6. ego trip
7. doggy bag
8. childproof
9. brown-bagging
10. straight up

Graduate Level

11. Underhanded or unsportsmanlike conduct (D.P.).
12. An overhead metal bar on dune buggies or race cars for protection in case of a turnover (R.B.).
13. A familiar object whose presence dispels anxiety (S.B.).
14. A film characterized by nudity and sexual situations (S.F.).
15. A derived product; a byproduct (S.O.).
16. A shot in basketball in which the ball is thrown down through the basket (D.S.).
17. A professional athlete who is free to negotiate with any team (F.A.).
18. To destroy oneself (S.D.).
19. A fall from a surfboard (W.O.).
20. A fight (P.U.).

11. dirty pool
12. roll bar
13. security blanket
14. skin flick
15. spinoff
16. dunk shot
17. free agent
18. self-destruct
19. wipeout
20. punchup

Ph. D. Level

21. To be uncooperative, obstructive, or evasive (S.W.).
22. An important-sounding word used to impress laymen (B.W.).
23. Something received without charge (F.B.).
24. A motion picture film that is stopped to appear as a static picture (F.F.).
25. Lacking importance, trivial, insignificant (M.M.).
26. A highly publicized event of little interest (N.E.).
27. Something that is dull or boring (D.V.).
28. A quick temper (S.F.).
29. To put an end to by severe criticism (S.D.).
30. A parody or takeoff (S.U.).

21. stone-wall
22. buzz word
23. freebee
24. freeze-frame
25. Mickey Mouse
26. nonevent
27. Dullsville
28. short fuse
29. shoot down
30. sendup

CURRENT WORDS III
All answers are a single word. The first letter of the answer is provided.

Freshman Level

1. Markedly or exaggeratedly masculine (M).
2. To expose one's genitals suddenly and briefly (F).
3. A weak or ineffectual person (W).
4. One who is unusually strange or queer (W).
5. A red mark produced in lovemaking by sucking the skin (H).
6. Showing signs of tension or uneasiness (u).
7. A feeling of boredom or general disatisfaction (B).
8. The human buttocks (B).
9. To throw up, to vomit (B).
10. An athlete, especially a school athlete (J).

1. macho
2. flash
3. wimp
4. weirdo
5. hickey
6. uptight
7. blahs
8. buns
9. barf
10. jock

Graduate Level

11. One who takes a militant attitude and advocates action (H).
12. To promote or publicize extravagantly (H).
13. A clumsy and awkward person (K).
14. Having bizarre or unconventional tastes especially in sex (K).
15. A stimulant drug (U).
16. To remove income to avoid paying taxes (S).
17. Out of one's mind, crazy (B).
18. To remove a recorded sound from a videotape (B).
19. Unprofessional, amateurish (B).
20. Influence, pull, power to affect something (C).

11. hawk
12. hype
13. klutz
14. kinky
15. upper
16. skim
17. bonkers
18. blip
19. bush
20. clout

Ph. D. Level

21. To eat between meals (N).
22. Being in a dirty, uncared for condition (G).
23. The place at which two systems meet and interact (I).
24. An award of honor (K).
25. A pointed witty remark or retort, a dig (Z).
26. To talk indecisively, equivocate (W).
27. A jail or prison (S).
28. Extraordinarily successful (B).
29. Deceptive or foolish talk (J).
30. To cause illegally obtained money to appear legitimate by passing it through a third party (L).

21. nosh
22. grungy
23. interface
24. kudo
25. zinger
26. waffle
27. slammer
28. boffo
29. jive
30. launder

HEADWEAR

Freshman Level

1. A headdress that symbolizes sovereignty.
2. A covering for the head and back of the neck, sometimes forming part of a garment.
3. A protective covering for the head.
4. A broad-brimmed hat popular in Mexico.
5. A cloth worn twisted about the head.
6. A Scots cap with a tight headband and full, flat top.
7. Man's silk hat with a tall cylindrical crown and narrow brim.
8. A close-fitting off-the-face hat.
9. A small brimless cap, often decorated with a button.
10. An outdoor headpiece for children usually tied under the chin.

1. crown
2. hood
3. helmet
4. sombrero
5. turban
6. tam-o'-shanter (tam)
7. top hat
8. toque
9. beanie
10. bonnet

Graduate Level

11. A brimless tapering felt cap with a tassel.
12. A waterproof hat with a brim over the neck.
13. A soft felt hat with a brim and a crown creased lengthwise.
14. Brimless headgear, usually visored.
15. A hat woven from leaves of a tree of central and South America.
16. A close-fitting hoodlike knitted cap covering the head, neck, and part of the shoulders
17. A decorative ornament worn by women on formal occasions.
18. A stiff hat with a curved narrow brim and a round crown.
19. A soft flat cap originating in the Basque regions of France and Spain.
20. A broad-brimmed cowboy hat with a high crown.

11. fez
12. sou' wester
13. fedora
14. cap
15. panama hat
16. balaclava
17. tiara
18. derby or bowler
19. beret
20. Stetson

Ph. D. Level

21. A small, snug brimless cap often worn indoors.
22. A light black lace scarf often worn over the head and shoulders of women in Latin American and Spain.
23. A wreath or garland for the head.
24. A small brimless hat with a flat top.
25. A man's hat with a low, flat crown and usually a turned-up brim
26. A close-fitting cap or hood worn by nuns under a veil.
27. A woman's small helmetlike hat.
28. A monk's hood.
29. A tall fur cap worn by British guardsmen.
30. A net or bag worn to keep a woman's hair in place.

21. skullcap
22. mantilla
23. chaplet
24. pillbox
25. pork-pie
26. coif
27. cloche
28. cowl
29. busby
30. snood

HORSE AND HORSE-RACING TERMS

Freshman Level

1. A race in which two horses finish in a tie.
2. The total number of horses in a race.
3. A horse that has never won a race.
4. The official time scheduled for a race to begin.
5. To withdraw a horse from a race in which it was entered.
6. A young female horse before sexual maturity.
7. Any young horse less than one year old.
8. A castrated male horse.
9. A sexually mature female horse.
10. A stallion used for breeding.

1. dead heat
2. field
3. maiden
4. post time
5. scratch
6. filly
7. foal
8. gelding
9. mare
10. stud (horse)

Graduate Level

11. The probable betting odds on the morning of the race.
12. The weight that a horse carries in a race.
13. The official who assigns the weight a horse must carry.
14. A system where a bettor must pick the winner in the first and second races.
15. To change suddenly into a gallop from a trot or pace.
16. The straightaway on the side of the track opposite the finish line or post.
17. A horse that has passed its first January 1.
18. Any untamed western horse.
19. The mother of a foal.
20. Any forward movement such as walking or galloping.

11. morning line
12. impost
13. handicapper
14. daily double
15. break
16. backstretch
17. yearling
18. bronco (bronc)
19. dam
20. gait

Ph. D. Level

21. The father of a foal.
22. Riding equipment such as the bridle and saddle.
23. The fenced-in area where the horses are saddled.
24. Officials who may disqualify a horse.
25. Any objection raised after a race.
26. A horse that runs in a claiming race.
27. A small-priced or favorite horse.
28. A race of more than a mile.
29. A race of a mile or less.
30. An apprentice jockey who gets a weight allowance.

21. sire
22. tack
23. paddock
24. stewards
25. inquiry
26. plater
27. chalk
28. route
29. sprint
30. bug boy

TEXTILES/FABRICS

Freshman Level

1. The soft hair from the fleece of sheep.
2. A course fabric made of jute or hemp; used for bagging.
3. A synthetic material used for women's stockings.
4. The soft fibrous material obtained from the plant.
5. Literally the "king's cloth."
6. A strong cotton used for overalls.
7. A fine natural fiber produced by the larvae of certain worms.
8. A heavy cloth used for sails, tents, etc.
9. Cheap printed cotton cloth.
10. A fabric woven from the fibers of flax.

1. wool
2. burlap
3. nylon
4. cotton
5. corduroy
6. denim
7. silk
8. canvas
9. calico
10. linen

Graduate Level

11. A fabric with a glossy face and a dull back.
12. A leather having a soft, napped finish.
13. A soft fabric used for warm undergarments.
14. A cellulose material used in tire cords and garments.
15. A thin fabric, usually striped, with a crinkled surface.
16. A soft woolen cloth of Scots origin.
17. A fabric with a rough, nubby surface; named after a Chinese province.
18. A fine wool obtained from goats from the Himalayan region.
19. A cloth made from the hair of goats or rabbits of the same name.
20. A firm, twilled worsted fabric often used for coats.

11. satin
12. suede
13. flannel
14. rayon
15. seersucker
16. tweed
17. shantung
18. cashmere
19. angora
20. gabardine

Ph. D. Level

21. A cotton fabric woven in solid colors, checks, plaids, etc.
22. A soft, fuzzy cord used for bedspreads, fringes, etc.
23. A fabric with a smooth, almost shiny surface used for sportswear.
24. A sheer lightweight fabric (also a cooking term).
25. A strong, close-woven fabric (often used for raincoats), named because it was made in Avignon, a papal residence.
26. A plain-weave cotton fabric originally made in Iraq.
27. A cotton fabric, usually glazed and printed in bright colors.
28. A fine, plain-woven, somewhat stiff fabric used in women's party frocks.
29. A closely woven cotton fabric without gloss; used for sheeting.
30. A twilled fabric characterized by a diagonal rib on both sides; used for suits, coats, and dresses.

21. gingham
22. chenille
23. sharkskin
24. chiffon
25. poplin
26. muslin
27. chintz
28. taffeta
29. percale
30. serge

RELIGIOUS GROUPS

Freshman Level

1. A group who believe in adult baptism by total immersion.
2. They avoid all ritual and refer to themselves as Friends.
3. The Church of Jesus Christ of Latter Day Saints.
4. The movement founded by John Wesley in 1738.
5. These Gospel preachers can be Low, High, or Middle churchmen.
6. American sects that observe Saturday as the true Sabbath.
7. A denomination founded by Mary Baker Eddy (1821–1910).
8. They see themselves as "the Lord's organization." Abel was the first one.
9. "Speaking in tongues" is a feature of their meetings.
10. This group grew out of Christian mission meetings held by the Rev. William Booth.

1. Baptists
2. Quakers
3. Mormons
4. Methodism
5. Evangelists
6. Adventists
7. Christian Science
8. Jehovah's Witnesses
9. Pentecostalism
10. Salvation Army

Graduate Level

11. No special doctrines but a belief in the single personality of God.
12. The oldest sect of Nonconformists who hold that each congregation should be independent.
13. The religion of Celtic Britain and Gaul.
14. The religion of Tibet.
15. A secret society preaching the immense latent potential of the mind.
16. A revivalist group calling themselves The United Society of believers in Christ's Second Appearing.
17. A major Muslim sect opposed to the orthodox Sunnites.
18. A faith which teaches the unity of all religions and the unity of mankind.
19. A sect of Russian origin. They protest materialism by walking about naked.
20. A community of the Punjab. The hair is never cut and usually hidden under a turban.

11. Unitarianism
12. Congregationalists
13. Druidism
14. Lamaism
15. Rosicrucians
16. Shakers
17. Shiites (Shia)
18. Bahai faith
19. Doukhobors
20. Sikhism

Ph. D. Level

21. A sect of Muslim Shiites that terrorized Persia and Syria in the Middle Ages.
22. A denomination formed in the U.S.A. by John Thomas.
23. A Jewish sect which may have influenced the teachings of Jesus.
24. A sun religion which for two centuries rivaled Christianity.
25. The state religion of Persia prior to Islam.
26. An Indian sect based on "ahimsa," the sacredness of all life.
27. A sect of Egyptian Christians.
28. The branch of Protestantism founded by Jean Chauvin.
29. A member of the Church of England.
30. A religion that began with the publication of A.j. Davis' *Nature's Divine Revelations* (1847).

21. Assassins
22. Christadelphians
23. Essenes
24. Mithraism
25. Zoroastrianism
26. Jainism
27. Coptic Church
28. Calvinism
29. Anglican
30. Spiritualism

IDEAS AND BELIEFS

Freshman Level

1. The therapeutic effects of implanting needles in the body.
2. Its main pursuit was the transmutation of metals.
3. A belief that heavenly bodies influence human affairs.
4. A mythical continent said to have lain between Europe and America.
5. Detection of underground water by holding a stick.
6. The removal of an evil spirit by a ritual or prayer.
7. The practice of curing physical and mental ills by supernatural power.
8. Eternal life.
9. The belief that the Pope, when speaking on matters of faith or morals, is not subject to error.
10. A noisy type of spirit which throws things about—possibly a rare but natural phenomenon.

1. Acupuncture
2. Alchemy
3. Astrology
4. Atlantis
5. Dowsing
6. Exorcism
7. Faith healing
8. Immortality
9. Papal infallibility
10. Poltergeist

Graduate Level

11. Black magic or sorcery by women.
12. A Hindu technique for freeing the mind from the senses.
13. The need to establish an autonomous Jewish homeland.
14. Name for medicine men who used magical arts to cure ills.
15. A name for any ideal society.
16. The communication between minds other than by the ordinary senses.
17. The ability to "see" objects or events not discernible by others by reason of space, time, or other causes.
18. The Chinese *Book of Changes*.
19. The supposed ability of some men to transform themselves into wolves.
20. The belief that the Great Pyramid at Giza can reveal important truths.

11. Witchcraft
12. Yoga
13. Zionism
14. Shamans
15. Utopia
16. Telepathy
17. Clairvoyance
18. I Ching
19. Lycanthropy
20. Pyramidology

Ph. D. Level

21. A society founded in 1884 to ensure gradual introduction of socialist practices.
22. The traditional code of honor of the Samurai.
23. A late eighteenth century artistic movement that replaced formalism with imaginative emotionalism.
24. A widespread secret organization of English origin.
25. A secret society founded in 1776 to combat ignorance.
26. A branch of fringe medicine whose motto is "like cures like."
27. A group who vandalized machinery fearing it would destroy their livelihood.
28. The branch of psychology that said the whole was greater than the sum of its parts.
29. This group followed the Beat Generation of the 1940s and 50s.
30. A quasi-philosophical system started by Ron Hubbard.

21. Fabian Society
22. Bushido
23. Romanticism
24. Freemasonry
25. Illuminati
26. Homoeopathy
27. Luddites
28. Gestalt psychology
29. Flower people (Love Generation)
30. Scientology (dianetics)

THEORIES OF PHILOSOPHY

Identify the term used to describe the theory (all are -isms).

Freshman Level

1. The rejection of the concept of God.
2. The position that we can never know ultimate answers to fundamental inquiries.
3. Any system that holds that all will work out for the best.
4. The belief that all is doomed to evil.
5. A method that makes practical consequences the test of truth.
6. The theory that reason alone can arrive at basic reality.
7. Assertion of a belief without authoritative support.
8. The belief that the universe follows a predetermined pattern.
9. The doctrine that physical well-being is all important.
10. The doctrine that pleasure is the highest good.

1. Atheism
2. Agnosticism
3. Optimism
4. Pessimism
5. Pragmatism
6. Rationalism
7. Dogmatism
8. Determinism
9. Materialism
10. Hedonism

Graduate Level

11. Any system that regards human interests as paramount.
12. The belief that the serving of one's own interests is paramount.
13. The principle of acting in the interests of others.
14. The doctrine that no facts can be certainly known.
15. The theory that truth lies midway between dogmatism and skepticism.
16. Belief in an ultimate reality that transcends human experience.
17. Acceptance of the concept of God as a workable hypothesis.
18. The belief that God is identical with the universe.
19. The theory that there is an ultimate reality in which all differences are reconciled.
20. Rejection of the concept of the absolute.

11. Humanism
12. Egoism
13. Altruism
14. Skepticism
15. Criticism
16. Transcendentalism
17. Theism
18. Pantheism
19. Absolutism
20. Relativism

Ph. D. Level

21. Theory that reality is only appearance.
22. Belief that the world consists of two radically independent and absolute elements— e.g., good and evil.
23. Belief that there are more than two irreducible components of reality.
24. Denial of objective universal values; the self is the ultimate reality.
25. The theory that the will is the determining factor in the universe.
26. Belief in only one ultimate reality, whatever its nature.
27. Belief that the universe is composed of distinct and indivisible units.
28. Belief that withdrawal from the physical world is the highest good.
29. Rejection of all a priori knowledge in favor of experience and induction.
30. Any system that regards thought as the basis of knowledge.

21. Phenomenalism
22. Dualism
23. Pluralism
24. Existentialism
25. Voluntarism
26. Monism
27. Atomism
28. Asceticism
29. Empiricism
30. Idealism

FOREIGN PHRASES AND WORDS

Give the English meaning for each foreign language word or phrase.

Freshman Level

1. Petite
2. Per diem
3. Apropos
4. Au revoir
5. Tête-à-tête
6. Modus operandi
7. Status quo
8. Nom de plume
9. Per se
10. En passant

1. Small
2. By the day
3. With respect to, suitably
4. Till we meet again
5. An intimate conversation between two people
6. Method of operating
7. The existing condition
8. Pen name
9. By itself
10. In passing

Graduate Level

11. A la mode
12. Entre nous
13. En masse
14. A priori
15. Tout ensemble
16. De facto
17. Esprit de corps
18. En route
19. Pièce de resistance
20. Table d'hôte

11. After the fashion
12. Between ourselves
13. In the mass
14. From cause to effect
15. The whole taken together
16. Actually
17. Animating spirit of a collective body
18. On the road
19. The main dish of a meal
20. A course meal served at a fixed price

Ph. D. Level

21. Ex post facto
22. Mal de mer
23. De trop
24. Déclassé
25. Comme il faut
26. Prima facie
27. Ex officio
28. Pro tempore
29. Ad valorem
30. Bon mot

21. From what is done afterward
22. Seasickness
23. Out of place; superfluous
24. Degraded from one's class in society
25. As it should be
26. At first view
27. By virtue of an office
28. Temporarily
29. According to the value
30. Witticism

WORDS OF FOREIGN ORIGIN

All answers are one word. The last two letters of the answer are provided—e.g., First appearance before the public: -ut. *Answer*: debut.

Freshman Level

1. Remains, fragments: -is.
2. An exhibition by a medium: -ce.
3. A male body servant: -et.
4. Behind the times: -sé.
5. The select people: -te.
6. Showing lack of experience: -ve.
7. Against: -us.
8. Influence derived from success: -ge.
9. A disclosure of something discreditable: -sé.
10. One's employment record: -mé.

1. Debris
2. Séance
3. Valet
4. Passé
5. Elite
6. Naive
7. Versus
8. Prestige
9. Exposé
10. Résumé

Graduate Level

11. Bored, indifferent: -sé.
12. A burlesque on recent events: -ue.
13. There! Behold! -là.
14. Originality plus style: -ic.
15. Style of hairdress: -re.
16. One who knows the details of a fine art: -ur.
17. The attendants of a person of prominence: -ge.
18. A person of the middle class: -is.
19. A prima donna: -va.
20. The principal course at a meal: -ee.

11. Blasé
12. Revue
13. Voilà
14. Chic
15. Coiffure
16. Connoisseur
17. Entourage
18. Bourgeois
19. Diva
20. Entree

Ph. D. Level

21. Vague discontent resulting from inactivity: -ui.
22. Strong mental leaning or attraction: -nt.
23. Giving zest, having an agreeably tart taste: -nt.
24. A clique, a small select circle of congenial persons: -ie.
25. An amateur or a dabbler in art: -te.
26. Delicate skill: -se.
27. Born: -eé.
28. One under the care and protection of another: -gé.
29. List of dramas, songs, etc., ready for performance: -re.
30. A group combined to foster special interests: -oc.

21. Ennui
22. Penchant
23. Piquant
24. Coterie
25. Dilettante
26. Finesse
27. Née
28. Protégé
29. Repertoire
30. Bloc

HOMOPHONES I

The meanings are provided. Name the sound-alike words—e.g. One plus one: more than enough. *Answer*: two, too.

Freshman Level

1. Single thing, opposite of lost
2. Two of a kind, a fruit
3. In this place, to listen to
4. Window glass, suffering
5. Cost of travel, just
6. An opening, entire
7. Simple, a tool
8. Falling water, term of a ruler
9. A fragment, freedom from war
10. Owed, condensed moisture

1. one, won
2. pair, pear
3. here, hear
4. pane, pain
5. fare, fair
6. hole, whole
7. plain, plane
8. rain, reign
9. piece, peace
10. due, dew

Graduate Level

11. To inscribe by hand, a ceremony
12. A victim, to beseech
13. Gifts, bearing
14. Finely ground meal, a blossom
15. Part of a chimney, short for "influenza"
16. An underground worker, under full age
17. An exercise for study, to decrease
18. That which one borrows, solitary
19. A part in a play, a list
20. To lift, to level to the ground

11. write, rite
12. prey, pray
13. presents, presence
14. flour, flower
15. flue, flu
16. miner, minor
17. lesson, lessen
18. loan, lone
19. role, roll
20. raise, raze

Ph. D. Level

21. Only, the immortal spirit
22. To appear, a joining
23. To quote, vision
24. A blood vessel, a weathercock
25. To swing back and forth, to relinquish
26. Audibly, sanctioned
27. To give up, that from which anything is grown
28. Rough, a way
29. To disturb, a state of development
30. A frame of iron bars, eminent

21. sole, soul
22. seem, seam
23. cite, sight
24. vein, vane
25. wave, waive
26. aloud, allowed
27. cede, seed
28. coarse, course
29. faze, phase
30. grate, great

HOMOPHONES II

Replace the word "blank" in each sentence with a pair of sound-alikes—e.g., I can't *blank* the *blank* from here. *Answer:* see, sea.

Freshman Level

1. The *blank* said that she had *blank* the bed.
2. He *blank* up the *blank* balloon.
3. I can't *blank* you from *blank*.
4. I put *blank* books over *blank*.
5. The *blank* boys *blank* all the hamburgers.
6. She's *blank* young to have *blank* teen-age children.
7. He turned *blank* when he saw the hole in the *blank*.
8. The people sitting in the first two *blank* received a *blank*.
9. The soldier *blank* her ring all during the *blank*.
10. I can't *blank* to lose more *blank*.

1. maid, made
2. blew, blue
3. hear, here
4. their, there
5. eight, ate
6. too, two
7. pale, pail
8. rows, rose
9. wore, war
10. wait, weight

Graduate Level

11. The *blank* dress will be ruined if there's a *blank* in the sleeve.
12. Barbara *blank* she has a *blank* for news.
13. Most postal workers who deliver the *blank* are *blank*.
14. A toy *blank* is no good; you need a *blank* one to catch big fish.
15. The *blank* was added incorrectly by *blank* of the students.
16. I yelled "whoa" at the *blank* until I became *blank*.
17. If you *blank* carefully your answers will be *blank*.
18. You are not *blank* to talk *blank* during the exam.
19. They wanted a house where they could *blank* the *blank*.
20. He *blank* the ball down *blank* the hoop.

11. whole, hole
12. knows, nose
13. mail, male
14. reel, real
15. sum, some
16. horse, hoarse
17. write, right
18. allowed, aloud
19. see, sea
20. threw, through

Ph. D. Level

21. They write *blank* like *blank*.
22. The higher airplane *blank* seems *blank* to me.
23. The *blank* on the ocean liners are kept busy during a *blank*.
24. It would be *blank* if the *blank* on my barbecue never needed to be cleaned.
25. She *blank* away from the wild party because she's a *blank* person.
26. The school *blank* said he believed in the *blank* of fair play.
27. The thief hid his *blank* of jewels and *blank* in the attic.
28. I don't believe in hunting and I *blank* that his *blank* escapes.
29. It would be quite a *blank* to jump over a fence eight *blank* in height.
30. I had already *blank* that *blank* three times so I left the theater.

21. prose, pros
22. fare, fair
23. crews, cruise
24. great, grate
25. stayed, staid
26. principal, principle
27. cache, cash
28. pray, prey
29. feat, feet
30. seen, scene

ONOMATOPOEIC EXCLAMATIONS IN COMIC BOOKS/PAPERS

Identify the expression from the meaning. (Alternate answers may be possible.)

Freshman Level

1. To express disgust or to indicate the sound of a grunt.
2. To express sudden pain.
3. The sound made by the throat in swallowing as a sign of surprise, etc.
4. To indicate a loud shattering sound as glass breaking.
5. To indicate a sucking noise in the process of eating or drinking.
6. To indicate a loud laugh; a guffaw.
7. To indicate a laugh in a high voice, a titter.
8. To indicate a short metallic sound as a coin dropped.
9. To indicate the sound of a small object falling into water.
10. To indicate a sharp metallic sound as a bullet striking a rock.

1. Ugh!
2. Ouch! or Ow!
3. Gulp!
4. Crash!
5. Slurp!
6. Hee-haw!
7. Tee-hee!
8. Clink! or clank!
9. Kerplop or kerplunk
10. Ping!

Graduate Level

11. To indicate pleasure, surprise, or strong feeling.
12. To indicate a loud sound like a gunshot or explosion.
13. To indicate mild incredulity, disappointment, disgust or remonstrance.
14. Used reduplicatively to indicate a laugh.
15. To indicate the deep resonant sound of a bell.
16. To indicate the sound of something flattening on impact.
17. To express various emotions as astonishment, pain, or desire.
18. To indicate the sound of a car or motorcycle engine being revved.
19. To catch the breath as an expression of shock, concern, or emotion.
20. To indicate a dull thump as a shoe dropped on the floor.

11. Wow!
12. Bang! or boom!
13. Aw!
14. Yuk, yuk
15. Bong!
16. Splat!
17. Oh!
18. Vroom! vroom!
19. Gasp!
20. Clunk! or thud!

Ph. D. Level

21. A gurgling sound as liquid from a bottle with intermittent air blockage.
22. To indicate a ringing metallic sound.
23. To indicate sound made by a person shot, stabbed, etc.
24. To indicate the sound of a cannon being fired.
25. To indicate the sound of crushing as boots on gravel, or snow.
26. To indicate the sound of pain or strain.
27. To indicate the sound of a bat hitting a baseball.
28. To indicate one is considering something said.
29. To indicate the sound of machine-gunfire.
30. To indicate the sound made to get one's attention discreetly.

21. Glug!
22. Clang!
23. Aaach! or eeeeh!
24. Blam! or boom!
25. Kerr-unch!
26. Groan!
27. Crack!
28. Hmmm!
29. Rat-tat-tat-tat!
30. Pssst!

DEVIL'S DICTIONARY
The meaning is given but the answer may surprise you—e.g., in bad company. *Answer*: alone.

Freshman Level

1. A temporary insanity curable by marriage.
2. A person who talks when you want him to listen.
3. A substitute for the whip of the slave driver.
4. The patriotic art of lying for one's country.
5. A stench in the ear. The chief product of civilization.
6. To ask that the laws of the universe be annulled.
7. A period of cheating between two periods of war.
8. One skilled in the circumvention of the law.
9. A person more interested in himself than me.
10. An instrument that employs the friction of a horse's tail on the entrails of a sheep.

1. love
2. bore
3. debt
4. diplomacy
5. noise
6. pray
7. peace
8. lawyer
9. egotist
10. fiddle

Graduate Level

11. A statement of belief inconsistent with one's own opinion.
12. The civility of envy.
13. Conspiciously miserable.
14. An agreeable sensation arising from contemplating another's misery.
15. A member of the unconsidered or negligible sex.
16. Evident to one's self and to nobody else.
17. Dumb and illiterate.
18. A synonym for "husband."
19. Linen used at funerals to conceal a lack of tears.
20. A master, a mistress, and two slaves, making in all, two.

11. absurdity
12. congratulations
13. famous
14. happiness
15. male
16. self-evident
17. truthful
18. brute
19. handkerchief
20. marriage

Ph. D. Level

21. A proponent of the doctrine that black is white.
22. Certain abstentions.
23. A dead sinner revised and edited.
24. Mistaken at the top of one's voice.
25. Acceptable hypocrisy.
26. In politics the party that prevents the government from governing.
27. An illness affecting high public officials who want to go fishing.
28. In Christian countries, the day after the baseball game.
29. A shackle for the free.
30. A despot whom the wise ridicule and obey.

21. optimist
22. virtues
23. saint
24. positive
25. politeness
26. opposition
27. overwork
28. Monday
29. habit
30. fashion

CLICHES
Complete the expression.

Freshman Level: Provide the final word.

1. Method in one's ———
2. Never a dull ———
3. Up the creek without a ———
4. Take the bull by the ———
5. Milk of human ———
6. Talk through one's ———
7. Flash in the ———
8. Hook, line, and ———
9. Cool as a ———
10. Beat around the ———

1. madness
2. moment
3. paddle
4. horns
5. kindness
6. hat
7. pan
8. sinker
9. cucumber
10. bush

Graduate Level: Provide the final *two* words.

11. Too funny ———
12. Too little ———
13. Throw in ———
14. Too numerous ———
15. Turn over a ———
16. Sight for ———
17. Once in a ———
18. Paint the ———
19. Penny for ———
20. Lend a ———

11. for words
12. too late
13. the towel
14. to mention
15. new leaf
16. sore eyes
17. blue moon
18. town red
19. your thoughts
20. helping hand

Ph. D. Level: Provide the final *three* words.

21. More than ———
22. Handwriting ———
23. In on ———
24. Easier ———
25. Breathe a ———
26. All over ———
27. Matter of ———
28. Throw caution ———
29. When all is ———
30. No sooner ———

21. meets the eye
22. on the wall
23. the ground floor
24. said than done
25. sigh of relief
26. but the shouting
27. life and death
28. to the winds
29. said and done
30. said than done

STINKY PINKIES

Rhyming pairs—e.g., television set: b.t. *Answer*: boob tube.

Freshman Level

1. A tardy spouse	l.m.	1. late mate
2. A sharp operator	w.d.	2. wheeler-dealer
3. A two-way radio	w.t.	3. walkie-talkie
4. Very loyal	t.b.	4. true blue
5. Conservative elderly person	f.d.	5. fuddy-duddy
6. A nursery rhyme egg	H.D.	6. Humpty-Dumpty
7. Short and plump	r.p.	7. roly-poly
8. Mischievous behavior	h.p.	8. hanky-panky
9. Flashy, exciting display	r.d.	9. razzle-dazzle
10. Meaningless ritual	m.j.	10. mumbo jumbo

Graduate Level

11. A flavor of ice cream	t.f.	11. tutti-frutti
12. The basic questions	n.g.	12. nitty-gritty
13. Confusion, turmoil	h.b.	13. hurly-burly
14. An airline pilot	f.g.	14. fly guy
15. Jazz piano playing	b.w.	15. boogie-woogie
16. Every which way	h.s.	16. helter-skelter
17. Randomly	w.n.	17. willy-nilly
18. Cheerful father	g.d.	18. glad dad
19. Funniest joke	b.j.	19. best jest
20. A hobo in the rain	d.t.	20. damp tramp

Ph. D. Level

21. An inexperienced monarch	g.q.	21. green queen
22. Expensive lager	d.b.	22. dear beer
23. A barrel organ	h.g.	23. hurdy-gurdy
24. Undecorated locomotive	p.t.	24. plain train
25. Breakfast fish exporter	k.s.	25. kipper shipper
26. A fat poet	l.b.	26. lard-bard
27. Escaped fowl	l.g.	27. loose goose
28. A faster clergyman	g.v.	28. quicker vicar
29. A lollipop dropped at the beach	s.c.	29. sandy candy
30. A happy German	M.J.	30. Merry Jerry

SOMETHING IN COMMON
Each set of four words shares something in common—e.g., foot, eel, vacuum, Hawaii. *Answer:* double vowels.

Freshman Level

1. raccoon, settee, embarrass, bassoon.
2. willow, museum, pump, yesterday.
3. youth, melt, usher.
4. assess, giggling, preference, intimidation.
5. select, tramp, trace, golden.
6. radar, laser, scuba.
7. silent, tinsel, enlist, listen.
8. level, redder, rotator, mom.
9. expunge, erase, raze, nullify.
10. fix, live, vile, exit.

1. Two pairs of double letters.
2. Begin and end with same letter.
3. Begin with a pronoun.
4. One letter appears four times.
5. New word when first letter removed.
6. Each is an acronym.
7. Anagrams of each other.
8. Same forward and backward.
9. Synonyms of each other.
10. Letters that are Roman numerals.

Graduate Level

11. irate, scatter, bath, millionaire.
12. thorn, teas, shout, stew.
13. Booth, Bottoms, Bridges.
14. horn, pommel, skirt, seat.
15. tops, earth, anger, ought.

16. Marvel, Octopus, Decent, Septic.
17. begger, appease, plumber, breadth.
18. honest, often, asinine, outwork.
19. sum, win, ring, all.
20. wound, wind, minute, bass.

11. Contain names of animals.
12. Anagrams for north, east, south, west.
13. Surnames of actors.
14. Parts of a saddle.
15. New word when last letter is shifted to front.

16. Begin with abbreviation for month.
17. Contain names of food.
18. Contain names of numbers.
19. Words are part of the four seasons.
20. Have two direct pronunciations.

Ph. D. Level

21. tea, sea, are, why.
22. TAX, FAIL, COURT, MIND.

23. star, parts, drawer, diaper.
24. banana, fine, hug, luck.

25. diesel, boycott, lynch, watt.
26. WOW, MOM, TOOT, AHA.
27. FEAT, WEEK, FIVE, MILE.
28. liquid, orange, widow, lemon.
29. rain, pure, reign, pains.
30. begins, almost, chin, abhor.

21. Homophones of letters t,c,r,y.
22. First and last letters are state abbreviations.
23. Form new words when reversed.
24. last letter of word immediately precedes first letter of word in alphabet.
25. Eponyms: people's names.
26. Appear the same in a mirror.
27. Have no curved letters.
28. All are difficult to rhyme.
29. Acronyms of country names.
30. Letters are in alphabetical order.

UNCOMMON BEGINNINGS

The first two letters of the answer are provided. They are unusual letter combinations.

Freshman Level

1.	Oh	A branch of the Mississippi River.	1. Ohio River
2.	Wy	One of the Rocky Mountain states.	2. Wyoming
3.	Od	An instrument used to measure distance.	3. Odometer
4.	Cz	A European country.	4. Czechoslovakia
5.	Oa	Any watered spot in the desert.	5. Oasis
6.	Rh	A French river flowing into the Mediterranean.	6. Rhone
7.	Zi	A semiprecious stone.	7. Zircon
8.	Gu	A country and capital with the same name.	8. Guatemala
9.	Gn	An african antelope also known as a wildebeest.	9. Gnu
10.	Zu	Switzerland's largest city.	10. Zurich

Graduate Level

11.	Ty	A region including part of western Austria and northern Italy.	11. Tyrol
12.	Za	The second largest city in Yugoslavia.	12. Zagreb
13.	Dj	Capital of Indoesia	13. Djakarta
14.	Io	This sea is the deepest part of the Mediterranean Sea.	14. Ionian Sea
15.	Dn	A major river of European U.S.S.R.	15. Dnieper
16.	Iw	Site of Joe Rosenthal's 1945 Pulitzer-winning photograph.	16. Iwo Jima
17.	Ku	An oil-rich country.	17. Kuwait
18.	Zu	A brave group of African natives.	18. Zulus
19.	Sr	Home of the Tamils.	19. Sri Lanka
20.	Rw	Landlocked central African country.	20. Rwanda

Ph. D. Level

21.	Iz	A Turkish port of the Aegean Sea.	21. Izmir
22.	Lh	The holy city of Tibet.	22. Lhasa
23.	Ob	Bavarian village noted for its Passion Plays.	23. Oberammergau
24.	Pt	Grouselike birds found in Alaska and Greenland.	24. Ptarmigans
25.	Ts	Tidal wave known by this Japanese word for "storm wave."	25. Tsunami
26.	Ob	A black glass formed when volcanic lava cools suddenly.	26. Obsidian
27.	Xe	Colorless, odorless, gas that is part of atmosphere.	27. Xenon
28.	Ze	Any warm, gentle western breeze.	28. Zephyr
29.	Qa	Persian Gulf country whose capital is Doha.	29. Qatar
30.	Zu	An area of the Netherlands now called the Ijsselmeer.	30. Zuider Zee

ABBREVIATIONS
Give the full form of each abbreviation.

Freshman Level

1. PBS	1. Public Broadcasting Service
2. RV	2. Recreational vehicle
3. PG	3. Parental guidance
4. MVP	4. Most valuable player
5. R & B	5. Rhythm and blues
6. R & D	6. Research and development
7. DH	7. Designated hitter
8. VAT	8. Value-added tax
9. DMZ	9. Demilitarized zone
10. ETV	10. Educational television

Graduate Level

11. EEC	11. European Economic Community
12. AIDS	12. Acquired Immune Deficiency Syndrome
13. CB	13. Citizens band
14. LED	14. Light-emitting diode
15. MOR	15. Middle of the road
16. MIA	16. Missing in action
17. OD	17. Overdose
18. ABM	18. Antiballistic missile
19. CPR	19. Cardio-pulmonary resuscitation
20. RDA	20. Recommended dietary allowance

Ph. D. Level

21. SIDS	21. Sudden Infant Death Syndrome
22. ESL	22. English as a second language
23. REM	23. Rapid eye movement
24. PCB	24. Polychlorinated biphenyl
25. SAT	25. Scholastic Aptitude Test
26. PCV valve	26. Positive crankcase ventilation valve
27. FET	27. Federal Excise Tax
28. ISBN	28. International Standard Book Number
29. IUD	29. Intrauterine device
30. SHC	30. Spontaneous human combustion

WORD JUGGLING I

Freshman Level: Fill in the blank with an anagram of the underlined word.

1. I <u>hate</u> the ——of the summer.
2. John <u>agrees</u> that the wheels need more——.
3. I don't <u>recall</u> leaving the tools in the——.
4. New <u>emigrants</u> have been ——into the country.
5. To <u>infer</u> that he had a ——collection was wrong.
6. The <u>fighter</u> plane attacked the——train.
7. She is <u>trifling</u> with your emotions by——.
8. He <u>indeed</u>——stealing the money.
9. He <u>earned</u> everyone's respect as he——middle age.
10. The <u>state</u> government leaves a bad——in my mouth.

1. heat
2. grease
3. cellar
4. streaming
5. finer
6. freight
7. flirting
8. denied
9. neared
10. taste

Graduate Level: Each pair of words is identical except for the middle letter.

11. The —y— lived in a large —n—.
12. The —b— soldiers tried to —p— the government troops.
13. The —s— display will be shown —t— in the day.
14. Her —v— lived in a —w— apartment.
15. The —a— was so intense it almost burned my —e—.
16. A —i— of the whip directed the entire —o—.
17. Don't —a— me by always using the wrong —n—.
18. A —f— of the soldiers were covered in —l—.
19. You must be —e— to be able to —a— other's work.
20. The football —a— sat on the —u— and watched TV.

11. mayor, manor
12. rebel, repel
13. laser, later
14. lover, lower
15. flash, flesh
16. flick, flock
17. tease, tense
18. fifth, filth
19. adept, adapt
20. coach, couch

Ph. D. Level: Fill in the blanks with words that are spelled the same but pronounced differently—
e.g. There was a——in her eye when she saw the——in her coat. *Answer* tear.

21. He——the bandage around the——.
22. I——to carry all that ——to the dump.
23. The palace——is so impressive it will——you.
24. It took me a——to focus the microscope on the—— organism.
25. Put the——in the barn before you——the field.
26. My arm felt even——after I had done the exercise a——of times.
27. The musician put away his——and went fishing for——.
28. There will be a——if the prisoners don't stay in a ——.
29. You must——when you meet the princess with the yellow——in her hair.
30. I can't——it up in this strong——.

21. wound
22. refuse
23. entrance
24. minute
25. sow
26. number
27. bass
28. row
29. bow
30. wind

WORD JUGGLING II

Freshman Level: Find the hidden word in each sentence—e.g., "Now here is a good idea," he said. *Answer:* nowhere.

1. My neighbor decided to paint his bar red.
2. The men tally their golf scores after each hole.
3. In jury trials the foreman delivers the verdict.
4. Either buy a new suit or wear your old one.
5. There is just ice in the freezer, nothing else.
6. The book is ideal for ages six to ten.
7. She has ten dollars more than her son.
8. I will beg one of the soldiers to help us.
9. I slander only those who slander me.
10. Babe Ruth was never able to bat ten home runs in a row.

1. barred
2. mentally
3. injury
4. suitor
5. justice
6. forages
7. hasten
8. begone
9. islander
10. batten

Graduate Level: Make a new word by adding a second word consisting of the number of letters indicated—e.g., Bet (3). *Answer:* betray.

11. ant (3)
12. decor (3)
13. heat (3)
14. prose (4)
15. idea (4)
16. reap (4)
17. side (4)
18. arc (5)
19. pronoun (5)
20. rest (6)

11. anther
12. decorate
13. heathen
14. prosecute
15. idealist
16. reappear
17. sidereal
18. archives
19. pronouncement
20. restoration

Ph. D. Level: Put the same letters in each blank. The number of letters on each word is given—e.g., We seem to <u>2</u> <u>6</u> trouble because you're <u>8</u> badly. *Answer:* be having, behaving.

21. The <u>7</u> doctor was <u>3</u> <u>4</u> to operate.
22. The <u>9</u> was told to <u>7</u> <u>2</u> hand in his resignation.
23. An <u>6</u> <u>2</u> <u>4</u> surrounded by water.
24. We <u>6</u> that <u>1</u> <u>5</u> of such magnitude was amoral.
25. Did you <u>6</u> that it was <u>3</u> <u>3</u> but water that he slipped on?
26. The <u>7</u> pleased for assistance <u>2</u> <u>5</u> terms.
27. The <u>6</u> will be dealt with <u>2</u> <u>4</u> trials.
28. His <u>6</u> was so sore he couldn't keep <u>2</u> <u>4</u>.
29. The priest carried <u>1</u> <u>5</u> <u>6</u> the aisle.
30. The <u>8</u> said that with more <u>4</u> <u>4</u> will lay more eggs.

21. notable, not able
22. inspector, inspect or
23. island, is land
24. agreed, a agreed
25. notice, not ice
26. invalid, in valid
27. injury, in jury
28. instep, in step
29. a cross, across
30. heathens, heat hens

DON'T BE SHEEPISH
Identify the animal related to each animal adjective

Freshman Level

1. Canine	1. doglike
2. Elephantine	2. elephantlike
3. Serpentine	3. serpentlike
4. Feline	4. catlike
5. Asinine	5. asslike
6. Bovine	6. cowlike
7. Leonine	7. lionlike
8. Porcine	8. piglike
9. Piscine	9. fishlike
10. Viperine	10. viperlike

Graduate Level

11. Ovine	11. sheeplike
12. Aquiline	12. eaglelike
13. Equine	13. horselike
14. Caprine	14. goatlike
15. Lupine	15. wolflike
16. Anguine	16. snakelike
17. Murine	17. mouselike
18. Ursine	18. bearlike
19. Vulpine	19. foxlike
20. Lacertine	20. lizardlike

Ph. D. Level

21. Accipitrine	21. hawklike
22. Cervine	22. deerlike
23. Lemurine	23. lemurlike
24. Pavonine	24. peacocklike
25. Anserine	25. gooselike
26. Suine	26. swinelike
27. Lutrine	27. otterlike
28. Sulline	28. hoglike
29. Ranine	29. froglike
30. Taurine	30. bull-like

WORD BITS

Provide a word that contains the given letters in the given order and without letters between. The answer must have other letters both before and after the given cluster—e.g., kg. *Answer:* backGammon, or backGround, or blackGuard.

Freshman Level

1. uxu
2. ajo
3. yra
4. hao
5. nted
6. uco
7. cheo
8. rju
9. necd
10. scet

1. Luxury
2. Cajole
3. Tyrant
4. Chaos
5. Antedote
6. Bucolic
7. Luncheon, truncheon
8. Perjury
9. Anecdote
10. Ascetic

Graduate Level

11. lego
12. ltp
13. utho
14. ygm
15. pule
16. ostl
17. mmac
18. ckney
19. sote
20. oerc

11. Allegory
12. Saltpeter
13. Authority
14. Pygmy
15. Opulent
16. Jostle
17. Immaculate
18. Hackneyed
19. Esoteric
20. Coerce

Ph. D. Level

21. wkw
22. nimic
23. cissi
24. sthu
25. ocra
26. agia
27. nvei
28. asci
29. ncar
30. aran

21. Awkward
22. Inimical
23. Vicissitude
24. Posthumous
25. Procrastinate
26. Plagiarism
27. Inevigle
28. Irascible
29. Incarcerate
30. Harangue

5 / MUSIC

MUSICAL QUESTIONS

Given the artist and the year the song was a hit complete the song title. Each title is a question.

Freshman Level

1. Dionne Warwick — 1968 — "Do You Know——" — 1. The Way to San Jose?
2. Rod Stewart — 1979 — "Do Ya Think——" — 2. I'm Sexy?
3. Beatles — 1964 — "Do You Want to——" — 3. Know a Secret?
4. Peggy Lee — 1969 — "Is That——" — 4. All There Is?
5. Tom Jones — 1965 — "What's New——" — 5. Pussycat?
6. Sammy Davis Jr. — 1962 — "What Kind of——" — 6. Fool Am I?
7. Elvis Presley — 1960 — "Are You——" — 7. Lonesome Tonight?
8. Lonnie Donegan — 1970 — "Does Your Chewing Gum——" — 8. Lose Its Flavor (On the Bedpost Over Night)?
9. Olivia Newton-John — 1975 — "Have You Never——" — 9. Been Mellow?
10. Bee Gees — 1971 — "How Can You Mend——" — 10. A Broken Heart?

Graduate Level

11. Bee Gees — 1977 — "How Deep Is——" — 11. Your Love?
12. Tony Orlando and Dawn — 1973 — "Say, Has Anybody Seen——" — 12. My Sweet Gypsy Rose?
13. Kingston Trio — 1962 — "Where Have All——" — 13. The Flowers Gone?
14. Connie Francis — 1958 — "Who's—— — 14. Sorry Now?
15. Frankie Lyman and the Teenagers — 1956 — "Why Do Fools——" — 15. Fall in Love?
16. Dupress featuring Joey Vann — 1963 — "Why Don't You——" — 16. Believe Me?
17. Shirelles — 1961 — "Will You Love——" — 17. Me Tomorrow?
18. Lovin' Spoonful — 1966 — "Did You Ever Have to——" — 18. Make Up Your Mind?
19. Ricky Nelson — 1957 — "Have I Told You——" — 19. Lately That I Love You?
20. Creedence Clearwater Revival —— — 1971 — "Have You Ever Seen——" — 20. the Rain?

Ph. D. Level

21. Bobby Freeman — 1958 — "Do You Want——" — 21. To Dance?
22. Hurricane Smith — 1973 — "Oh, Babe, ——" — 22. What Would You Say?
23. Three Degrees — 1974 — "When Will I——" — 23. See You Again?
24. Tony Orlando and Dawn — 1973 — "Who's in the——" — 24. Strawberry Patch with Sally?
25. Creedence Clearwater Revival — 1970 — "Who'll Stop——" — 25. the Rain?
26. Poppy Family featuring Susan Jacks — 1970 — "Which Way——" — 26. You Goin' Billy?
27. Johnny Mathis — 1963 — "What Will——" — 27. Mary Say?
28. Sonny and Cher — 1966 — "What Now——" — 28. My Love?
29. Robert Flack and Donny Hathaway — 1972 — "Where Is——" — 29. the Love?
30. Joni James — 1955 — "How Important——" — 30. Can It Be?

COLE PORTER

Freshman Level: Complete the song title.

1. "You'd Be So Nice to———"
2. "What Is This Thing———"
3. "I Get a Kick———"
4. "In the Still———"
5. "I've Got You———"
6. "My Heart Belongs———"
7. "From This———"
8. "Get Out———"
9. "It's All Right———"
10. "I Concentrate———"

1. Come Home To.
2. Called Love?
3. out of You
4. of the Night
5. Under My Skin
6. to Daddy
7. Moment On
8. of Town
9. with Me
10. on You

Graduate Level: Provide the next three words of the lyrics.

11. "I Love Paris in the winter———"
12. "The eyes, the arms, the ———"
13. "For you and I have a guardian angel on high, with ———"
14. "People say in Boston even———"
15. "In the roaring traffic's boom, In the silence of———"
16. "Flying too high with some guy in the sky, Is my idea of———"
17. "You're the Nile, You're the———"
18. "It was just one of those nights, Just one of———"
19. "It brings back the sound of music so tender, it brings back a night———"
20. "But each time I do, just the thought of you makes me stop, ———"

11. when it drizzles
12. mouth of you
13. nothing to do
14. beans do it
15. my lonely room
16. nothing to do
17. Tow'r of Pisa
18. those fabulous flights
19. of tropical splendor
20. Before I begin

Ph. D. Level: Name the song that contains the given lyrics.

21. "Like the beat, beat, beat of the tom-tom."
22. "Birds do it, Bees do it."
23. "Who's prepared to pay the price, For a trip to paradise?"
24. "You're a melody, From a symphony by Strauss."
25. "If we'd thought a bit of the end of it, When we started painting the town."
26. "And here we are, planning to love forever, and promising never to part."
27. "So swell to keep ev'ry home-fire burning for."
28. "The skies are clear, And if you want to go walking, dear."
29. "Life's great, life's grand."
30. "If you're ever in a jam, Here I am."

21. "Night and Day"
22. "Let's Do It"
23. "Love for Sale"
24. "You're the Top"
25. "Just One of Those Things"
26. "Begin the Beguine"
27. "Easy To Love"
28. "It's De-Lovely"
29. "Ridin' High"
30. "Friendship"

TOP RECORDINGS—1984
Name the artist(s).

Freshman Level: Gold Singles

1. "Against All Odds (Take a Look at Me Now)"
2. "Girls Just Want to Have Fun"
3. "Jump"
4. "I Just Called to Say I Love You"
5. "Karma Chameleon"
6. "To All the Girls I've Loved Before"

7. "Uptown Girl"
8. "I Feel for You"
9. "Footloose"
10. "Let's Go Crazy"

1. Phil Collins
2. Cyndi Lauper
3. Van Halen
4. Stevie Wonder
5. Culture Club
6. Julio Iglesias and Willie Nelson
7. Billy Joel
8. Chaka Khan
9. Kenny Loggins
10. Prince

Graduate Level: Platinum Albums

11. "Roll On"
12. "Tonight"
13. "Born in the U.S.A."
14. "Pipes of Peace"
15. "She's So Unusual"
16. "Waking up With the House on Fire"
17. "Stay Hungry"
18. "Outlandos D'Amour"
19. "What About Me"
20. "Undercover"

11. Alabama
12. David Bowie
13. Bruce Springsteen
14. Paul McCartney
15. Cyndi Lauper
16. Culture Club
17. Twisted Sister
18. Police
19. Kenny Rogers
20. The Rolling Stones

Ph. D. Level: Platinum Albums

21. "Heartbeat City"
22. "Seven and the Ragged Tire"
23. "Reach the Beach"
24. "Poncho and Lefty"

25. "Rebel Yell"
26. "Grace Under Pressure"
27. "Animalize"
28. "Signs of Life"
29. "The Principle of Moments"
30. "Make It Big"

21. The Cars
22. Duran, Duran
23. The Fixx
24. Merle Haggard and Willie Nelson
25. Billy Idol
26. Rush
27. Kiss
28. Billy Squier
29. Robert Plant
30. Wham!

GRAMMY AWARD WINNERS
Name the artist(s).

Freshman Level: Records

1.	1984 "What's Love Got to Do With It"	1.	Tina Turner
2.	1983 "Beat It"	2.	Michael Jackson
3.	1975 "Love Will Keep Us Together"	3.	Captain and Tennille
4.	1972 "The First Time Ever I Saw Your Face"	4.	Roberta Flack
5.	1970 "Bridge over Troubled Waters"	5.	Simon and Garfunkel
6.	1969 Aquarius/Let the Sunshine In"	6.	5th Dimension
7.	1968 "Mrs. Robinson"	7.	Simon and Garfunkel
8.	1966 "Strangers in the Night"	8.	Frank Sinatra
9.	1962 "I Left My Heart in San Francisco"	9.	Tony Bennett
10.	1961 "Moon River"	10.	Henry Mancini

Graduate Level: Records

11.	1980 "Sailing"	11.	Christopher Cross
12.	1979 "What a Fool Believes"	12.	The Doobie Brothers
13.	1978 "Just the Way You Are"	13.	Billy Joel
14.	1977 "Hotel California"	14.	Eagles
15.	1974 "I Honestly Love You"	15.	Olivia Newton John
16.	1973 "Killing Me Softly With His Song"	16.	Roberta Flack
17.	1971 "It's Too Late"	17.	Carole King
18.	1967 "Up, Up and Away"	18.	5th Dimension
19.	1965 "A Taste of Honey"	19.	Herb Alpert
20.	1963 "The Days of Wine and Roses"	20.	Henry Mancini

Ph. D. Level: Albums

21.	1984 "Can't Slow Down"	21.	Lionel Ritchie
22.	1983 "Thriller"	22.	Michael Jackson
23.	1979 "52nd Street"	23.	Billy Joel
24.	1978 "Saturday Night Fever"	24.	Bee Gees
25.	1977 "Rumors"	25.	Fleetwood Mac
26.	1976 "Songs in the Key of Life"	26.	Stevie Wonder
27.	1968 "By the Time I Get to Phoenix"	27.	Glen Campbell
28.	1971 "Tapestry"	28.	Carole King
29.	1967 "Sgt. Pepper's Lonely Hearts Club Band"	29.	The Beatles
30.	1965 "September of My Years"	30.	Frank Sinatra

70's ROCK n' ROLL

Freshman Level

1. This group was formed by former members of The Byrds, The Hollies, and Buffalo Springfield.
2. His back-up band is the E Street Band.
3. Davie Jones changed his name to this.
4. This Pink Floyd album spent more weeks in the top 200 chart than any other.
5. This Englishman was born Reginald Dwight.
6. The Jefferson Airplane changed their name to this.
7. Their albums include *Desperado*.
8. He fronted The Faces.
9. Her back-up band was called The Stone Poneys.
10. His 1972 hit single was *Superstition*.

1. Crosby, Stills, and Nash
2. Bruce Springsteen
3. David Bowie
4. "Dark Side of the Moon"
5. Elton John
6. Jefferson Starship
7. The Eagles
8. Rod Stewart
9. Linda Ronstadt
10. Stevie Wonder

Graduate Level

11. He was the front man for the English band Roxy Music.
12. This shock-rockers real name is Vincent Furnier.
13. This was Bob Marley's back-up band.
14. Flutist Ian Anderson fronted this English band.
15. Stevie Nicks and Lindsey Buckingham joined them.
16. This English band's albums include *Crime of the Century*.
17. This band was originally fronted by David Lee Roth.
18. This English band's albums include Brain Salad Surgery.
19. He is known as Slowhand.
20. These Englishmen penned "Smoke on the Water."

11. Brian Ferry
12. Alice Cooper
13. The Wailers
14. Jethro Tull
15. Fleetwood Mac
16. Supertramp
17. Van Halen
18. Emerson, Lake, and Palmer
19. Eric Clapton
20. Deep Purple

Ph. D. Level

21. He topped the singles charts with "American Pie."
22. These southern-rockers disbanded after a plane crash killed key members.
23. This band was formed by former members of Free, King Crimson, and Mott the Hoople.
24. The Silver Bullet Band was his back-up group.
25. Their hits include "We're an American Band."
26. His band was The Mothers of Invention.
27. The band Chicago shortened its name from this.
28. His back up band was called Crazy Horse.
29. This American band's songs include "Dream On" and "Walk This Way."
30. They were originally billed as the New Yardbirds.

21. Don McLean
22. Lynyrd Skynyrd
23. Bad Company
24. Bob Seger
25. Grand Funk Railroad
26. Frank Zappa
27. Chicago Transit Authority
28. Neil Young
29. Aerosmith
30. Led Zeppelin

CLASSICAL COMPOSERS

Freshman Level

1. This Russian composed the ballet *The Nutcracker*.
2. The Austrian composer of "Tales from the Vienna Woods."
3. He composed the opera *The Magic Flute*.
4. The French composer of "Bolero."
5. The German composer of *A Midsummer Night's Dream*.
6. Hungarian composer of *The Merry Widow*.
7. The composer of the opera *Hansel and Gretel*.

8. American composer of *West Side Story*.
9. Composer of the first musical to win a Pulitzer Prize, *Of Thee I Sing*.
10. Bach's Toccata and Fugue in D Minor is the theme for this classic horror film.

1. Peter Tchaikovsky
2. Johann Strauss, Jr.
3. W. Amadeus Mozart
4. Maurice Ravel
5. Felix Mendelssohn
6. Franz Lehar
7. Englebert Humperdinck
8. Leonard Bernstein
9. George Gershwin
10. *Phantom of the Opera*

Graduate Level

11. American best known for his "Fanfare for the Common Man."
12. Strauss's *Also Sprach Zarathustra* is heard in this sci-fi film.

13. This Italian's most famous work is *The Four Seasons*.
14. German composer commonly known for "Cradle Song."
15. German composer of the "Hallelujah Chorus."
16. Name the Kurt Weill/Bertollt Brecht opera that includes "Mack the Knife."
17. This U.S. conductor-composer specialized in Wagnerian opera.
18. Hungarian-born U.S. composer best known for his operettas, including *The Desert Song*.
19. As a youth, this composer studied briefly with Mozart and Haydn.
20. German composer and husband of the legendary cabaret singer Lotte Lenya.

11. Aaron Copland
12. *2001: A Space Odyssey*
13. Antonio Vivaldi
14. Johannes Brahms
15. George F. Handel
16. *The Threepenny Opera*
17. Walter Damrosch
18. Sigmund Romberg.
19. Ludwig van Beethoven
20. Kurt Weill

Ph. D. Level

21. Richard Wagner married the daughter of this Hungarian composer.
22. He dominated Italian opera during the late nineteenth century.
23. English composer of *The Fairy Queen Suite*.
24. This composer was nicknamed the Red Priest.
25. Composer of the operetta, *Orpheus in the Underworld*.
26. Russian composer of the opera *The Snow Maiden*.
27. This Austrian composer began creating German lieder in 1814.
28. Italian composer best known for *Pagliacci*.
29. This Russian pianist-composer emigrated to the U.S.A. in 1918.
30. Austrian composer-conductor known for Romantic symphonies employing large numbers of musicians and singers.

21. Franz Liszt
22. Giuseppe Verdi
23. Henry Purcell
24. Antonio Vivaldi
25. Jacques Offenbach
26. Rimsky-Korsakov
27. Franz Schubert
28. R. Leoncavallo
29. S. Rachmaninoff
30. Gustav Mahler

MUSICAL INSTRUMENTS
Identify the musical instrument (no repeat answers).

Freshman Level

 1. Felt-covered hammers strike upon steel wires.
 2. A stretched membrane is struck with sticks, hands, etc.
 3. Angels pluck it.
 4. The instrument of cowboys and rock stars.
 5. The Pied Piper's instrument.
 6. Four strings and a bow, and held against the shoulder.
 7. Single-reed mouthpiece, finger holes, and keys.
 8. A long narrow-bored metal tube whose pitch is varied by valves.
 9. A wide-bore bass instrument whose pitch is varied by valves.
10. Pipes and reeds sounded by compressed air.

 1. piano
 2. drum
 3. harp
 4. guitar
 5. flute
 6. violin/viola
 7. clarinet
 8. trumpet
 9. tuba
10. organ

Graduate Level

11. This brass instrument derives from a huntsman's horn.
12. Invented in Belgium by Antoine Sax.
13. Strumming instrument thought to have originated in Africa.
14. Wooden bars graduated in length and struck with mallets.
15. Like the head of a drum with jingles in the rim.
16. A fretted neck, a pear-shaped body, and eight strings.
17. Its name sounds like an English tramp.
18. Held between the knees, four strings, tuned an octave lower than the viola.
19. Concave metal plates clashed together.
20. A flat saucerlike disk struck with a hammer.

11. French horn
12. saxophone
13. banjo
14. xylophone
15. tamborine
16. mandolin
17. oboe
18. cello
19. cymbals
20. gong

Ph. D. Level

21. A keyboard whose strings are plucked instead of struck.
22. A large, low-pitched double-reed woodwind instrument.
23. A metal bar bent to have three sides and struck with a rod.
24. Located at the back of a dictionary.
25. Forerunner of the piano, brass pins strike horizontal strings.
26. Like a trumpet without keys or valves.
27. Harplike with a sounding box, used by the Greeks.
28. A small flute pitched an octave higher than the ordinary flute.
29. A set of bells tuned to a scale.
30. Metal reeds in slots in a frame, played by blowing.

21. harpsichord
22. bassoon
23. triangle
24. zither
25. clavichord
26. bugle
27. lyre
28. piccolo
29. chimes
30. harmonica (mouth organ)

GEOGRAPHICAL SONGS
Complete the song title with a place name.

Freshman Level

1. "I Left My Heart In———"
2. "Do You Know the Way to———"
3. "Yellow Rose of———"
4. "———On My Mind"
5. "April In ———"
6. "The ——— Waltz"
7. "The Night the Lights Went Out in ———"
8. "It's a Long Way to ———"
9. "Moon Over ———"
10. "There'll Always Be An ———"

1. San Francisco
2. San Jose
3. Texas
4. Georgia
5. Paris
6. Tennessee
7. Georgia
8. Tipperary
9. Miami
10. England

Graduate Level

11. "Rose of ——— Square"
12. "Girl From ———"
13. "Hotel ———"
14. "The ——— Choo Choo"
15. "By the Time I Get to ———"
16. "Weekend in ———"
17. "Slow Boat to ———"
18. "Moonlight in ———"
19. "My Old ——— Home"
20. "——— Concerto"

11. Washington
12. Ipanema
13. California
14. Chattanooga
15. Phoenix
16. New England
17. China
18. Vermont
19. Kentucky
20. Warsaw

Ph. D. Level: The artist who had a hit with the song is provided.

21. Fats Domino: "Walking to ———"
22. Joni Mitchell: "Free Man in ———"
23. B.J. Thomas: "Eyes of a ——— Woman"
24. Gene Pitney: "Twenty Four Hours From ———"
25. Paper Lace: "The Night ——— Died"
26. Mountain: "——— Queen"
27. Kenny Ball & His Jazzmen: "Midnight in ———"
28. Gladys Night & the Pips: "Midnight Train to ———"
29. Bee Gees: "The Lights Went Out In ———"
30. Johnny Horton: "North to ———"

21. New Orleans
22. Paris
23. New York
24. Tulsa
25. Chicago
26. Mississippi
27. Moscow
28. Georgia
29. Massachusetts
30. Alaska

6 / GEOGRAPHY

GENERAL I

Freshman Level

1. This country occupies the northeast corner of Africa.
2. The smallest of the Scandinavian countries.
3. The most westerly country in the West Indies.
4. In 1997 this area will be returned to China.
5. The southernmost Central American country.
6. This country occupies the western part of the Iberian Peninsula.
7. It extends further north than any other European country.
8. This country is over ten times as long as it is wide.
9. The Hindus consider this river to be sacred.
10. The desert in this country is called the Outback.

1. Egypt
2. Denmark
3. Cuba
4. Hong Kong
5. Panama
6. Portugal
7. Norway
8. Chile
9. Ganges
10. Australia

Graduate Level

11. Most of the apostles came from towns around this sea.
12. This African nation has the same name as an old English coin.
13. Name the five Gulf States.

14. Name the five states bordering on the Pacific Ocean.

15. This U.S. city has been called the City of Seven Hills.
16. Name the islands on which Napoleon (a) was born and (b) died.
17. The Indians called this lake Gitche Gumee.
18. Name the sandiest of all deserts.
19. This, the northernmost of all deserts, is covered with snow in the winter.
20. What is the foehn?

11. Sea of Galilee
12. Guinea
13. Florida, Alabama, Texas, Mississippi, Louisiana
14. Washington, Oregon, Alaska, California, Hawaii
15. San Francisco
16. Corsica (a) St. Helena (b)
17. Lake Superior
18. Arabian Desert
19. Gobi Desert
20. A wind

Ph. D. Level

21. The Mosquito Coast is on the east coast———.

22. What western hemisphere country has an area called Mesopotamia?
23. This tiny republic claims to be Europe's oldest state.
24. This republic occupies the third largest island in the Mediterranean.
25. The name of this palace comes from the Arabic Kalat-Alhamra meaning "red castle."
26. For years this country was known as the Hermit Kingdom
27. A narrow waterway called the Golden Horn flows through it.
28. The section around the western end of this lake is called the Golden Horseshoe.
29. What is the claim to fame of Montana's Flathead Lake?

30. The leader of this new state named the country after himself (1932).

21. Nicaragua and Honduras
22. Argentina
23. San Marino
24. Cyprus
25. The Alhambra
26. Korea
27. Istanbul
28. Lake Ontario
29. Largest freshwater lake west of Mississippi River
30. Saudi Arabia (Saud)

GENERAL II

Freshman Level

1. The country between the Arabian Sea and Bay of Bengal.
2. The only U.S. state borderng only one other state.
3. What European capital is farthest south?
4. What European capital is farthest west?
5. A country with both an Atlantic and Indian Ocean coast.
6. What continent is closest to Antarctica?
7. This country has three capital cities; one legislative, one administrative, and one judicial.
8. The largest city south of the equator.
9. This country's name means "little Venice."
10. How many countries are in Central America?

1. India
2. Maine
3. Athens
4. Reykjavik
5. South Africa
6. South America
7. South Africa
8. São Paulo
9. Venezuela
10. Seven

Graduate Level

11. The poorest nation in the western hemisphere.
12. The Galapagos Islands belong to this country.
13. In what country is the world's southernmost city?
14. Europe's two smallest independent states.
15. The most southerly capital city.
16. In 1985 this country had the largest foreign debt, $100 billion.
17. The only British soil occupied by Germany in WW II.
18. Through what Asian country does the equator pass?
19. Washington, D.C., and this European capital are both near 39° N.
20. What mainland European capital city is farthest north?

11. Haiti
12. Ecuador
13. Chile (Punta Arenas)
14. Vatican City, Monaco
15. Wellington, N.Z.
16. Brazil
17. Channel Islands
18. Indonesia
19. Lisbon
20. Helsinki

Ph. D. Level

21. The Central American country with only a Pacific coast.
22. The largest city in Africa.
23. The two largest cities in the western hemisphere.
24. The South American country with a Pacific and Caribbean coast.
25. The African country with the largest population.
26. This country was formerly called British Honduras.
27. What two countries share the island of New Guinea?

28. What sea covers the largest area?
29. Asia is the largest continent. What continent ranks second.
30. What country ranks seventh in size but second in population?

21. El Salvador
22. Cairo
23. New York, Mexico City
24. Colombia
25. Nigeria
26. Belize
27. Indonesia, Papua New Guinea
28. Philippine Sea
29. Africa
30. India

CAPITALS AND COUNTRIES

Name the country in which the given capital city is located.

Freshman Level

1. Vienna
2. Helsinki
3. Tokyo
4. Madrid
5. Havana
6. Budapest
7. Kingston
8. Warsaw
9. Seoul
10. Beirut

1. Austria
2. Finland
3. Japan
4. Spain
5. Cuba
6. Hungary
7. Jamaica
8. Poland
9. South Korea
10. Lebanon

Graduate Level

11. Prague
12. Lima
13. Baghdad
14. Damascus
15. Buenos Aires
16. Canberra
17. Stockholm
18. Lisbon
19. Tripoli
20. Belgrade

11. Czechoslovakia
12. Peru
13. Iraq
14. Syria
15. Argentina
16. Australia
17. Sweden
18. Portugal
19. Libya
20. Yugoslavia

Ph. D. Level

21. Reykjavik
22. Rangoon
23. Islamabad
24. Wellington
25. Santiago
26. San Salvador
27. Sofia
28. Rabat
29. Caracas
30. Bogota

21. Iceland
22. Burma
23. Pakistan
24. New Zealand
25. Chile
26. El Salvador
27. Bulgaria
28. Morocco
29. Venezuela
30. Colombia

RIVERS
The longest river in the country is given. Name the country.

Freshman Level

1.	Mississippi	1.	U.S.A.
2.	Mackenzie	2.	Canada
3.	Amazon	3.	Brazil, Peru
4.	Murray-Darling	4.	Australia
5.	Nile	5.	Egypt, Sudan
6.	Seine	6.	France
7.	Rio Grande (Rio Bravo)	7.	Mexico
8.	Yangtze (Chang Jiang)	8.	China
9.	Shannon	9.	Ireland
10.	Jordan	10.	Jordan, Israel

Graduate Level

11.	Severn	11.	England (U.K.)
12.	Orinoco	12.	Venezuela
13.	Po	13.	Italy
14.	Indus	14.	Pakistan
15.	Mekong	15.	Laos, Kampuchea
16.	Tigris	16.	Iraq
17.	Niger	17.	Niger, Nigeria, Mali
18.	Tagus	18.	Portugal
19.	Congo	19.	Zaire
20.	Rhine	20.	West Germany, Switzerland

Ph. D. Level

21.	Vistula	21.	Poland
22.	Elbe	22.	East Germany
23.	Black	23.	Jamaica
24.	Orange	24.	South Africa, Lesotho
25.	Ebro	25.	Spain
26.	Euphrates	26.	Syria
27.	Victoria-Nile	27.	Uganda
28.	Volga	28.	U.S.S.R. (European)
29.	Ganges	29.	Bangladesh, India
30.	Ob	30.	U.S.S.R. (Asian)

SOUTH OF THE BORDER

Name the country that is to the south of the given country.

Freshman Level

1. Canada
2. Switzerland
3. Denmark
4. U.S.A.
5. Lebanon
6. Venezuela
7. France
8. Nepal
9. United Kingdom
10. Mongolia

1. U.S.A.
2. Italy
3. West Germany
4. Mexico
5. Israel
6. Brazil
7. Spain
8. India
9. France
10. China

Graduate Level

11. Iraq
12. Mexico
13. Poland
14. Ecuador
15. Bulgaria
16. Afghanistan
17. Guyana
18. Egypt
19. Syria
20. Paraguay

11. Saudi Arabia
12. Guatemala
13. Czechoslovakia
14. Peru
15. Greece/Turkey
16. Pakistan
17. Brazil
18. Sudan
19. Jordan
20. Argentina

Ph. D. Level

21. Malaysia
22. Nicaragua
23. Romania
24. Laos
25. Angola

26. Botswana
27. Albania
28. Honduras
29. Luxembourg
30. Hungary

21. Indonesia
22. Costa Rica
23. Bulgaria
24. Cambodia
25. Namibia (Southwest Africa)
26. South Africa
27. Greece
28. Nicaragua
29. France
30. Yugoslavia

EAST OF EDEN
Name the country that is east of the given country.

Freshman Level

1. Chile	1. Argentina
2. Portugal	2. Spain
3. Norway	3. Sweden
4. Libya	4. Egypt
5. Ireland	5. United Kingdom
6. Finland	6. U.S.S.R.
7. Pakistan	7. India
8. Iraq	8. Iran
9. Poland	9. U.S.S.R.
10. Greece	10. Turkey

Graduate Level

11. Israel	11. Jordan
12. Italy	12. Yugoslavia
13. Belgium	13. West Germany
14. Sweden	14. Finland
15. Lebanon	15. Syria
16. East Germany	16. Poland
17. Afghanistan	17. Pakistan
18. Denmark	18. Sweden
19. Haiti	19. Dominican Republic
20. Cambodia (Kampuchea)	20. Vietnam

Ph. D. Level

21. Hungary	21. Romania
22. Sudan	22. Ethiopia
23. Paraguay	23. Brazil
24. Chad	24. Sudan
25. El Salvador	25. Honduras
26. Colombia	26. Venezuela
27. Uganda	27. Kenya
28. Ecuador	28. Peru
29. Morocco	29. Algeria
30. Syria	30. Iraq

NATIONS
Provide one country for each clue. The first letter is provided.

Freshman Level: All countries have 6-letter names.

1. B	1. Brazil, Belize, Bhutan, Brunei
2. C	2. Canada, Cyprus
3. G	3. Greece, Guyana, Guinea, Gambia
4. M	4. Mexico, Monaco, Malawi
5. P	5. Poland, Panama
6. F	6. France
7. N	7. Norway
8. S	8. Sweden
9. T	9. Turkey, Tuvalu
10. I	10. Israel

Graduate Level: All countries have 5-letter names.

11. C	11. Chile, Congo
12. I	12. India, Italy
13. S	13. Spain, Sudan, Syria
14. B	14. Burma, Benin
15. E	15. Egypt
16. G	16. Ghana, Gabon
17. L	17. Libya
18. H	18. Haiti
19. J	19. Japan
20. K	20. Kenya

Ph. D. Level: All countries have 4-letter names.

21. C	21. Cuba
22. C	22. Chad
23. F	23. Fiji
24. I	24. Iran
25. I	25. Iraq
26. L	26. Laos
27. M	27. Mali
28. O	28. Oman
29. P	29. Peru
30. T	30. Togo

STRAITS AND SEAS

Name the two main land bodies separated by the strait or sea.

Freshman Level

1. Strait of Gibraltar
2. Strait of Dover
3. Bering Strait
4. Red Sea
5. Mediterranean Sea
6. Formosa Strait
7. Davis Strait
8. Straits of Florida
9. Aegean Sea
10. Strait of Juan de Fuca

1. Spain and Morocco
2. France and England
3. U.S.A. (Alaska) and U.S.S.R.
4. Africa and Asia (Saudi Arabia)
5. Europe and Africa
6. China and Taiwan (Formosa)
7. Canada and Greenland
8. U.S.A. (Florida) and Bahamas/Cuba
9. Greece and Turkey
10. Canada and U.S.A. (Washington state)

Graduate Level

11. Strait of Magellan
12. Korea Strait
13. Yucatan Strait
14. Strait of Hormuz
15. Cook Strait
16. Black Sea
17. Yellow Sea
18. Strait of Georgia
19. Hudson Strait
20. Tasman Sea

11. Tierra del Fuego and mainland South America
12. South Korea and Japan
13. Mexico and Cuba
14. Iran and United Arab Emirates
15. North Island and South Island (New Zealand)
16. U.S.S.R. and Turkey
17. Korea and China
18. Vancouver Island and Mainland Canada
19. Baffin Island and mainland Canada
20. New Zealand and Australia

Ph. D. Level

21. Strait of Belle Isle
22. Luzon Strait
23. Dardanelles Strait
24. Baltic Sea
25. Adriatic Sea
26. Caribbean Sea
27. Strait of Bonifacio
28. Palk Strait
29. Bass Strait
30. Ionian Sea

21. Island of Newfoundland and mainland Canada
22. Philippines and Taiwan (Formosa)
23. Turkey (Asia) and Turkey (Europe)
24. Sweden and Poland/U.S.S.R.
25. Italy and Yugoslavia
26. West Indies and Central America/South America
27. Corsica and Sardinia
28. Sri Lanka and India
29. Tasmania and mainland Australia
30. Greece and Italy

CITIES
The last two letters of each answer are the first two letters of the next answer—e.g., If one answer is Genoa, the next answer might be Oakland.

Freshman Level

1. Capital of Italy
2. City with the same name as the country.
3. Capital of Sri Lanka
4. Capital of Colombia
5. Washington City
6. City in India
7. City in Egypt
8. City in Michigan
9. City in Florida
10. City in Kansas

1. Rome
2. Mexico
3. Colombo
4. Bogota
5. Tacoma
6. Madras
7. Aswan
8. Ann Arbor
9. Orlando
10. Dodge

Graduate Level

11. Major city of southeast Florida
12. City of Minnesota
13. Capital of Pakistan
14. City in Australia
15. City in India
16. Japanese city
17. American borough
18. City in Alaska
19. City in Switzerland
20. City in Chile

11. Miami
12. Minneapolis
13. Islamabad
14. Adelaide
15. Delhi
16. Hiroshima
17. Manhattan
18. Anchorage
19. Geneva
20. Valparaiso

Ph. D. Level

21. Motor City
22. City in New York State
23. Capital of Venezuela
24. City in the Soviet Union
25. Capital of Turkey
26. Capital of Morocco
27. City in Georgia
28. City in west Florida
29. City in France
30. City in Turkey

21. Detroit
22. Ithaca
23. Caracas
24. Astrakhan
25. Ankara
26. Rabat
27. Atlanta
28. Tampa
29. Paris
30. Istanbul

THE STATES I

Name the state identified by the clue.

Freshman Level

1. The smallest in population.
2. Its highest point is a hilltop 345 feet above sea level.
3. The southernmost point in the United States.
4. The largest of all living things is here.
5. Largest state east of the Mississippi.
6. The easternmost state (not Alaska).
7. The longest toll road in the world.
8. The first atomic bomb explosion.
9. The only state named after a president.
10. The last state, alphabetically speaking.

1. Alaska
2. Florida
3. Hawaii
4. California
5. Georgia
6. Maine
7. New York
8. New Mexico
9. Washington
10. Wyoming

Graduate Level

11. The nation's longest freshwater shoreline.
12. The home of shoofly pie and Amish farmers.
13. Most arid of all the states.
14. The middle state of the three on the west coast.
15. The first state alphabetically.
16. The smallest state.
17. The most densely populated state.
18. Its name means Land of the Red People.
19. Mormons settled here.
20. Silt from thirty-one states ends up here.

11. Michigan
12. Pennsylvania
13. Nevada
14. Oregon
15. Alabama
16. Rhode Island
17. New Jersey
18. Oklahoma
19. Utah
20. Louisiana

Ph. D. Level

21. Open-pit mining created the world's biggest man-made hole.
22. Mount Mitchell is the highest peak east of the Mississippi.
23. Near Rugby is the geographic center of North America.
24. The highest surface wind ever recorded, 231 mph, blew here in 1934.
25. The nation's only diamond mine.
26. This state compares itself to a diamond: tiny but valuable.
27. The Grand Canyon is located here.
28. At Arco in 1955 atomic energy was first used to supply electricity to an entire community.
29. Second after California for agriculture.
30. Site of "the bloodiest" one-day battle in U.S. history (Antietam, 22,700 casualties).

21. Minnesota
22. North Carolina
23. North Dakota
24. New Hampshire
25. Arkansas
26. Delaware
27. Arizona
28. Idaho
29. Iowa
30. Maryland

THE STATES II
Name the state identified by the clue.

Freshman Level

1. The second smallest state.
2. The only New England state lacking an ocean coastline.
3. The home of the first English settlement in North America.
4. Puget Sound is located in this state.
5. The last of the original thirteen colonies to be founded.
6. Home state of the Grand Ole Opry.
7. The site of the headwaters of the Mississippi River.
8. This state has more farmed area than any other state.
9. This state has the largest total black population.
10. The state with the highest mean elevation.

1. Delaware
2. Vermont
3. Virginia
4. Washington
5. Georgia
6. Tennessee
7. Minnesota
8. Texas
9. New York
10. Colorado

Graduate Level

11. Smallest state in the continental U.S. west of the Alleghenies.
12. The eighteenth state admitted to the union.
13. The Federal Government owns 87 percent of the land of this inland state.
14. The most rural state (over 90 percent of the land is in farms).
15. It leads in the production of paper and processed chicken.
16. The country's largest supplier of beer.
17. It leads in the production of the familiar flat tins of sardines.
18. It produces 97 percent of the nation's high-grade domestic bauxite ore.
19. The soil of this state is considered the finest in America.
20. It holds first place in apples, blueberries, and red raspberries.

11. Indiana
12. Louisiana
13. Nevada
14. North Dakota
15. Georgia
16. Wisconsin
17. Maine
18. Arkansas
19. Iowa
20. Washington

Ph. D. Level

21. This was the smallest in the Confederacy.
22. It ranks first nationally in lead mining.
23. Mount San Jacinto, the steepest mountain escarpment in the U.S.A.
24. Astoria, the Oldest American City West of the Missouri, is in this state.
25. The Vertical Assembly Building, the world's largest building in terms of enclosed space, is in this state.
26. There are more Basques in this state than any place other than their homeland.
27. The Civil War fiercely divided this state. Over 30,000 fought for the Confederacy. About 64,000 for the Union.
28. The Mormon Trail, Oregon Trail, and Pony Express all crossed this state.
29. Lawrence Welk and Peggy Lee were born in this state.
30. Its largest lake is Lake Eufaula.

21. South Carolina
22. Missouri
23. California
24. Oregon
25. Florida
26. Idaho
27. Kentucky
28. Nebraska
29. North Dakota
30. Oklahoma

CAPITALS AND STATES
Name the state in which the given state capital is located.

Freshman Level

1. Columbus
2. Hartford
3. Sacramento
4. Austin
5. Tallahassee
6. St. Paul
7. Charleston
8. Little Rock
9. Phoenix
10. Providence

1. Ohio
2. Connecticut
3. California
4. Texas
5. Florida
6. Minnesota
7. West Virginia
8. Arkansas
9. Arizona
10. Rhode Island

Graduate Level

11. Albany
12. Concord
13. Juneau
14. Raleigh
15. Lincoln
16. Cheyenne
17. Lansing
18. Jackson
19. Harrisburg
20. Santa Fe

11. New York
12. New Hampshire
13. Alaska
14. North Carolina
15. Nebraska
16. Wyoming
17. Michigan
18. Mississippi
19. Pennsylvania
20. New Mexico

Ph. D. Level

21. Boise
22. Salem
23. Olympia
24. Carson City
25. Dover
26. Montpelier
27. Pierre
28. Helena
29. Jefferson
30. Bismarck

21. Idaho
22. Oregon
23. Washington
24. Nevada
25. Delaware
26. Vermont
27. South Dakota
28. Montana
29. Missouri
30. North Dakota

ORIGINS OF STATE NAMES
All answers are state names.

Freshman Level

1. In honor of the first president of the country.
2. In honor of George II of England.
3. In honor of Louis XIV of France.
4. From an Indian word meaning Father of Waters.
5. From a English county.
6. From the country to the south of the United States.
7. In honor of Sir William Penn.
8. From the French meaning "green mountain."
9. In honor of Elizabeth, Virgin Queen of England.
10. Meaning "land of Indians."

1. Washington
2. Georgia
3. Louisiana
4. Mississippi
5. New Hampshire
6. New Mexico
7. Pennsylvania
8. Vermont
9. Virginia, West Virginia
10. Indiana

Graduate Level

11. From the Spanish meaning "feast of flowers."
12. In honor of Henrietta Marie (Queen of Charles I).
13. First used to distinguish the mainland from the offshore islands.
14. In honor of the English Duke of York.
15. In honor of Charles I of England.
16. From one of the English Channel Islands.
17. From the Greek island of the same name.
18. From the Spanish meaning "mountain."
19. From an Indian word meaning "great river."
20. Means Gem of the Mountains.

11. Florida
12. Maryland
13. Maine
14. New York
15. North/South Carolina
16. New Jersey
17. Rhode Island
18. Montana
19. Ohio
20. Idaho

Ph. D. Level

21. From the Spanish for "snowcapped."
22. From an Indian word meaning "great lake."
23. From an Indian word meaning "beside the long tidal river."
24. From the Spanish "ruddy" or "red."
25. From an Indian word meaning, "mountains and valleys alternating."
26. From a tribe name meaning "people of the mountains."
27. From an Indian word meaning "friends."
28. From an Indian word meaning "great land" or "mainland."
29. From an Indian word meaning "little spring."
30. From an imaginary island in a Spanish book.

21. Nevada
22. Michigan
23. Connecticut
24. Colorado
25. Wyoming
26. Utah
27. Texas
28. Alaska
29. Arizona
30. California

LARGE U.S. CITIES
Identify the city from its location.

Freshman Level

1. Northwest Georgia south of the Appalachian Mountains.
2. North-central Colorado on South Platte River.
2. 2,397 miles southwest of San Francisco.
4. At junction of the Clear and West forks of the Trinity River about thirty miles west of Dallas.
5. Between Santa Monica and San Pedro bays.
6. North-central Utah at the foot of the Wasatch Range.
7. Central Ohio on Scioto River.
8. South Carolina on peninsula between Ashley and Cooper Rivers.
9. Southeastern Wisconsin on Lake Michigan.
10. New Jersey on Passaic River.

1. Atlanta
2. Denver
3. Honolulu
4. Fort Worth
5. Los Angeles
6. Salt Lake City
7. Columbus
8. Charleston
9. Milwaukee
10. Newark

Graduate Level

11. Tennessee on Cumberland River.
12. Virginia at mouth of Chesapeake Bay.
13. Rhode Island at the head of the Narragansett Bay.
14. Missouri near junction of Mississippi and Missouri Rivers.
15. Texas about 190 miles west of Houston.
16. West-central California on a peninsula across from Oakland.
17. West coast of Florida at mouth of Hillsboro River.
18. Alabama in the Jones Valley at the foot of Red Mountain.
19. Minnesota on both sides of the Mississippi River.
20. Oregon near the junction of the Willamette and Columbia rivers.

11. Nashville
12. Norfolk
13. Providence
14. St. Louis
15. San Antonio
16. San Francisco
17. Tampa
18. Birmingham
19. Minneapolis
20. Portland

Ph. D. Level

21. At the mouth of the Genesee River on Lake Ontario.
22. Ninety miles northeast of San Francisco.
23. At the junction of the Minnesota River with the Mississippi.
24. Arizona on the Salt River.
25. New Mexico on the upper Rio Grande.
26. Ohio, on the Cuyahoga River.
27. Texas on the Colorado River.
28. On Cook Inlet west of the Chugach Mountains.
29. On the Mississippi River about eighty-five miles northwest of New Orleans.
30. California, about 100 miles south of Los Angeles.

21. Rochester
22. Sacramento
23. St. Paul
24. Phoenix
25. Albuquerque
26. Akron
27. Austin
28. Anchorage
29. Baton Rouge
30. San Diego

BUILDINGS: The U.S.A. and Canada

Freshman Level

1. The tallest building in the world from 1932 to 1971.
2. This Chicago building is currently the world's tallest.
3. These twin towers dominate the New York City skyline.
4. This railway station has the world's largest indoor clock (N.Y.C.).
5. The most elegant of the casinos in Las Vegas.
6. It preceded the Empire State as the world's tallest building.
7. The ceremonial capital of the political world (N.Y.C.).
8. Building located at 1600 Pennsylvania Avenue in Washington, D.C.
9. The Declaration of Independence was signed here.
10. The largest ground area covered by any office building.

1. Empire State Building
2. Sear's Tower
3. World Trade Center
4. Grand Central Station
5. Caesar's Palace
6. Chrysler Building
7. U.N. Building
8. The White House
9. Independence Hall
10. The Pentagon

Graduate Level

11. This museum was one of the last works of Frank Lloyd Wright.
12. This cinema in Los Angeles dates from the heyday of Hollywood.
13. This arena in New Orleans was completed in 1975.
14. The world's largest Gothic cathedral (N.Y.C.).

15. This wedge-shaped building was New York's first skyscraper.
16. This shopping center is Toronto's major tourist attraction.
17. This rambling "mystery" house is in San Jose, California.
18. This multilevel modular apartment complex was an Expo 67 attraction.
19. Toronto's new domed stadium has a retractable roof.
20. In addition to the Sear's Tower, Chicago has two buildings over 1,000 feet in height. Name either.

11. Guggenheim Museum
12. Mann's/Grauman's Chinese Theater
13. Louisiana Superdome
14. Cathedral of St. John the Divine
15. The Flatiron Building
16. Eaton Center
17. Winchester House
18. Habitat
19. The Sky Dome
20. Standard Oil; John Hancock Center

Ph. D. Level

21. The world's largest commercial hotel building (N.Y.C.).
22. The world's largest private house (Asheville, N.C.).
23. The most expensive private house ever built (San Simeon, California).
24. This hotel in Quebec City stands on a hilltop site.
25. San Francisco's tallest building.
26. Canada's tallest building (Toronto).
27. The world's tallest hotel (Atlanta, Georgia).

28. The world's largest casino (Atlantic City, New Jersey).
29. This government building has an imposing cast-iron dome.
30. The world's largest department store (N.Y.C.).

21. Waldorf-Asoria
22. Biltmore House
23. Hearst Castle
24. Chateau Frontenac
25. Transamerica Pyramid
26. First Canadian Place
27. Peachtree Center Plaza Hotel
28. Resorts International
29. Capitol Building
30. Macy's

BUILDINGS OF THE WORLD

Freshman Level

1. This building dominates the Acropolis in Athens.
2. The best known and most impressive monument of Roman architecture.
3. India's most renowned monument.
4. Australia's best-known architectural gem.
5. The premier church of Roman Catholic Christendom.
6. The official residence of French kings, 1682– 1790.
7. Chapel in Vatican used for papal elections.
8. A fortified enclosure in Moscow.
9. The burial place of Britain's honored civilian dead.
10. Sir Christopher Wren's masterful London cathedral.

1. Parthenon
2. The Colosseum
3. Taj Mahal
4. Sydney Opera House
5. St. Peter's Basilica
6. Palace of Versailles
7. Sistine Chapel
8. The Kremlin
9. Westminster Abbey
10. St. Paul's Cathedral

Graduate Level

11. The Mona Lisa is in this museum.
12. A moorish fortified palace overlooking the city of Grenada.
13. The residence of the Royal Family in London.
14. The most important church of the Byzantine Empire for nearly 1000 years.
15. French cathedral noted for its stained glass and magnificent sculptures.
16. This British royal residence is the world's largest inhabited castle.
17. This cathedral and its shrine were the destination of Geoffrey Chaucer in his most famous book.
18. The most important Islamic shrine outside Mecca.
19. Paris cathedral noted for a huge rose window and flying buttresses.
20. A famous opera house in Milan, Italy.

11. The Louvre
12. The Alhambra
13. Buckingham Palace
14. Hagia Sophia
15. Chartres
16. Windsor Castle
17. Canterbury Cathedral
18. Dome of the Rock, Jerusalem
19. Notre Dame
20. La Scala

Ph. D. Level

21. Venetian church with an oriental, fairy-tale appearance.
22. This palace at Knossos, Crete, has inverted columns.
23. The great temple in Cambodia built for the deified spirit of a dead king.
24. The best preserved Roman building, built by Hadrian as a temple to all the known gods.
25. The largest palace, the Imperial Palace in Peking, is in an area known as the ——
26. This English palace is perhaps the most famous "Oriental" building in Europe.
27. This was the seat of government and residence of principal magistrate of the Republic of Venice.
28. This onion-domed church in Moscow was built by Ivan the Terrible.
29. This museum in Istanbul was once the home of the Turkish Sultan.
30. Third largest church in Europe. Its roof has 135 spires each bearing a statue.

21. St. Marks
22. Minoan Royal Palace
23. Angkor Wat
24. Pantheon
25. Forbidden City
26. Brighton Pavilion
27. Doge's Palace
28. St. Basil's
29. Topkapi Palace
30. Milan Cathedral

STATUES AND MONUMENTS

Freshman Level

1. These ancient "wonders of the world" still stand.
2. This Pacific Island is noted for its giant stone heads.
3. The world's largest triumphal arch.
4. America's most famous statue.
5. The world's tallest full-figure statue is that of "The Motherland" in this country.
6. This tapered 555-foot shaft stands in Washington, D.C.

7. This massive work at Gizeh guards the pyramids.
8. This nude statue is Michelangelo's best known sculpture.
9. Rodin's sculpture of a pensive individual.
10. Rodin's sculpture of a couple embracing.

1. Pyramids
2. Easter Island
3. Arc de Triomphe, Paris
4. Statue of Liberty
5. U.S.S.R.
6. Washington Monument
7. The Sphinx
8. "David"
9. "The Thinker"
10. "The Kiss"

Graduate Level

11. The statue at water's edge in Copenhagen Harbor.
12. The armless figure of the Goddess of Love and Beauty.
13. The most famous prehistoric standing-stone monument in Europe.
14. The largest pyramid and the largest monument ever constructed is in this country.
15. The faces of four presidents are carved on this South Dakota site.
16. Name the four presidents.

17. Michelangelo's seated figure of a bearded visionary leader.
18. This Greek statue showed an athlete throwing a disc.

19. The statue of this seated president is by D. C. French.

20. The Roman fountain featured in *Three Coins in the Fountain*.

11. "The Little Mermaid"
12. "Venus de Milo"
13. Stonehenge
14. Mexico
15. Mount Rushmore
16. Washington, Jefferson, Lincoln, T. Roosevelt
17. "Moses"
18. "Discobolus (Discus Thrower)"
19. "Lincoln" (Lincoln Memorial)
20. Trevi Fountain

Ph. D. Level

21. Fountain of a small boy urinating (Belgium).
22. Michelangelo's sculpture of the dead Christ in Mary's lap.
23. Equestrian figures of Confederate leaders are carved in this Georgian site.
24. Name the three leaders depicted.

25. Cellini's masterpiece of a Greek hero holding up the head of Medusa.
26. J. Fraser's statue of an Indian warrior on a pony.
27. The head and arms of the "Victory of Samothrace" are missing. The statue is best known as ———.
28. The Terrace of Lions is on this Greek Island.
29. This Egyptian obelisk now stands in London.
30. The tallest monument is in the U.S.A. Name it.

21. "Mannekin Pis"
22. "Pietà"
23. Stone Mountain
24. J. Davis, R. E. Lee, T. E. Jackson
25. "Perseus"
26. "End of the Trail"
27. "Winged Victory"
28. Delos
29. Cleopatra's Needle
30. Gateway to the West Arch (St. Louis)

WALLS, TOWERS, BRIDGES, et al.

Freshman Level

1. The longest structure ever built.
2. This bridge spans a channel at the entrance of San Francisco Bay.
3. A famous Roman wall in northern Britain.
4. This bridge over the Thames has been replaced twice.
5. This type of bridge, named after its inventor, is useful for rapid military actions.
6. Spanning the East River, it was designated a national historic landmark in 1964.
7. The 984-foot tower was built for the World's Fair in 1889.
8. The most famous tower in the Bible.
9. Italy's most famous tower.
10. Title of 1957 film which won seven Oscars including Best Picture.

1. Great Wall of China
2. Golden Gate Bridge
3. Hadrian's Wall
4. London Bridge
5. Bailey Bridge
6. Brooklyn Bridge
7. Eiffel Tower
8. Tower of Babel
9. Leaning Tower of Pisa
10. Bridge on the River Kwai

Graduate Level

11. Two black granite walls in Washington, D.C., serve as a memorial to ———.
12. A tall monument in Trafalgar Square.
13. This bridge at the entrance to New York Harbor carries a double deck roadway.
14. It crosses the canal between the Doge's Palace and prison.
15. A bridge in Hartland, New Brunswick, holds this distinction.
16. The steps in Rome ascend past the house where Keats died.
17. The lower part of the wall is said to be from Herod's Temple.
18. This bridge in Scotland is the best known steel cantilever bridge.
19. Title of a novel by Thornton Wilder (1927).

20. The world's tallest free-standing structure.

11. Viet Nam War Veterans
12. Nelson's Monument
13. Verrazano-Narrows Bridge
14. Bridge of Sighs
15. Longest covered bridge
16. Spanish Steps
17. Wailing (Western) Wall
18. Firth of Forth Bridge
19. *Bridge of San Luis Rey*
20. CN Tower (Toronto)

Ph. D. Level

21. A 1,074-meter bridge connecting Europe and Asia.
22. It consists of a metal frame covered with bottles and china.
23. This bridge in Florence is lined with shops.
24. The Victor Emmanuel Monument in Rome is nicknamed the ———.
25. This "gate" was the main entrance to the Citadel at Mycenae.
26. This single-arched bridge crosses the Grand Canal in Venice.
27. The tallest chimney belongs to this company in Sudbury, Ontario.
28. This bridge, nicknamed Galloping Gertie, collapsed in 1940.
29. The Queen's Staircase, a flight of sixty-six steps, is in this city.
30. The longest bridge-tunnel system in the western hemisphere.

21. Bosporus Bridge
22. Watt's Tower, L.A.
23. Ponte Vecchio
24. Wedding Cake
25. The Lion Gate
26. Rialto Bridge
27. International Nickel Co.
28. Tacoma Narrows Bridge
29. Nassau
30. Chesapeake Bay Bridge-Tunnel

COUNTRIES

Freshman Level: Complete the name of the country.

1. S———land
2. I———land
3. T———land
4. P———land
5. N———land
6. N———lands
7. Al———ia
8. Au———ia
9. An———a
10. Ar———a

1. Switzerland, Swaziland, Scotland
2. Ireland or Iceland
3. Thailand
4. Poland
5. New Zealand
6. Netherlands
7. Albania or Algeria
8. Australia or Austria
9. Andorra
10. Argentina, Arabia

Graduate Level: Complete the name of the country.

11. B———ia
12. C———ia
13. E———ia
14. I———ia
15. L———ia
16. M———ia
17. S———ia
18. T———
19. Y———ia
20. Z———ia

11. Bolivia or Bulgaria
12. Cambodia, Colombia, Czechoslovakia
13. Ethiopia
14. India or Indonesia
15. Liberia
16. Malaysia or Mauritania
17. St. Lucia, Saudi Arabia, Somalia, or Syria
18. Tanzania or Tunisia
19. Yugoslavia
20. Zambia

Ph. D. Level: What country's name is an anagram for the given word?

21. Rain
22. Pure
23. Pains
24. Chain
25. Reign
26. Serial
27. Also
28. Moan
29. Mail
30. Plane

21. Iran
22. Peru
23. Spain
24. China
25. Niger
26. Israel
27. Laos
28. Oman
29. Mali
30. Nepal

NATIONAL FLAGS

Freshman Level

1. Red with a hammer, sickle, and star.
2. A red maple leaf at the center.
3. Fifty stars plus thirteen red and white stripes.
4. Three vertical bands: blue, white, red from left to right.
5. A large red circle on a white field.
6. A square red flag with a large white cross.
7. Green with a sword and an inscription.
8. White with two horizontal blue stripes and a blue Star of David in the center.
9. A yellow diamond shape with a globe in it, on a green field.
10. Red with a large gold star and four smaller gold stars.

1. U.S.S.R.
2. Canada
3. U.S.A.
4. France
5. Japan
6. Switzerland
7. Saudi Arabia
8. Israel
9. Brazil
10. China

Graduate Level

11. The blue ensign with six white stars.
12. Three vertical bands: green, white, red from left to right.
13. The combined crosses of St. George, St. Andrew and St. Patrick
14. A white star and crescent on a red field.
15. A gold cross on a blue field.
16. White with a blue and red yin and yang symbol.
17. Two horizontal bands: top white, bottom red.
18. A large gold star centered on a red field.
19. Red and white bands with a cypress tree in the center.
20. Nine blue and white stripes with a white cross in the upper left corner.

11. Australia
12. Italy
13. United Kingdom
14. Turkey
15. Sweden
16. South Korea
17. Poland
18. Viet Nam
19. Lebanon
20. Greece

Ph. D. Level

21. The blue ensign with four red stars.
22. Red, yellow, green bands with a large *R* in the center.
23. Three vertical bands: green, white, orange from left to right.
24. White with a yellow map and olive branches.
25. Three horizontal bands: orange, white, blue, top to bottom and three smaller flags in the center.
26. Three horizontal bands: red, white, black, top to bottom.
27. Green with a large red circle in the center.
28. Three horizontal bands, orange, white, green from top to bottom, plus a wheel in the center.
29. Three horizontal bands, red, white, blue, top to bottom.
30. Three horizontal bands, blue, white, blue, top to bottom.

21. New Zealand
22. Rwanda
23. Ireland
24. Cyprus
25. South Africa
26. Iraq
27. Bangladesh
28. India
29. Netherlands or Luxembourg
30. Argentina

WORLD RANKINGS
Name the country that leads the world in the given category.

Freshman Level

1.	Tea consumption	1.	U.K.
2.	Gold production	2.	South Africa
3.	Coffee production	3.	Colombia
4.	Rice production	4.	China
5.	Wool production	5.	Australia
6.	Wine production	6.	France
7.	Ship production	7.	Japan
8.	Passenger car production	8.	U.S.A.
9.	Steel production	9.	U.S.S.R.
10.	Petroleum reserves	10.	Saudi Arabia

Graduate Level

11.	Rubber production	11.	Malaysia
12.	Cement production	12.	U.S.S.R.
13.	Cheese production	13.	Netherlands
14.	Television set production	14.	Japan
15.	Radio production	15.	Hong Kong
16.	Beer production	16.	Luxembourg
17.	Fish catch	17.	Japan
18.	Educational expenditure per pupil	18.	Sweden
19.	Aluminum production	19.	U.S.A.
20.	Iron production	20.	U.S.S.R.

Ph. D. Level

21.	Salt production	21.	Bahamas
22.	Diamond production	22.	Zaire
23.	Peanut production	23.	India
24.	Size of merchant marine	24.	Liberia
25.	Film production	25.	India
26.	Number of film theaters	26.	U.S.S.R.
27.	Crime rate	27.	Lebanon
28.	Crude petroleum production	28.	U.S.S.R.
29.	Average annual rate of inflation	29.	Chile
30.	GNP per capita	30.	Kuwait

GEOGRAPHICAL NOURISHMENT

Provide a food or beverage to complete the name of the dish or beverage. (No repeat answers please.)

Freshman Level

1. Yorkshire——
2. Brussels——
3. Boston——
4. Idaho——
5. Worcestershire——
6. Black Forest——
7. Swiss——
8. Irish——
9. French——

10. Spanish——

1. pudding
2. sprouts
3. beans, cream pie
4. potatoes
5. sauce
6. cake
7. cheese/steak/chocolate
8. stew, coffee
9. fries, onion soup, toast, dressing
10. onion, coffee, omelet, rice

Graduate Level

11. Scotch——
12. Cayenne——
13. Welsh——
14. Peking——
15. Salisbury——
16. Thousand Island——
17. Lima——
18. Virginia——
19. Waldorf——
20. Polish——

11. whiskey, eggs
12. pepper
13. rabbit
14. duck
15. steak
16. dressing
17. beans
18. ham
19. salad
20. sausage

Ph. D. Level

21. Hungarian——
22. —— Kiev
23. —— Newburg
24. English——
25. London——
26. Madeira——
27. Bavarian——
28. Manhattan or New England——
29. Swedish——
30. Nanaimo——

21. goulash
22. chicken
23. lobster
24. muffins, trifle
25. broil
26. wine
27. cream
28. clam chowder
29. meatballs
30. bars

7 / DAYS AND DATES

EVENTS OF THE TWENTIETH CENTURY

Freshman Level

1. 1902: End of war in South Africa. It was known as the———.
2. 1903: The Wright Brothers' flight at this North Carolina site.
3. 1905: He published his special theory of relativity.
4. 1908: The first of these cars rolled off the line in Detroit.
5. 1908: He became the first black heavyweight champion.
6. 1910: French physicist designed this new type of sign.
7. 1911: He became the first president of the Chinese Republic.
8. 1914: This war began.
9. 1917: Revolution in this country.
10. 1919: This peace treaty followed WWI.

1. Boer War
2. Kitty Hawk
3. Albert Einstein
4. Model-T Fords
5. Jack Johnson
6. Neon sign
7. Dr. Sun Yat-sen
8. WWI
9. Russia
10. Treaty of Versailles

Graduate Level

11. 1920: The U.S.A. rejected membership in this organization.
12. 1922: This Egyptian tomb was unearthed.
13. 1926: He became the 124th emperor of Japan.
14. 1928: Scottish bacteriologist discovered this.
15. 1929: The stock market crash preceded this.
16. 1931: Japan occupied this region.
17. 1933: He became chancellor of Germany.
18. 1936: This civil war broke out.
19. 1939: WWII began when Germany attacked———.
20. 1941: This event brought the U.S.A. into WWII.

11. League of Nations.
12. King Tutankhamen
13. Hirohito
14. Penicillin
15. Great Depression
16. Manchuria
17. Adolf Hitler
18. Spanish Civil War
19. Poland
20. Pearl Harbor bombing

Ph. D. Level

21. 1942: This physicist produced an atomic chain reaction.
22. 1949: This defensive organization was formed.
23. 1953: This Soviet leader died.
24. 1957: This, the first artificial earth satellite, was launched.
25. 1958: France's Fifth Republic is established under President———.
26. 1967: Israel defeated Arab states in this war.
27. 1968: Soviet troops invaded this country.
28. 1969: He was first to walk on the moon.
29. 1971: East Pakistan became the independent state of———.
30. 1974: President Nixon resigned as a result of this———.

21. Enrico Fermi
22. NATO
23. Joseph Stalin
24. Sputnik
25. Charles de Gaulle
26. Six-Day War
27. Czechoslovakia
28. Neil Armstrong
29. Bangladesh
30. Watergate Scandal

EVENTS OF THE NINETEENTH CENTURY

Freshman Level

1. 1803: The U.S. doubled in size under this president.
2. 1804: He was crowned Emperor of France.
3. 1805: Nelson won a major battle here.
4. 1812: Napoleon invaded this country.
5. 1812: The War of 1812 was fought between these two countries.
6. 1815: Napoleon was defeated here.
7. 1819: America acquired this area from Spain.
8. 1819: The *Savannah* became the first steamship to———.
9. 1824: His Ninth Symphony was first performed.
10. 1829: George Stephenson's *Rocket* was successful. It was a———.

1. Thomas Jefferson
2. Napoleon
3. Trafalgar
4. Russia
5. U.S.A., England
6. Waterloo
7. Florida
8. Cross the Atlantic
9. Beethoven
10. Steam locomotive

Graduate Level

11. 1833: The British Empire abolished this in its colonies.
12. 1839–1842: This war took place in China.
13. 1844: Samuel Morse invented the———.
14. 1853: Commodore Perry opened up trade with———.
15. 1854: This war began when Britain and France declared war on Russia.
16. 1859: He published *On the Origin of Species.*
17. 1861: Civil War broke out in this country.
18. 1862: This French author published *Les Misérables.*
19. 1863: This act freed most American slaves.
20. 1864: This French chemist discovered a process to retard spoilage of beverages.

11. Slavery
12. Opium War
13. Telegraph
14. Japan
15. Crimean War
16. Charles Darwin
17. U.S.A.
18. Victor Hugo
19. Emancipation Proclamation
20. Louis Pasteur

Ph. D. Level

21. 1865: This racist organization was founded in Tennessee.
22. 1865: He took the first steps to introduce antiseptic surgery.
23. 1866: He invented dynamite.
24. 1867: This emperor of Mexico was executed.
25. 1869: This canal opened for traffic.
26. 1877: Thomas Edison invented this.
27. 1887: *A Study in Scarlet* was published. It was the first———.
28. 1895: He invented the wireless telegraph.
29. 1896: He devised the I.Q. test.
30. 1898: Pierre and Marie Curie discovered this.

21. Ku Klux Klan
22. Joseph Lister
23. Alfred Nobel
24. Maximilian
25. Suez Canal
26. Phonograph
27. Sherlock Holmes novel.
28. Marconi
29. Alfred Binet
30. Radium

EVENTS OF THE EIGHTEENTH CENTURY

Freshman Level

1. 1701–1714: The war of Spanish———.
2. 1703: This Russian city (now Leningrad) was founded.
3. 1704: Britain took possession of this strategic site.
4. 1707: These two European countries were constitutionally united.
5. 1714: George I succeeded Anne, establishing this house on the English throne.
6. 1721–1742: Ministry of Britain's "first prime minister." Name him.
7. 1726: Swift published this book.
8. 1728: He crossed the strait between Siberia and Alaska.
9. 1738: He began Methodist revivals.
10. 1740–1786: Period of this man's reign in Prussia.

1. Succession
2. St. Petersburg
3. Gibraltar
4. England, Scotland
5. House of Hanover
6. Robert Walpole
7. *Gulliver's Travels*
8. Vitus Bering
9. John Wesley
10. Fredrick the Great

Graduate Level

11. 1750: Death of this German composer.
12. 1756–1763: Period of this war in Europe.
13. 1757: Victory of Clive at Plassey laid foundation of British power in———.
14. 1759: Britain's defeat of France at this site signaled the collapse of French power in North America.
15. 1759: This writer published *Candide.*
16. 1762–1796: Period of this leader's rule in Russia.
17. 1762: This writer published *The Social Contract.*
18. 1768–1769: His voyages of discovery in Pacific and Antarctic waters.
19. 1769: He patented the first efficient condensing steam engine.
20. 1770: Hargreaves patented this.

11. J. Sebastian Bach
12. Seven Year's War
13. India
14. Quebec
15. Voltaire
16. Catherine the Great
17. Rosseau
18. Captain Cook
19. James Watt
20. Spinning jenny

Ph. D. Level

26. 1774: A congress made up of delegates from all the colonies except Georgia.
22. 1776: He published *The Wealth of Nations.*
23. 1783: This treaty ended American Revolutionary War.
24. 1788: The first Europeans settled here.
25. 1789: This revolution began.
26. 1791: This act created Upper and Lower Canada.
27. 1794: He patented the cotton gin.
28. 1796: He successfully tested vaccination.
29. 1798: The Romantic movement in English poetry began with publication of lyrical ballads by———.
30. 1799: He became the First Consul of France.

21. The First Continental Congress
22. Adam Smith
23. Treaty of Paris
24. Australia
25. French Revolution
26. Constitutional Act
27. Eli Whitney
28. Edward Jenner
29. Wordsworth or Coleridge
30. Napoleon

EVENTS OF THE SEVENTEENTH CENTURY

Freshman Level

1. 1603: James I became King of England following her death.
2. 1606: Dutch navigator Willem Jansz discovered this continent.
3. 1607: First English settlement in Virginia was founded here.
4. 1608: This French explorer founded Quebec.
5. 1611: This translation of the Bible was issued.
6. 1613: This dynasty was founded in Russia.
7. 1616: Death of this literary genius.
8. 1618: Outbreak of this lengthy war.
9. 1620: Pilgrims founded this colony.
10. 1624: Dutch founded this colony, which is now New York.

1. Elizabeth I
2. Australia
3. Jamestown
4. Champlain
5. King James version
6. Romanov
7. Shakespeare
8. Thirty Years' War
9. Plymouth, Massachusetts
10. New Amsterdam

Graduate Level

11. 1624: He became the chief minister of France.
12. 1628: He published his discovery of the circulation of blood.
13. 1629: Giovanni Bernini was appointed chief architect of this building.
14. 1630: Puritans founded this city.
15. 1634: He founded a refuge colony in Maryland for Roman Catholic settlers.
16. 1640: Portugal gained independence from this country after sixty years of rule.
17. 1642: He discovered New Zealand.
18. 1642: This Italian physicist died and this great English scientist was born.
19. 1644: End of this Chinese dynasty.
20. 1649: This English king was beheaded.

11. Richelieu (Jean du Plessis)
12. William Harvey
13. St. Peters, Rome
14. Boston
15. Lord Baltimore
16. Spain
17. Abel Tasman
18. Galileo Galilei, Isaac Newton
19. Ming
20. Charles I

Ph. D. Level

21. 1652: Cape Town was founded by this nation.
22. 1664: France formed this trading company.
23. 1666: This city was destroyed by fire.
24. 1670: This colony in South Carolina was founded.
25. 1681: He received land grant comprising present Pennsylvania, all of Delaware, and a large slice of Maryland.
26. 1683: Taiwan became part of———.
27. 1681: This building in Athens was badly damaged during a bombardment.
28. 1689: He became the sole czar of Russia (to 1725).
29. 1689: Enactment of this bill in England.
30. 1694: This famous bank was created.

21. Dutch
22. French East Indian Company.
23. London
24. Charleston
25. William Penn
26. China
27. Parthenon
28. Peter the Great
29. Bill of Rights
30. Bank of England

EVENTS OF THE SIXTEENTH CENTURY

Freshman Level

1. 1507: First use of this name on a map.
2. 1509: He became king of England (to 1547).
3. 1509: Sebastian Cabot discovered this bay.
4. 1513: He crossed Panama and reached the Pacific.
5. 1513: He wrote *The Prince.*
6. 1515: He became king of France (to 1547).
7. 1517: He launched the Protestant Reformation.
8. 1517: Egypt was conquered by the———.
9. 1517: The Spanish began their conquest of———.
10. 1519: This Italian genius died.

1. America
2. Henry VIII
3. Hudson Bay
4. Balboa
5. Machiavelli
6. Francis I
7. Luther
8. Turks
9. Mexico
10. Leonardo da Vinci

Graduate Level

11. 1520: He became the Ottoman sultan (to 1566).

12. 1522: He began the first circumnavigation of the globe.
13. 1532: Portuguese established permanent settlement in this western country.
14. 1533: He began his reign in Russia (to 1584).
15. 1535: Cartier discovered this river.
16. 1535: He captured the Inca capital.
17. 1539: He began exploration of southeastern U.S.A. for Spain.
18. 1540: He began exploration of northern Mexico and U.S. Southwest for Spain.
19. 1543: His work laid the cornerstones of modern astronomy.
20. 1555: Peace of Augsburg temporarily setteled conflict between these two groups in Germany.

11. Suleiman I (The Magnificent)
12. Magellan
13. Brazil
14. Ivan IV (the Terrible)
15. St. Lawrence
16. Pizarro
17. De Soto
18. Coronado
19. Copernicus
20. Catholics and Protestants

Ph. D. Level

21. 1564: Death of this Italian sculptor, painter, architect.
22. 1565: This, the oldest U.S. city, was founded.
23. 1571: Manila came under the control of this country.
24. 1572: This group was massacred on St. Bartholomew's Day.
25. 1580: He completed the first British circumnavigation of the globe.
26. 1582: This new calendar was established.
27. 1588: This naval victory by Britain.

28. 1589: Henry IV became king of France, establishing this dynasty.
29. 1598: Edict of Nantes granted rights to———.
30. 1600: This company was founded in London.

21. Michelangelo
22. St. Augustine
23. Spain
24. French Protestants
25. Drake
26. Gregorian calendar
27. Defeat of Spanish Armada
28. Bourbon
29. Huguenots
30. British East India Company

JANUARY EVENTS

Freshman Level

1. January 1 is New Year's Day. Name the song associated with New Years.
2. On January 3, 1959, the forty-ninth state became a reality.
3. January 8, 1935, was the birthday of this rock legend.
4. January 14, 1875, was the birthday of this doctor who founded a hospital in Africa.
5. January 19, 1807, the birthday of this Confederate general.
6. This *Casablanca* star was born on January 23, 1899.
7. On January 27, 1858, this city was chosen to be Canada's capital city.
8. On January 30, 1649, this king was beheaded.
9. On January 20, 1948, this leader was assassinated.
10. On January 15, 1929, this civil rights leader was born.

1. "Auld Lang Syne"
2. Alaska
3. Elvis Presley
4. Albert Schweitzer
5. Robert E. Lee
6. H. Bogart
7. Ottawa
8. Charles I
9. M. Gandhi
10. M. Luther King, Jr.

Graduate Level

11. January 13, 1984, is the date on which the composer of the song "Oh Susanna" died. Name him.
12. The first meeting of this prestigious body took place on January 10, 1946.
13. This U.S. president was born on January 9, 1913.
14. This Russian leader died on January 21, 1924.
15. On January 26, 1788, a shipload of British convicts arrived at Botany Bay in this country.
16. On January 27, 1756, this musical genius was born in Salzburg, Austria.
17. Name the tragedy that took place on January 28, 1986.
18. On January 20, 1841, this city was ceded to Britain at the end of the Opium War.
19. This black American scientist died on January 5, 1943, at Tuskegee, Alabama.
20. The author of the Winnie-the-Pooh stories was born on January 18, 1882.

11. Stephen Foster
12. U.N. General Assembly
13. R. Nixon
14. N. Lenin
15. Australia
16. W. A. Mozart
17. *Challenger* exploded
18. Hong Kong
19. George Washington Carver
20. A. A. Milne

Ph. D. Level

21. January 17, 1706, was the birthday of the author of *Poor Richard's Almanack*. Name him.
22. January 11, 1815, was the birthday of Canada's first prime minister. Name him.
23. The Beehive State achieved statehood on January 4, 1896.
24. The Feast of Epiphany is on January 6. What Shakespearean title refers to Epiphany Eve?
25. The 18th Amendment was passed on January 16, 1919. What did it do?
26. January 20 is an important date for all U.S. Presidents. Why?
27. On January 22, 1901, this British monarch died.
28. January 25, 1759, was his, the Plowman Poet's, birthday.
29. On January 29, 1861, the Sunflower State achieved statehood.
30. On January 16, 1942, this movie star was killed in a plane crash while on a war-bond drive.

21. Ben Franklin
22. Sir John A. Macdonald
23. Utah
24. *Twelfth Night*
25. Brought in Prohibition.
26. Inauguration Day
27. Queen Victoria
28. Robert Burns
29. Kansas
30. Carole Lombard

FEBRUARY EVENTS

Freshman Level

1. What special day is February 2?
2. What special day is February 14?
3. What day is Leap Year Day?
4. What president was born on February 6, 1911, in Illinois.
5. He became the Cuban leader on February 16, 1958.
6. Born on February 10, 1893, he made the song "Inka Dinka Doo" one of his trademarks.
7. This famous aviator was born on February 4, 1902.
8. One of baseball's greatest heroes was born on February 6, 1895, in Baltimore. Name him.
9. On February 24, 1946, he was elected president of Argentina.
10. On February 26, 1815, Napoleon escaped from this island.

1. Groundhog Day
2. Valentine's Day
3. February 29
4. R. Reagan
5. Fidel Castro
6. Jimmy Durante

7. Charles Lindbergh
8. Babe Ruth

9. Juan Peron
10. Elba

Graduate Level

11. On February 9, 1861, Jefferson Davis became president of———.
12. What date in 1732 was Washington's actual birthday?
13. February 12, 1809, was this president's birthday.
14. February 15 is Remember the Maine Day. What was the *Maine*?
15. She was kidnapped on February 4, 1974.
16. On February 3, 1894, this U.S. artist, noted for his illustrations on magazine covers, was born.
17. On February 1, 1935, this dam began operation.
18. This Italian opera singer was born on February 25, 1873.
19. This actress was born on February 27, 1932, in England.
20. This slogan has appeared on page one of *The New York Times* since February 10, 1897.

11. Confederacy

12. February 22
13. A. Lincoln
14. U.S. battleship

15. Patty Hearst
16. Norman Rockwell

17. Boulder/Hoover
18. Enrico Caruso
19. Elizabeth Taylor
20. "All the News That's Fit to Print"

Ph. D. Level

21. February 9, 1773, was the birthday of the ninth president. Name him.
22. This man was marooned on an island for four years until rescued on February 1, 1709.
23. On February 11, 1929, the Treaty of Lateran created———.
24. On February 1, 1896, he discovered X-rays.
25. This youth organization was incorporated on February 8, 1910.
26. By Presidential Proclamation February 1 is National———Day.
27. On February 1, 1865, the 13th Amendment was passed. What did it do?
28. By Presidential Proclamation February is American——— Month.
29. What was founded in Ripon, Wisconsin, on February 28, 1854.
30. Born on February 11, 1847, he said, "Genius is one percent inspiration and ninety-nine percent perspiration."

21. William Henry Harrison

22. Alexander Selkirk

23. Vatican City
24. W. Roentgen
25. Boy Scouts of America

26. Freedom
27. Abolished slavery

28. Heart

29. Republican Party
30. Thomas Edison

MARCH EVENTS

Freshman Level

1. March 10, 1797. This city became the capital of New York State.
2. March 12, 1933. President F. D. Roosevelt made the first of his radio speeches known as———.
3. March 18, 1937. She began her solo attempt to circle the world.
4. March 23, 1775. He delivered his "Liberty or Death" speech.
5. March 25, 1821. This country gained its independence from Turkey.
6. March 24, 1874. Birth date of this magician and escape artist.
7. March 30, 1981. He said, "I am in control."
8. March 27, 1978. The worst air disaster in history took place here.
9. March 30, 1867. The U.S. made this important purchase.
10. March 28, 1979. A nuclear power plant accident took place here.

1. Albany
2. fireside chats
3. Amelia Earhart
4. Patrick Henry
5. Greece
6. Harry Houdini
7. Alexander Haig
8. Canary Islands
9. Alaska
10. Three Mile Island, Pa.

Graduate Level

11. March 25, 1975. This Saudi Arabian king was killed by his nephew.
12. March 13, 1519. He landed in Mexico.
13. March 15, 44 B.C. He was assassinated.
14. March 9, 1860. These two ships battled against each other.
15. March 1, 1954. This was tested at Bikini Atoll.
16. March 3, 1847. Birth date of inventor born in Scotland.
17. March 19, 1813. Birth date of this Scottish physician and explorer.
18. March 16, 1968. This atrocity took place in Vietnam.
19. March 6, 1475. Birth date of this Italian painter, sculptor, architect.
20. March 3, 1853. Birth date of this Dutch painter noted for his use of brilliant colors.

11. King Faisal
12. Hernando Cortez
13. Julius Caesar
14. *Monitor, Merrimack*
15. H-bomb
16. Alexander Bell
17. David Livingstone
18. My Lai Massacre
19. Michelangelo
20. Vincent Van Gogh

Ph. D. Level

21. March 18, 1837. Birth date of 22nd and 24th U.S. president. Name him.
22. March 5, 1836. The siege here ended.
23. March 6, 1957. The Gold Coast became independent and was renamed———.
24. March 7, 1857. The Supreme Court ruled against this black slave.
25. March 9, 1934. Birth date of the first man to travel in space. Name him.
26. March 13, 1781. Sir William Herschel discovered this planet.
27. March 25, 1306. He was installed as King of Scotland.
28. March 29, 1971. He was found guilty of the My Lai Massacre.
29. March 29, 1951. They were found guilty of spying.
30. March 31, 1976. The New Jersey Supreme Court ruled that her respirator could be turned off.

21. Grover Cleveland
22. Alamo
23. Ghana
24. Dred Scott
25. Yuri Gagarin
26. Uranus
27. Robert Bruce
28. William Calley
29. Rosenbergs
30. Karen Quinlan

APRIL EVENTS

Freshman Level

1. April 1, 1948. The U.S.S.R. began its blockade of this city.
2. April 9, 1865. What happened at Appomattox?

3. April 15, 1452. Birth date of the "Mona Lisa" artist.
4. April 16, 1889. Birth date of the Little Tramp.
5. April 14, 1865. Assassination of this man.
6. April 18, 1906. What American tragedy took place?

7. April 29, 1945. He committed suicide.
8. April 21, 1918. This air ace was shot down.

9. April 23, 1564. Birth date of this literary genius.
10. April 27, 1822. Birth date of the 18th U.S. President.

1. Berlin
2. Lee surrendered to Grant

3. Leonardo da Vinci
4. Charlie Chaplin
5. Abraham Lincoln
6. San Francisco earthquake

7. Adolf Hitler
8. Manfred von Richthofen (Red Baron)

9. William Shakespeare
10. Ulysses Grant

Graduate Level

11. April 14, 1912. 1,517 people perished in this tragedy.
12. April 6, 1909. He reportedly reached the North Pole.
13. April 5, 1976. This wealthy recluse died.
14. April 3, 1860. The first ride of this mail service took place.
15. April 3, 1882. This man was killed by Robert Ford.
16. April 2, 1512. Florida was discovered by this explorer.
17. April 30, 1975. This country surrendered.
18. April 30, 1803. The U.S.A. completed this transaction.
19. April 28, 1789. This marine rebellion took place.
20. April 21, 753 B.C. The traditional date of the founding of this city.

11. *Titanic* sunk
12. Robert Peary
13. Howard Hughes
14. Pony Express
15. Jesse James
16. Ponce de Leon
17. South Vietnam
18. Louisiana Purchase
19. Mutiny on the *Bounty*.
20. Rome

Ph. D. Level

21. April 27, 1521. This explorer was killed in the Philippines.
22. April 26, 1986. A nuclear accident occurred in this Soviet city.
23. April 26, 1894. Rudolf Hess's birthday. He died in this prison.
24. April 30, 1939. This fair opened.
25. April 25, 1959. This waterway opened.
26. April 26, 1964. Tanganyika and Zanzibar merged to form this country.
27. April 24, 1895. Joshua Slocum became the first person to do this.
28. April 17, 1961. This ill-fated invasion took place.
29. April 23, 1616. This Spanish writer died at age sixty-nine.
30. April 25, 1908. Birth date of this CBS broadcaster noted for dramatic and accurate broadcasts from London during the WW II Blitz.

21. Ferdinand Magellan
22. Chernobyl
23. Spandau
24. New York World's Fair
25. St. Lawrence Seaway
26. Tanzania

27. Sail solo around the world.
28. Bay of Pigs
29. Miguel de Cervantes
30. Ed Murrow

MAY EVENTS

Freshman Level

1. May 6, 1954. He broke the 4-minute mile barrier.
2. May 28, 1940. This famous evacuation began.
3. May 6, 1895. Birth date of this romantic idol of the 1920s.
4. First Saturday in May. This event takes place at Churchill Downs.
5. May 18, 1980. This volcano erupted.
6. May 24, 1883. This bridge over the East River opened.
7. The last Monday in May in the U.S. is———.
8. May 14, 1948. This country declared its independence.
9. May 18, 1974. India became the sixth nation to acquire this.
10. May 23, 1934. This pair of bank robbers was killed.

1. Roger Bannister
2. Dunkirk
3. Rudolph Valentino
4. Kentucky Derby
5. Mount St. Helens
6. Brooklyn Bridge
7. Memorial Day
8. Israel
9. Atomic bomb
10. Bonnie and Clyde

Graduate Level

11. May 25, 1936. This man began his streak of six world records in two days.
12. May 22, 1960. Israel announced the capture of this man.
13. May 28, 1934. Five daughters were born into this Canadian family.
14. May 20–21, 1927. Lindbergh made his historic flight in this plane.
15. May 9, 1945. What special day was it?
16. May 6, 1937. This disaster occurred at Lakehurst, New Jersey.
17. May 5, 1961. He became the first American in space.
18. May 29, 1953. Hillary and Tensing conquered this.
19. May 27, 1937. This American bridge opened.
20. May 7, 1915. This ship was torpedoed and sank.

11. Jesse Owens
12. Adolf Eichmann
13. Dionne
14. *Spirit of St. Louis*
15. V-E Day
16. *Hindenburg* exploded
17. Alan Shepard
18. Mount Everest
19. Golden Gate Bridge
20. *Lusitania*

Ph. D. Level

21. May 23, 1701. He was hanged on questionable piracy charges.
22. May 25, 1941. This German battleship sank Britain's largest battleship, the *Hood*.
23. May 19, 1536. This woman was executed.
24. May 8, 1902. This volcano on Martinique erupted.
25. May 29, 1630. The English monarchy was restored after Cromwell. Who became king?
26. May 10, 1869. What event occurred on this date at Promontory Point, Utah?
27. May 7, 1954. The French lost this major battle.
28. May 2, 1863. This military leader was shot by mistake by his own men.
29. May 2, 1670. This company was formed.
30. May 1, 1960. His U-2 spy plane was shot down over the U.S.S.R.

21. Captain Kidd
22. The *Bismarck*
23. Anne Boleyn
24. Mount Pelee
25. Charles II
26. Railroad link (golden spike)
27. Dien Bien Phu
28. Stonewall Jackson
29. Hudson Bay Company
30. Francis Gary Powers

APRIL 15, THE TITANIC SINKS

Freshman Level

1. What was the *Titanic*'s planned destination?
2. It departed from this English port.
3. How many voyages had the *Titanic* completed prior to the disaster?
4. In 1987 a safe from the *Titanic* was opened on television. Who hosted the show?
5. At approximately what time did the collision occur?
6. To what line did the *Titanic* belong?
7. The *Titanic* was first to use this new distress signal.
8. There were over 2,200 on board. About how many perished?
9. Walter Lord's famous book was titled———.
10. Lord's second *Titanic* book (1986) was titled———.

1. New York City
2. Southhampton
3. None (maiden voyage)
4. Telly Savalas
5. Midnight
6. White Star Line
7. SOS
8. 1,500
9. *A Night to Remember*
10. *The Night Lives On*

Graduate Level

11. In what year did the disaster occur?
12. A priceless jeweled copy of this book went down with the ship.
13. What other problem had the *Titanic* had during its entire voyage?
14. Where are the graves of the unclaimed corpses that were recovered?
15. What occurred in September 1985?
16. The supposed rule for placing passengers on lifeboats was———?
17. Name the male star of the 1953 film, *Titanic*.
18. It could have been worse. How?
19. What was unusual about one of the four huge funnels?
20. What part did Fred Fleet play in the disaster?

11. 1912
12. The *Rubaiyat*
13. A fire in coal bunker
14. Halifax
15. *Titanic* located and photographed.
16. "Women and children first"
17. Clifton Webb
18. *Titanic* was only two-thirds full.
19. It was a dummy.
20. Sighted the iceberg

Ph. D. Level

21. In 1898 a novel was written about a huge ship that hit an iceberg on its maiden voyage and sank. What was the ship called?
22. Thomas Andrews perished. Who was he?
23. This famous millionaire also perished.
24. What was the name of the *Titanic*'s sister ship?
25. Name the first ship to reach the scene.
26. This nearby ship made no attempt to reach the wreck.
27. What role did the ship *Mackay-Bennett* play in the disaster?
28. What was the captain's name?
29. What was omitted from the launching of the *Titanic*?
30. What song was the orchestra playing as the ship sank?

21. *Titan*
22. The *Titanic*'s builder
23. John Jacob Astor
24. *Olympic*
25. The *Carpathia*
26. The *Californian*
27. Recovered bodies
28. Edward Smith
29. A christening ceremony
30. "Autumn"

V-J DAY

Freshman Level

1. What do the letters V-J stand for?
2. What was the date of V-J day?
3. On August 6 an atomic bomb was dropped on this city.
4. This president made the decision to drop the bomb.
5. What type of plane carried the bomb?
6. Who was the Emperor of Japan at the time?
7. On August 9 a second bomb was dropped on this city.
8. Also on August 9 the U.S.S.R. began hostilities against Japan by invading———.
9. Name the project that produced the atomic bomb.
10. Who headed the project?

1. Victory over Japan
2. September 2, 1945
3. Hiroshima
4. Harry Truman
5. B-29 (Superfortress)
6. Hirohito
7. Nagasaki
8. Manchukuo (Manchuria)
9. Manhattan Project
10. Robert Oppenheimer

Graduate Level

11. Where did the Japanese sign the terms of surrender?
12. Who signed on behalf of the Allies?

13. Where was the battleship at the time?
14. On March 16 this tiny island was captured, placing the Allies' planes within 750 miles of Tokyo.
15. The next island to fall was about 350 miles from Japan. It was———.
16. In a desperate attempt to stem the tide, these suicide pilots were used.
17. Translate the word "Kamikaze."
18. In this proclamation of July 26 the Allied Powers called for "unconditional surrender."
19. On August 10 Japan agreed to surrender but made this sole condition.
20. The Allies replied that the Emperor's fate would be decided by the———.

11. Battleship *Missouri*
12. Gen. Douglas MacArthur
13. Tokyo harbor
14. Iwo Jima

15. Okinawa

16. Kamikaze

17. Divine Wind
18. Potsdam Proclamation

19. Emperor remain as sovereign ruler.
20. Japanese people

Ph. D. Level

21. The atomic bomb had been successfully tested at this site.

22. What was the name of the plane that dropped the bomb?
23. What was the Hiroshima bomb nicknamed?
24. What was the Nagasaki bomb nicknamed?
25. What role did Paul Tibbets, Jr., play in the victory?
26. The point on the ground directly above or below the point of detonation is called———.
27. The planned invasion of the Japanese home islands in November was given this code name.
28. How was the news of the surrender given to the Japanese people?
29. The only Axis head of government to be hanged by the Allies was———.
30. The U.S. officially ended its war with Japan on April 28, 19——.

21. Alamogordo, New Mexico
22. *Enola Gay*
23. Little Boy
24. Fat Man
25. Piloted the *Enola Gay*
26. Ground Zero

27. Operation Olympic

28. Emperor on radio

29. Hideki Tojo

30. 1952

AVIATION FIRSTS

Freshman Level

1. 1903 The Wright Brothers made their famous first flight in this plane.
2. 1927 Lindbergh's accomplishment.
3. 1987 This plane made the first nonstop flight around the world without refueling.
4. 1926 He made the first flight over the North Pole.
5. 1919 John Alcock and Arthur Whitten Brown's accomplishment.
6. 1932 She made the first transatlantic solo flight by a woman.
7. 1949 A Boeing B-50A Superfortress accomplished this.
8. 1980 First man-powered craft to fly across English channel.
9. 1978 The first successful transatlantic balloon flight.
10. 1929 Richard Byrd was first to do this.

1. *Flyer*
2. First solo transatlantic flight
3. *Voyager*
4. Richard Byrd
5. First nonstop trans-atlantic flight
6. Amelia Earhart
7. First round-the-world flight.
8. *Gossamer Albatross*
9. *Double Eagle II*
10. Fly over South Pole

Graduate Level

11. 1782 The Montgolfier brother's accomplishment.
12. 1900 First flight of rigid-frame airships designed by this German.
13. 1921 First use of this nonflammable gas in a balloon.
14. 1922 Harold Harris became first member of Caterpillar Club. Membership is limited to people who have had———.
15. 1976 First regularly scheduled SST (supersonic transport) flight in this plane.
16. 1977 The *Gossamer Condor*, the first successful———.
17. 1933 He made the first round-the-world solo flight.
18. 1939 The German Heinkel HE178 made the first———.
19. 1947 Capt. Chuck Yeager flew the X-1 rocket plane in this first.
20. 1910 Lt. Eugene Ely took off from the *Birmingham* to make the first flight———.

11. First balloon ascension
12. Ferdinand von Zeppelin
13. Helium
14. Life saved by parachute
15. Concorde
16. man-powered aircraft
17. Wiley Post
18. turbojet flight
19. First piloted supersonic flight
20. from shipboard

Ph. D. Level

21. 1937 German pilot Hanna Reitsch made the first successful flight in a———.
22. 1952 A BOAC DeHavilland Comet was used for the first———.
23. 1797 André-Jacques Garnerin bravely did this first.
24. 1980 A balloon, *Joy of Sound*, made the first successful———.
25. 1984 *Rosie O'Grady's Balloon of Peace* made the first———.
26. 1932 Ruth Rowland Nichols became the first woman———.
27. 1909 Louis Bleriot made the first flight———.
28. 1910 Baroness Raymonde de la Roche became the first———.
29. 1908 Unfortunately Thomas Selfridge became the first———.
30. 1980 The *Solar Challenger* made the first———.

21. Helicopter
22. Jetliner service
23. First parachute jump
24. Balloon flight over North Pole
25. Solo transatlantic balloon flight
26. Airline pilot
27. Across English Channel
28. Licensed woman pilot
29. Airplane fatality
30. Long-distance solar-powered flight.

IT HAPPENED HERE
What event took place at the given time and place?

Freshman Level

1.	July 29, 1981	St. Paul's Cathedral	1. Charles and Di wedding
2.	December 22, 1984	New York subway	2. Bernard Goetz shooting
3.	December 8, 1980	Outside Dakota Hotel, New York	3. John Lennon shot
4.	April 14, 1865	Ford Theater, Washington, D.C.	4. Lincoln assassinated
5.	December 3, 1984	Union Carbide plant, Bhopal, India	5. Toxic gas fumes kill over 2,500 people
6.	May 13, 1981	St. Paul's Square	6. John Paul II shot
7.	July 27, 1934	Outside Biograph Theater, Chicago	7. John Dillinger killed
8.	February 14, 1929	2122 North Clark Street, Chicago	8. St. Valentine's Day Massacre
9.	June 5, 1944	Omaha Beach, France	9. D-Day landings
10.	June 17, 1972	Democratic National Committee Headquarters, Washington, D.C.	10. Watergate break-in

Graduate Level

11.	June 5, 1968	Ambassador Hotel, Los Angeles	11. R. Kennedy assassinated
12.	April 15–17, 1969	600-acre farm of Max Yasgur in Bethel, New York	12. Woodstock Music Festival
13.	March 30, 1981	Outside Washington Hilton Hotel	13. President Reagan shot
14.	November 22, 1963	411 Elm Street, Dallas, Texas	14. Oswald shot Kennedy
15.	August 4, 1944	263 Princengracht, Amsterdam	15. Anne Frank arrested
16.	April 4, 1968	Lorraine Motel, Memphis	16. Martin Luther King, Jr. assassinated
17.	August 8, 1969	10050 Cielo Drive, Los Angeles	17. Sharon Tate murdered
18.	October 23, 1983	Aviation Safety Building, Beirut	18. 241 marines killed in bomb attack
19.	May 28, 1987	Red Square, Moscow	19. Cessna plane landed
20.	May 29, 1985	Heysel Stadium, Brussels	20. Soccer riot (thirty-eight killed)

Ph. D. Level

21.	October 31, 1984	1 Safdarjang Road, New Delhi	21. Indira Gandhi assassinated
22.	May 4, 1985	Bitburg military cemetery, Germany	22. President Reagan lays wreath
23.	July 30, 1975	Manchus Red Fox Restaurant, Detroit	23. Hoffa disappeared
24.	September 18, 1975	625 Morris Street, San Francisco	24. Patty Hearst found
25.	May 15, 1972	Laurel Shopping Center, Laurel, Md.	25. George Wallace shot
26.	February 21, 1965	Audubon Ballroom, New York	26. Malcolm X assassinated
27.	August 4, 1892	92 Secord St., Fall River, Massachusetts	27. Lizzie Borden murders
28.	October 8, 1871	558 DeKoven Street, Chicago	28. Mrs. O'Leary's barn (Chicago fire).
29.	September 5, 1921	St. Francis Hotel, San Francisco	29. Fatty Arbuckle scandal
30.	August 5, 1962	12305 Fifth Helena Dr., Los Angeles	30. Marilyn Monroe died

174 DAYS AND DATES

EASTER

Freshman Level

1. What flower is associated with Easter?
2. This symbol of life is closely identified with Easter.
3. This animal, a symbol of fertility, is associated with Easter.
4. What is the Sunday prior to Easter Sunday called?
5. What city did Jesus enter on the Sunday prior to Easter Sunday?
6. What means of transportation did he use?
7. How many people partook of the Last Supper.
8. What act of humility did Christ perform at the Last Supper?
9. Who painted the famous fresco "The Last Supper"?
10. The Last Supper is comemmorated by what Christian holiday?

1. Lily
2. Egg
3. Rabbit
4. Palm Sunday
5. Jerusalem
6. An ass
7. Thirteen
8. Washed disciples' feet
9. Leonardo da Vinci
10. Holy Thursday or Maundy Thursday

Graduate Level

11. This disciple betrayed Jesus.
12. Where was Jesus at the time of the betrayal?
13. What did the betrayer receive for his treachery?
14. This Roman governor judged Jesus.
15. He was forced to carry the cross for Jesus.
16. The people demanded this man's release.
17. Name the hill on which Jesus was crucified?
18. This disciple denied that he knew Jesus.
19. This man claimed the body of Jesus.
20. Who was first to see Jesus on Easter Sunday?

11. Judas
12. Gethsemane
13. Thirty pieces of silver
14. Pontius Pilate
15. Simon of Cyrene
16. Barabbas
17. Golgotha (Calvary)
18. Peter
19. Joseph of Arimathaea
20. Mary Magdalene

Ph. D. Level

21. The angel told the woman to tell the disciples that Jesus would meet them in———.
22. When Jesus appeared to the disciples, one of them was absent and didn't believe the news. Name the doubter.
23. What was eventually done with the thirty pieces of silver?
24. What does the word "Golgotha" mean?
25. What Christian sacrament was inaugurated at the Last Supper?
26. By what name is the Wednesday of Holy Week known?
27. What was Judas' other name?
28. What are "Judas slits" or "Judas holes"?
29. What special Jewish feast was the Last Supper?
30. Why is it called the Passover?

21. Galilee
22. Thomas
23. Used to buy a potter's field
24. The place of a skull
25. Eucharist
26. Spy Wednesday
27. Iscariot
28. Peepholes in prison doors
29. The Passover Feast
30. The Angel of Death passed over the families of Israelites

8 / POTLUCK

KID'S STUFF

Freshman Level

1. He had a horse named Pokey.
2. What color is the Cookie Monster?
3. This cereal goes "snap, crackle, pop."
4. "Horseless carriages" are now called ———.
5. Which of the Seven Dwarfs didn't speak?
6. This nanny could slide up the bannister.
7. Name the male rabbit in the movie *Bambi*.
8. He wanted to be a real live boy.
9. He sings, "It's a Beautiful Day in the Neighborhood."
10. What are you doing when you "double Dutch"?

1. Gumby
2. Blue
3. Rice Krispies
4. Cars (automobiles)
5. Dopey
6. Mary Poppins
7. Thumper
8. Pinocchio
9. Mr. Rogers
10. Skipping rope

Graduate Level

11. What animals starred in *The Secret of NIMH*?
12. In the movie *Poltergeist*, the house was built on top of a ———.
13. The Caped Crusader is better known as ———.
14. He was the science officer on *Star Trek*.
15. This green doll lights up when you hug it.
16. What company makes a personal computer called the Macintosh?
17. This boy played with Winnie-the-Pooh.
18. How many dice are used to play Yahtzee?
19. In Stratego you try to capture this piece to win.
20. Lee Iacocca works for this company.

11. Rats
12. Graveyard (cemetery)
13. Batman
14. Spock
15. Glo Worm
16. Apple

17. Christopher Robin
18. Five
19. The Flag
20. Chrysler

Ph. D. Level

21. Peter Pan wanted Wendy to sew this back on.
22. In chess, the proper name for the "horse" is ———.
23. Name the two major leagues of baseball.

24. In this science-fiction movie Sting portrayed a character named Feyd.
25. Who portrayed Chachi on TV's *Happy Days*?
26. What sport has the same name as an insect?
27. Name the two sports in which the ball can be dribbled.
28. *The Sword in the Stone* is about this person.
29. What was the name of the Volkswagen Beetle in *The Love Bug*?
30. What was the name of the boy who found E.T.?

21. His shadow
22. Knight
23. American and National Leagues
24. *Dune*

25. Scott Baio
26. Cricket
27. Basketball, soccer
28. King Arthur
29. Herbie
30. Elliot

GAMES
Identify the game.

Freshman Level

1. Chance and Community Chest
2. Checkmate
3. Colonel Mustard
4. Baby Boomer Edition
5. Three No Trump
6. The dungeonmaster

7. The left bower
8. Crowned
9. Fifteen-two, fifteen-four
10. Marbles on a six-pointed star

1. Monopoly
2. Chess
3. Clue
4. Trivial Pursuit
5. Bridge
6. Dungeons and Dragons
7. Euchre
8. Checkers
9. Cribbage
10. Chinese checkers

Graduate Level

11. Bombs and the flag
12. A triple letter square
13. Slide
14. A royal flush
15. Twenty-eight rectangular tiles
16. Clue: Dracula; answer: vampire
17. Art Linkletter's image is on the $100 bill
18. The players break up monopolies
19. First to get all four men home by exact count wins
20. Words in pantomine

11. Stratego
12. Scrabble
13. Sorry
14. Poker
15. Dominoes
16. Password
17. The Game of Life
18. Anti-Monopoly
19. Parcheesi
20. Charades

Ph. D. Level

21. Buying and selling famous paintings
22. Bearing off
23. Armies and forty-two territories of the world
24. Groups of tiles called a pung
25. A deck in which the suits are colors, and there are no face cards.
26. The success formula is made up of money, fame, happiness
27. "Give" and "Take" cards
28. Gambling at the Racetrack or at the Stock Market
29. A variation of Parcheesi with "shortcuts"
30. Often called the oriental chess

21. Masterpiece
22. Backgammon
23. Risk
24. Mah-Jongg
25. Rook
26. Careers
27. Easy Money
28. Ratrace
29. Aggravation
30. Go

FAMOUS HORSES: Real and fictional

Freshman Level

1. A large wooden horse built by the Greeks.
2. Roy Roger's palomino horse.
3. The Lone Ranger's white stallion.
4. Gene Autry's horse.
5. A winged horse of Greek mythology.
6. A race-horse nicknamed Big Red.
7. The last horse to win the Triple Crown (1978).
8. The race horse belonging to Velvet in National Velvet.
9. Ken's horse on the Goose Bar Ranch on TV.
10. A horse created by author Anna Sewell.

1. Trojan horse
2. Trigger
3. Silver
4. Champion
5. Pegasus
6. Man-o'-War
7. Affirmed
8. Pi or Pie (Piebald)
9. Flicka (My Friend Flicka)
10. Black Beauty

Graduate Level

11. The only army survivor of Custer's Last Stand.
12. Napoleon's stallion at Waterloo.
13. Robert E. Lee's horse during the Civil War.
14. The first racehorse to win more than a million dollars.
15. The first Triple Crown winner (1919).
16. Hopalong Cassidy's horse.
17. The Wonder Horse of cowboy star Tom Mix.
18. The Cisco Kid's horse.
19. The horse had the title role in this 1979 movie about a boy and his horse.
20. A film was made about this Australian horse in 1983.

11. Comanche
12. Marengo
13. Traveler
14. Citation
15. Sir Barton
16. Topper
17. Tony
18. Diablo
19. *Black Stallion*
20. Phar Lap

Ph. D. Level

21. Caligula made this horse a consul.
22. The Duke of Wellington's horse at Waterloo.
23. It carried Mohammed from earth to the seventh heaven.
24. The winner of the first Kentucky Derby.
25. General Grant's horse during the Civil War.
26. Three English thoroughbreds were the ancestors of nearly all modern race horses. Name one.
27. Alexander the Great's horse.
28. The riderless horse at JFK's funeral.
29. The horse of British outlaw Dick Turpin.
30. The horse of Achilles.

21. Incitatus
22. Copenhagen
23. Al Borak
24. Aristides
25. Cincinnati
26. Eclipse, Herod, Matchem
27. Bucephalus
28. Black Jack
29. Black Bess
30. Xanthus

FORTS AND CAMPS

Freshman Level

1. The U.S. gold deposit is here (Kentucky).
2. A major resort city 40 kilometers north of Miami.
3. One of the largest industrial cities in Texas.
4. The official retreat of the U.S. president.
5. The setting for the 1980 movie *Friday the 13th*.
6. Whose law begins, "Worship God, seek beauty, give service"?
7. This fort in New Jersey is a center for Army basic training.
8. Capital city of the island of Martinique.
9. The Civil War started here.
10. In the 1962 hit song "Hello Muddah, Hello Faddah" Allan Sherman writes home from this camp.

1. Fort Knox
2. Fort Lauderdale
3. Fort Worth
4. Camp David
5. Camp Crystal Lake
6. Camp Fire Girls
7. Fort Dix
8. Fort-de-France
9. Fort Sumter
10. Camp Granada

Graduate Level

11. Comic strip character Beetle Bailey was posted here.
12. The second largest city in Indiana.
13. This fort on Lake Champlain was a stronghold during the Revolutionary War.
14. U.S. Army fort where Sergeant Bilko was stationed.

15. Paul Newman starred in this 1981 film.

16. A five-mile-long racetrack in a Stephen Foster song.
17. Confederate fort in Tennessee where Buckner surrendered to Grant.
18. A west-coast city in Southern Florida.
19. City in Arkansas at the Oklahoma state line.
20. Military post where Private Gomer Pyle was stationed.

11. Camp Swampy
12. Fort Wayne
13. Fort Ticonderoga

14. Fort Baxter and/or Camp Fremont
15. *Fort Apache, The Bronx*
16. Camptown Racetrack
17. Fort Donelson

18. Fort Myers
19. Fort Smith
20. Camp Henderson

Ph. D. Level

21. Fort located in Adventureland at Disneyworld, Florida.
22. Fort located in Adventureland at Disneyland California.
23. This fort stood at the present site of Kingston, Ontario.
24. Camp headed by Bill Murray in the 1974 movie *Meatballs*.
25. U.S. Army camp where Bill Murray took basic training in *Stripes* (1981).
26. The Statue of Liberty is on this fort.
27. This national monument off Florida's southern tip was used as a prison.
28. The site of the U.S. Army infantry center in Georgia.
29. Fort in Dakota Territory from which Custer departed in 1876.
30. This Montana dam was on the very first cover of *Life* magazine (1936).

21. Fort Sam Clemens
22. Fort Wilderness
23. Fort Frontenac
24. Camp North Star
25. Fort Arnold

26. Fort Wood
27. Fort Jefferson

28. Fort Benning
29. Fort Abraham Lincoln
30. Fort Peck Dam

RELIGION

Freshman Level

1. Who named the first woman, Eve?
2. Solomon was David's son. Who was Solomon's mother?
3. Joseph Smith founded this religious sect in 1830.
4. In 1858 Bernadette Soubrious witnessed a supernatural event at this site.
5. On what day did God create the sun, moon, and stars?
6. The Jewish New Year is called———.
7. What country has the largest Muslim population?
8. This religious faith forbids the eating of pork.
9. Other than the Old Testament, name the major book of Jewish thought.
10. The Society of Friends is commonly called———.

1. Adam
2. Bathsheba
3. Mormons
4. Lourdes (France)
5. Fourth day
6. Rosh Hashanah
7. Indonesia
8. Islam (Muslim)
9. Talmud (law and traditions)
10. Quakers

Graduate Level

11. What are the two main branches of the Islamic faith?
12. Who was the ancient Egyptian god of the sun?
13. Zacharias and Elisabeth were his parents.
14. For whom is the empty seat at the Passover seder?
15. This is the month during which the Muslims fast.
16. In what city is the Kaaba, the most sacred Muslim sanctuary?
17. This priest was a missionary to the leper colony in Molokai, Hawaii.
18. Mohammed's flight to Medina is known by this name.
19. Moses received the Ten Commandments on top of this mountain.
20. He was converted on the road to Damascus.

11. Sunnite and Shi'ites
12. Ra
13. John the Baptist
14. Prophet Elijah
15. Ramadan
16. Mecca
17. Father Joseph Damien
18. Hegira
19. Mount Sinai
20. Saint Paul

Ph. D. Level

21. What is Nicholas Breakspear's claim to fame?
22. What does "Kyrie Eleison" mean?
23. The Adi Granth is a holy book of this religious group.
24. He introduced The Book of Common Prayer in 1549.
25. Hagiographs are holy writings of this religion.
26. These ancient Hindu scriptures are written in an old form of Sanskrit.
27. What saint translated the Vulgate?
28. He is reputed to be the author of the Imitation of Christ.
29. Quetzalcoatl was a feathered serpent worshipped by the ———.
30. What is the oldest major religion?

21. Only Englishman to be Pope
22. Lord, Have Mercy
23. Sikh
24. King Edward VI
25. Jewish
26. Vedas
27. Saint Jerome
28. Thomas à Kempis
29. Toltecs and Aztecs
30. Hinduism

MONEY
All answers relate to money.

Freshman Level

1. This term denotes money that must be accepted for debts.
2. The Bible says this is the root of all evil.
3. The unfinished object on the back of the U.S. single.
4. The largest bill now circulated in the U.S.
5. What metal was removed from U.S. coins after 1965?
6. The American Express Card says this word distinguishes it from all others.
7. To start Monopoly each player receives this amount.
8. What is the rent on Boardwalk with one hotel?
9. If you said the secret word on *You Bet Your Life* you won ———.
10. Dr. Joyce Brothers won the top prize in the category of boxing on this show.

1. Legal tender
2. "the love of money"
3. Pyramid
4. $100
5. Silver
6. Member
7. $1,500.
8. $2,000.
9. $100
10. *The $64,000 Question*

Graduate Level

11. In the film *Cabaret* Sally Bowles sings this song.
12. This 1966 film made Clint Eastwood an international star.
13. What was the 1967 sequel called?
14. What is the price tag on Minnie Pearl's hat?
15. Arthur Hailey's best-seller about the banking industry.
16. The secretary for James Bond's boss is named ———.
17. The first film directed by Woody Allen (1969).
18. Karen Black, Sandy Dennis, and Cher star in this 1982 film.
19. Title of a 1959 movie about Red Nichols.
20. Total price paid for the Louisiana Purchase.

11. "Money, Money, Money"
12. *A Fistful of Dollars*
13. *For a Few Dollars More*
14. $1.98
15. *The Money Changers*
16. Miss Moneypenny
17. *Take the Money and Run*
18. *Come Back to the Five and Dime, Jimmy Dean, Jimmy Dean*
19. *Five Pennies*
20. $15 million.

Ph. D. Level

21. Shelley Long and Tom Hanks star in this film.
22. On this Canadian island there is a famous money pit.
23. The Bay City Roller's had this No. 9 hit song in 1976.
24. What does the C stand for in J. C. Penney?
25. The only film in which Edward G. Robinson costarred with James Cagney (1931).
26. This term refers to the cash in public hands and checking accounts in the U.S.A.
27. On many credit cards this word appears if you erase the signature panel.
28. Although nearly invisible the name of twenty-six U.S. States appear on this bill.
29. Name the three presidents whose portraits appear not only on the U.S. coins but also bills and savings bonds ———.
30. The portraits of only two nonpresidents have been featured on U.S. coins in circulation. Name them.

21. *The Money Pit*
22. Oak Island, Nova Scotia
23. "Money Money"
24. Cash
25. *Smart Money*
26. M1
27. Void
28. $5 bill
29. Washington, Jefferson, Lincoln
30. B. Franklin, Susan B. Anthony

AWARDS AND MEDALS
Identify the award or metal.

Freshman Level

1. Academy Awards
2. Emmy Awards
3. Grammy Awards
4. Blackwell's List
5. Clio Awards
6. Heisman Trophy
7. Pulitzer Prizes
8. Nobel Prizes

9. Man of the Year Award
10. Vezina Trophy

1. Outstanding achievements in the film industry
2. Outstanding achievements in the television industry
3. Outstanding achievements in the recording industry
4. Worst-dressed women
5. Excellence in advertising
6. Best college football player of the year
7. Journalism, letters, and music
8. Physics, chemistry, literature, peace, economics, medicine-physiology
9. Person having greatest influence on year (*Time* magazine)
10. Goalkeeper with fewest goals against (NHL)

Graduate Level

11. Patsy Awards
12. Hugo Awards
13. Obie Awards
14. Newbery Medal
15. Duke Kahanamoku Trophy
16. Lombardi Award
17. Eclipse Award
18. Golden Fleece Award
19. Stillman Award
20. George Foster Peabody Awards

11. Animals on television and in films
12. Outstanding science-fiction film or television programs
13. Excellence in off-Broadway theater
14. Distinguished contributions to children's literature.
15. Highest individual contribution to the sport of surfing
16. Nation's best linesman in college football
17. Individuals and horses for contribution to horseracing
18. Biggest waste of taxpayer's money
19. Animal saving human life or vice-versa
20. Outstanding service in field of broadcasting

Ph. D. Level

21. Wizard Award
22. Nebula Awards
23. Melville Cane Award
24. Grantland Rice Trophy
25. Winnie Award
26. Silver Buffalo
27. Reuben Award
28. The Roscoe
29. Silver Bowl
30. Spingarn Medal

21. Excellence in computer graphics
22. Outstanding science-fiction writing
23. American poetry
24. Best collegiate football team
25. Leading designer of American women's fashions
26. Committed service to young people (Boy Scouts of America)
27. Outstanding cartoonist of the year
28. Excellence in design of household furnishings and fixtures
29. Outstanding contributions to the world of dance
30. Highest achievement by a black American

WINTER OLYMPICS, 1988

Freshman Level

1. In what city were the 1988 winter olympics held?
2. In what Canadian province is the city located?
3. What country won the most medals?
4. What country was second in total medals won?
5. What country won the hockey gold?
6. All gold medals in hockey, but one, have been won by these three countries.
7. In 1936 this country won the hockey gold.
8. Name the large multiuse skating facility that was used.
9. What shape did the Olympic symbol take?

10. Who won the gold in men's figure skating?

1. Calgary
2. Alberta
3. U.S.S.R.
4. East Germany
5. U.S.S.R.
6. U.S.S.R., U.S.A., Canada
7. Great Britain
8. Saddledome
9. Snowflake or Maple Leaf
10. Brian Boitano (U.S.A.)

Graduate Level

11. This East German again won the women's figure skating gold.
12. Name one of the "demonstration events."

13. The biathlon combines these two skills.

14. Two falls dashed this U.S. speed skater's medal hopes.
15. What events took place at Nakiska?
16. This is the world's fastest self-propelled sport.
17. The single figure-skating consists of competition in three categories. Name them.

18. These warm winds affected the weather.
19. This Italian skier won two gold medals.
20. Name one of the events in which there are age restrictions.

11. Katarina Witt
12. Curling, free-style skiing, short-track skating
13. Target-shooting, cross-country skiing
14. Dan Jansen
15. Alpine skiing
16. Speed skating
17. Compulsory figures, short, and long programs
18. Chinooks
19. Alberto Tomba
20. Bobsled and luge

Ph. D. Level

21. Hockey uses a puck. Curling uses ———.
22. The mascots were students dressed up as ———.
23. What were the mascots named?
24. The Torch Relay was organized by this national oil company.
25. Debbie Thomas' license plate read SK8N4AU. Can you decipher it?
26. American Bonnie Blair's gold and bronze earned her this sobriquet.
27. Vreni Schneider won two golds in alpine skiing for this country.
28. Pairs champions Natalia Bestemianova and Andrei Bukin were known by this nickname.
29. What was the nickname of neophyte British ski jumper Eddie Edwards?
30. The 1992 winter Olympics will be held here.

21. Rocks or stones
22. Polar bears
23. Hidy and Howdy
24. Petro-Canada
25. Skating for Gold
26. Bonnie the Blue
27. Switzerland
28. B and B
29. The Eagle
30. Albertville, France

ALPHABET SOUP
Answers must begin with the given letter.

Freshman Level

1. A European country. **F**
2. A European country, **B**
3. A heavyweight boxing champion. **L**
4. A heavyweight boxing champion. **F**
5. An Academy Award winning movie. **S**
6. An Academy Award winning movie. **C**

7. A capital city. **D**
8. An NHL team name. **B**
9. An NHL team name. **C**
10. A country in the western hemisphere. **E**

1. France, Finland
2. Belgium, Bulgaria
3. Louis, Liston
4. Foreman, Frazier, Fitzsimmons
5. *Sting, Sound of Music*
6. *Cimarron, Calvalcade, Casablanca, Chariots of Fire*
7. Dublin, Damascus, Dakar, Dacca
8. Bruins, Blues, Black Hawks
9. Canadiens, Capitals, Canucks
10. Ecuador, El Salvador

Graduate Level

11. A heavyweight boxing champion. **B**
12. A heavyweight boxing champion. **M**
13. A capital city in Africa. **C**
14. A capital city in Asia. **S**
15. A country in South America. **P**
16. A president of the U.S.A. **C**
17. A president of the U.S.A. **P**
18. A fruit. **D**
19. A fruit. **T**
20. A musical instrument. **O**

11. Baer, Braddock, Burns
12. Marciano
13. Cairo, Cape Town
14. Singapore, Seoul
15. Peru, Paraguay
16. Carter, Coolidge, Cleveland
17. Polk, Pierce
18. Dates, damson
19. Tangerine
20. Organ, oboe

Ph. D. Level

21. An Academy Award winning movie. **D**
22. An Academy Award winning movie. **K**
23. An NHL team name. **S**
24. An NHL team name. **K**
25. A vegetable. **A**
26. A vegetable. **E**
27. A capital city. **O**
28. A U.S. state capital. **R**
29. A square on a Monopoly board. **S**
30. A North American mammal. **S**

21. *The Deer Hunter*
22. *Kramer vs. Kramer*
23. Sabres
24. Kings
25. Artichoke, asparagus
26. Endive, eggplant
27. Oslo, Ottawa
28. Richmond, Raleigh
29. St.Charles Place, States Avenue
30. Seal, skunk, squirrel

CORNY RIDDLES

Freshman Level

1. What type of house weighs the least?
2. What type of fish is the most valuable?
3. What horses keep late hours?
4. What pet is always on the floor?
5. What apple isn't an apple?
6. What kind of bell doesn't ring?
7. What kind of clothing is preferred by lawyers?
8. Carpenters don't like hitting these nails.
9. These socks can be found in your backyard.
10. This dog never barks.

1. A lighthouse
2. Goldfish
3. Nightmares
4. A carpet
5. Pineapple
6. A dumbbell
7. Lawsuits
8. Fingernails
9. Garden hose
10. Hot dog

Graduate Level

11. It's yours but other people use it more than you do.
12. How can you make seven even?
13. Why is a moon like a dollar?
14. How do you keep a rhinoceros from charging?

15. What do pigs write with?
16. What is dark but made by light?
17. What is in the middle of March?
18. What gets larger when you take more away?
19. Where do Eskimos keep their money?
20. What kind of tables do people eat?

11. Your name
12. Take away the "s".
13. It has four quarters
14. Take away its credit cards.
15. A pigpen
16. A shadow
17. The letter "r"
18. A hole
19. In snow banks
20. Vegetables

Ph. D. Level

21. What can you hold without touching it?

22. Who is buried in the tomb of Alexander the grape?
23. What is yellow and very dangerous?

24. Where was Solomon's temple located?
25. What has four legs and one foot?
26. What do beavers have that no other animals have?
27. When does eleven plus two equal one?
28. What has one horn and gives milk?
29. An athlete gets athlete's foot. What does an astronaut get?
30. What is worse than raining cats and dogs?

21. A meeting/conversation
22. Alexander the raisin
23. Shark-infested mustard
24. On his head
25. A bed
26. Baby beavers
27. At 11 o'clock
28. A milk truck
29. Missile toe
30. Hailing taxis

THREE OF A KIND
Identify what the three have in common.

Freshman Level

1. Huron, Superior, Erie
2. *Goldfinger, Octopussy, Thunderball*
3. St. Charles Place, Vermont Avenue, Marvin Gardens

4. Alfalfa, Buckwheat, Spanky
5. Flush, straight, full house
6. Bashful, Dopey, Grumpy

7. Incisors, cuspids, molars
8. Sapporo, Innsbruck, Calgary

9. The Joker, The Penguin, The Riddler
10. John, Thomas, Simon

1. Great Lakes
2. James Bond movies
3. Squares in game of Monopoly
4. *Our Gang* characters
5. Poker hands
6. Three of the seven Dwarfs
7. Teeth
8. Sites of winter Olympic games
9. Enemies of Batman
10. Apostles

Graduate Level

11. *Oliver, Rebecca, Marty*

12. Kizzy, Chicken George, Kunta Kinte
13. *Casablanca, The Big Sleep, The Caine Mutiny*

14. Manitoba, Alberta, Ontario
15. *Vertigo, Psycho, Marnie*
16. Catherine of Aragon, Catherine Howard, Catherine Parr
17. 3 red, 6 green, 8 black
18. Tiki Room, Jungle Cruise, Space Mountain
19. *The Stand, The Shining, The Dead Zone*
20. Whirlaway, Assault, Citation

11. Academy Awards winning movies
12. Characters in *Roots*
13. Humphrey Bogart movies
14. Provinces of Canada
15. Hitchcock films
16. Wives of Henry VIII
17. Pool balls
18. Disneyland attractions
19. Stephen King novels
20. Triple Crown winners

Ph. D. Level

21. Henry Wilson, Charles Curtis, Hannibal Hamlin

22. *I've Got a Secret, Keep Talking, The Joker's Wild*
23. Jack Haley, Ray Bolger, Bert Lahr
24. Cleopatra, Hannibal, Nero
25. *Clambake, Speedway, Charro!*
26. Joe Friday, Preston of the Yukon, Hans Schultz
27. Peepeye, Pipeye, Poopeye
28. Bobbie Joe, Billie Jo, Betty Jo

29. Ham, Shem, Japheth
30. Janus, Titan, Phoebe

21. Vice-presidents of the U.S.A.
22. TV game shows
23. In *Wizard of Oz* movie
24. Suicides
25. Elvis Presley movies
26. Sergeants
27. Popeye's nephews
28. Sisters on *Petticoat Junction*
29. Noah's sons
30. Moons of Saturn

SO I SAY

Provide the appropriate first name— e.g., So I say to the guy drinking America's favorite beer,———. *Answer*: Bud.

Freshman Level: So I say———

1. To the girl singing Christmas songs,———.
2. To the lady offering me an apple,———.
3. To the private detective,———.
4. To the man at the front door, "Welcome———".
5. To the girl eating oysters,———.
6. To the actor accepting the Academy Award,———.
7. To the woman threatening to take me to court,———.
8. To the little girl counting her coins,———.
9. To the guy who wants to open a gallery,———.
10. To the girl wanting to buy a pet,———.

1. Carol
2. Eve
3. Dick
4. Matt
5. Pearl
6. Oscar
7. Sue
8. Penny
9. Art
10. Kitten (Kitty)

Graduate Level

11. To the mountain climber,———.
12. To the little girl eating a biscuit,———.
13. To the woman about to pass the blessing,———.
14. To the German worker not wearing a hard hat,———.
15. To the geologist,———.
16. To the girl admiring the Scottish flowers,———.
17. To the lion tamer,———.
18. To the lady wearing the red gemstone broach———.
19. To the guy who forgot to bring his fishing pole,———.
20. To the bartender Mr. Collins,———.

11. Cliff
12. Cookie
13. Grace
14. Helmut
15. Rock
16. Heather
17. Leo
18. Ruby
19. Rod
20. Tom

Ph. D. Level

21. To the lawyer preparing the certificate of probate,———.
22. To the girl from the Old Dominion,———.
23. To the two men putting up the kitchen curtains,———.
24. To the gal begging for money,———.
25. To the boxer wearing the athletic support,———.
26. To the gas station attendant,———.
27. To the guy who just cut himself shaving,———.
28. To the girl arranging the green plants,———.
29. To the euchre player holding the right bower,———.
30. To the guy applying for the government subsidy,———.

21. Will
22. Virginia
23. Kurt 'n Rod
24. Charity
25. Jock
26. Phillip
27. Nick
28. Fern
29. Jack
30. Grant

WORD REBUSES

Freshman Level

1. cof fee
2. onalle
3. vgetebeals
4. June 6, June 6
5. ———it
6. mat mat mat mat
7. lips lips
8. f all
9. he ran nar eh
10. la - bor

1. coffee break
2. all in one
3. mixed vegetables
4. double date
5. blanket
6. format
7. tulips
8. fall apart
9. he ran forwards and backwards
10. division of labor

Graduate Level

11. job in job
12. docks docks
13. r/e/a/d/i/n/g
14. death life
15. ———program
16. symphon
17. rightstepdirection
18. cast cast cast cast
19. ha res
20. CtOaMxE

11. in between jobs
12. paradox
13. reading between the lines
14. life after death
15. space program
16. unfinished symphony
17. a step in the right direction
18. forecast
19. split hairs
20. income tax

Ph. D. Level

21. ed ot overs
22. amUous
23. eiln pu
24. ALL world
25. wether
26. jus 144 tice
27. timing tim ing
28. ecnalg
29. no ways it ways
30. sgeg

21. last of the red hot lovers
22. ambiguous
23. line up in alphabetical order
24. it's a small world after all
25. a bad spell of weather
26. a gross injustice
27. split-second timing
28. a backward glance
29. no two ways about it
30. scrambled eggs

CUSSED QUIZ

Freshman Level

1. What star is nearest to the earth?
2. What fruit has its seeds on the outside.
3. Niagara Falls is between these two lakes.

4. What mammal lives the longest?
5. Two is company. Three is a crowd. What are four and five?
6. What is considered to be the normal oral temperature?
7. What do these animals have in common: opposum, koala, wombat?
8. In *Hamlet*, Ophelia says of this herb, "That's for remembrance."
9. Elizabeth of York, wife of Henry VII, has had her portrait viewed by more people than any other queen. Why?
10. The first musical group to feature both John Lennon and Paul McCartney.

1. The sun
2. The strawberry
3. Lake Erie, Lake Ontario
4. Man
5. Nine
6. 98.6°F
7. Marsupials

8. Rosemary

9. Model for queen on playing cards
10. The Quarrymen

Graduate Level

11. Flying from Florida to the Panama Canal you head———.
12. Give three musical terms which can also be applied to baseball.

13. What word starts and ends with "und"?
14. In what country did India ink originate?
15. After the flood was over, Noah disgraced himself by———.
16. Riddle: Why is a room full of married couples like an empty room?
17. The first house numbers appeared in this city in 1463.
18. Name the two official daily newspapers of the U.S.S.R.

19. This London street is synonymous with English newspaper publishing.
20. This famous North American landmark moves backward constantly.

11. South and east
12. pitch, slide, run, tie, base (bass)
13. Underground
14. China
15. Getting drunk
16. There isn't a single person there
17. Paris
18. *Pravda (Truth), Izvestia (News)*
19. Fleet Street

20. Niagara Falls

Ph. D. Level

21. Who was the Merchant of Venice?
22. During what month is the earth closest to the sun?
23. What does a puddler do?

24. "Wait a moment." What is the time span of a moment?
25. When Casey came to bat, his team was losing. What was the score?
26. Sisters Mildred and Patty Hill wrote this song (1893).
27. Name the only U.S. president to die without leaving a will.
28. Aquavit has the flavor of———.
29. Japanese Junko Tabei was the first woman to———.
30. If you are convicted of embracery, what have you done?

21. Antonio (not Shylock)
22. January
23. Steelworker who melts steel.
24. 1½ minutes
25. 4 to 2

26. Happy Birthday to You
27. Lincoln
28. Caraway seeds
29. Climb Mount Everest
30. Tried to influence a judge or jury corruptly

TRUE OR FALSE
Fifteen of the statements are false. If false, provide an explanation if possible.

Freshman Level

1.	The African elephant sleeps standing up.	1.	True
2.	Turtles have no teeth.	2.	True
3.	Cat gut comes from cats.	3.	False (from sheep)
4.	Dogs sweat through their paws.	4.	True
5.	Panama hats originated in Panama.	5.	False (Ecuador)
6.	Teddy bears were named after President Theodore Roosevelt.	6.	True
7.	Jimmy Carter once claimed to have seen a UFO.	7.	True
8.	Women have two more ribs than men do.	8.	False (both have twelve)
9.	There is no soda in soda water.	9.	True
10.	The Canary Islands are named after birds.	10.	False (the bird canary was named after the islands)

Graduate Level

11.	Warm water freezes sooner than cold water.	11.	False
12.	Male ballet dancers don't dance on their toes.	12.	True
13.	Forks came into general use during the last century.	13.	True
14.	George Harrison was convicted of plagiarizing the tune for "My Sweet Lord."	14.	True
15.	Venetian blinds were invented in Venice.	15.	False (Japan)
16.	When your smoke detector begins to beep every few seconds, smoke is present.	16.	False (battery is weak)
17.	A woman who wears a size 36B bra has a larger breast than a woman who wears a size 34B.	17.	False (letter indicates breast size)
18.	Damascus is the world's oldest inhabited capital city.	18.	True
19.	Women's urinals were introduced in the U.S.A. in the 1930's.	19.	True
20.	A square halo in paintings depicts an unusually saintly living person.	20.	True

Ph. D. Level

21.	*A Midsummer Night's Dream* takes place during the summer.	21.	False (Spring)
22.	Chinese checkers originated in France.	22.	False (Sweden)
23.	Jesus' friends called him Jehovah.	23.	False (Joshua)
24.	The Thirty Years' War lasted thirty years.	24.	True
25.	The Battle of Bunker Hill was fought on Bunker Hill.	25.	False (Breed's Hill)
26.	The phrase, "Now is the time for all good men to come to the aid of the party" originated as a typing drill.	26.	True
27.	A higher rate of birth occurs during a full moon.	27.	False
28.	Camel's hair brushes are made of camel's hair.	28.	False (squirrel)
29.	Germany's *Oktoberfest* is celebrated in September.	29.	True
30.	There was one Texan survivor at the Alamo.	30.	False (six)

AND NOW FOR SOMETHING COMPLETELY DIFFERENT
Conversation catalysts. No answers are provided.

Freshman Level

1. What do the Chinese eat for breakfast?
2. Give your version of the most significant headline this century.
3. Was there ever a band of warrior women call Amazons?
4. Were chariot races once held in the Roman Colosseum?
5. Why do men have nipples?
6. What are you eating when you eat anchovies?
7. Name as many proverbs as you can.
8. Complete this sentence: There ought to be an award for————.
9. After whom is America named and why?
10. Do only humans truly laugh and cry?

Graduate Level

11. Who was the greatest athlete of the twentieth century?
12. Is it correct to say, "Try and finish it"?
13. Name eight parts of the body that are three-letter words.
14. Do porcupine "shoot" their quills?
15. How's your memory? State the Pythagorean Theorem.
16. At what time of day will the twenty-first century begin? Are you sure?
17. What prevents the federal government from printing all the money it needs?
18. How do you explain gravity? How does it work?
19. Should the Lord's Prayer be recited in schools?
20. Is midnight 12 A.M. or 12 P.M.?

Ph. D. Level

21. Do teachers stand for the national anthem in the staff room?
22. Briefly explain the main tenets of Communism.
23. If you dropped a ball down a hole that went right through the center of the earth, what would happen?
24. Why do the sun and moon look so much larger when they are near the horizon?
25. If God can do anything, could he create a stone so heavy that He couldn't lift it?
26. How is it possible to see through glass?
27. What do the numbers mean in 20/20 vision?
28. Where do houseflies go during the winter and how do they come back?
29. Mirrors reverse objects left to right. Why aren't objects reversed top to bottom?
30. According to the Bible, why didn't God want the people to build the Tower of Babel?

TWISTED TELEVISION PROGRAMS
One letter in each title has been changed. Correct the title.

Freshman Level

1. The Frying Nun
2. Sanford and Ron
3. Happy Ways
4. My Three Sins
5. The Old Couple
6. Cheeks
7. What's My Fine?
8. Adam's Bib
9. Kodak
10. Little Horse On The Prairie

1. *The Flying Nun*
2. *Sanford and Son*
3. *Happy Days*
4. *My Three Sons*
5. *The Odd Couple*
6. *Cheers*
7. *What's My Line?*
8. *Adam's Rib*
9. *Kojak*
10. *Little House On The Prairie*

Graduate Level

11. Have Fun Will Travel
12. One Way at a Time
13. Falcon Crust
14. Moonsighting
15. You Bet Your Wife
16. The Mud Squad
17. Food Times
18. The Price Is Light
19. Bet Smart
20. Your Hat Parade

11. *Have Gun Will Travel*
12. *One Day at a Time*
13. *Falcon Crest*
14. *Moonlighting*
15. *You Bet Your Life*
16. *The Mod Squad*
17. *Good Times*
18. *The Price Is Right*
19. *Get Smart*
20. *Your Hit Parade*

Ph. D. Level

21. Slipper
22. Growing Pawns
23. Wagon Trail
24. The Lone Boat
25. December Pride
26. The Tall Guy
27. Soup
28. Bag Town
29. Light Is Enough
30. House Walls

21. *Flipper*
22. *Growing Pains*
23. *Wagon Train*
24. *The Love Boat*
25. *December Bride*
26. *The Fall Guy*
27. *Soap*
28. *Big Town*
29. *Eight Is Enough*
30. *House Calls*